CONTENTS

The Scarecrow Author Bibliographies

1. John Steinbeck (Tetsumaro Hayashi). 1973.
2. Joseph Conrad (Theodore G. Ehrsam). 1969.
3. Arthur Miller (Tetsumaro Hayashi). 2d ed. due 1976.
4. Katherine Anne Porter (Waldrip & Bauer). 1969.
5. Philip Freneau (Philip M. Marsh). 1970.
6. Robert Greene (Tetsumaro Hayashi). 1971.
7. Benjamin Disraeli (R. W. Stewart). 1972.
8. John Berryman (Richard W. Kelly). 1972.
9. William Dean Howells (Vito J. Brenni). 1973.
10. Jean Anouilh (Kathleen W. Kelly). 1973.
11. E. M. Forster (Alfred Borrello). 1973.
12. The Marquis de Sade (E. Pierre Chanover). 1973.
13. Alain Robbe-Grillet (Dale W. Fraizer). 1973.
14. Northrop Frye (Robert D. Denham). 1974.
15. Federico García Lorca (Laurenti & Siracusa). 1974.
16. Ben Jonson (Brock & Welsh). 1974.
17. Four French Dramatists: Eugène Brieux, François de Curel, Emile Fabre, Paul Hervieu (Edmund F. SantaVicca). 1974.
18. Ralph Waldo Ellison (Jacqueline Covo). 1974.
19. Philip Roth (Bernard F. Rodgers, Jr.). 1974.
20. Norman Mailer (Laura Adams). 1974.
21. Sir John Betjeman (Margaret Stapleton). 1974.
22. Elie Wiesel (Molly Abramowitz). 1974.
23. Paul Laurence Dunbar (Eugene W. Metcalf, Jr.). 1975.
24. Henry James (Beatrice Ricks). 1975.
25. Robert Frost (Lentricchia & Lentricchia). 1976.
26. Sherwood Anderson (Douglas G. Rogers). 1976.
27. Iris Murdoch and Muriel Spark (Tominaga and Schneidermeyer). 1976.
28. John Ruskin (Kirk H. Beetz). 1976.
29. Georges Simenon (Trudee Young). 1976.

ROBERT FROST:

A Bibliography, 1913-1974

compiled by

Frank Lentricchia

and

Melissa Christensen Lentricchia

The Scarecrow Press, Inc.

Metuchen, N.J.   1976

cc

Library of Congress Cataloging in Publication Data

Lentricchia, Frank.
  Robert Frost : a bibliography, 1913-1974.

  (The Scarecrow author bibliographies ; no. 25)
  Includes index.
  1. Frost, Robert, 1874-1963--Bibliography.
I. Lentricchia, Melissa Christensen, joint author.
Z8317.78.L45 [PS3511.R94] 016.811'5'2   75-44093
ISBN 0-8108-0896-X

for

KELLY, KATE and DAVID

PREFACE

The work on this bibliography began casually, approximately seven years ago, as preparatory research on critical materials for Frank's book on Frost, <u>Robert Frost: Modern Poetics and the Landscapes of Self</u> (Durham: Duke University Press, 1975). Thanks to the work of one of his graduate assistants at UCLA, enough material was gathered to encourage us to continue the endeavor and to compile a substantial bibliography, one which scholars would find useful. We also felt compelled to proceed with what was often an arduous project by the lack of an extensive and up-to-date book on Frost in the field: though Clymer's bibliography is invaluable (and compiled with admirable care), it does not include work by and about Frost done in the past 39 years; and Donald Greiner's checklist is by design limited in its scope. In the late sixties both Reginald L. Cook (in <u>Sixteen Modern American Authors: A Survey of Research and Criticism</u>, ed. Jackson R. Bryer, Durham: Duke University Press, 1969) and Uma Parameswaram (in <u>Bulletin of Bibliography</u> 25 Jan.-April, May-Aug. 1967) made significant contributions to bibliographical work on Frost. But as Cook himself complains in the opening pages of his essay, "an extensive working bibliography is disappointingly unavailable."

We think the organization and contents of this book fulfill Cook's request for a "working" bibliography. The primary material--to which our approach is neither descriptive nor all-inclusive--has been separated from the secondary material. And within each of these broad areas are distinct sub-sections which--since we ourselves have been through some lists (particularly in the category of secondary material) comprised of a potpourri of reviews, articles and books--we believe will lend convenience to the researcher's task. Verifying the distinctions between general articles about Frost and reviews of his work was difficult in some instances. We believe, however, that we have successfully sorted out the mass of secondary material and that the time used to recheck entries will not have been wasted. Our inevitable concern over such matters may be further eased by the fact that bibliographical work can be (and often is) a minefield for making minor mistakes.

Most of what we have included are items one would expect to find in such a book: Frost's major publications and reviews thereof; books on Frost; parts of books on Frost; articles written abroad; dissertations and checklists. Those articles appearing in scholarly journals (e. g. , American Literature or Yale Review) have been distinguished from those published in popular magazines, newspapers, college newsletters, etc. In the section containing books about Frost we have added selected reviews of some of these works that we felt were of particular importance. (It is our opinion that many of these reviews appreciably stimulate and advance critical debate, and should be consulted by Frost scholars.) And at the request of our editors we have included a substantial list of Frost's uncollected poems and an appendix which outlines the bibliographical history of each of Frost's collected poems. We are pleased to acknowledge E. C. Lathem, whose edition of Frost's poems helped to make the compilation of such an appendix possible within a reasonable period of time.

Our intention has been to make available a usable bibliographical tool. We are well aware that a heavily secondary bibliography cannot be "complete" in any absolute sense of the word. Consequently, we acknowledge that, to some extent, the following lists are "selective. " We have tried, however, to provide students and critics of Frost with a nearly exhaustive bibliography.

M. C. L.
University of California, Irvine
May 1975

Part One: Primary Material

A. ROBERT FROST'S MAJOR PUBLICATIONS

1. BOOKS OF POETRY
(with contents)

1 Twilight. Lawrence, Mass. , 1894. Only two copies
   printed.
    Twilight
    My Butterfly
    Summering
    The Falls
    An Unhistoric Spot

2 A Boy's Will. London: David Nutt, 1913; New York:
   Holt, 1915.
    Into My Own
    Ghost House
    My November Guest
    Love and a Question
    A Late Walk
    Stars
    Storm Fear
    Wind and Window Flower
    To the Thawing Wind
    A Prayer in Spring
    Flower-Gathering
    Rose Pogonias
    Asking for Roses
    Waiting-Afield at Dusk
    In a Vale
    A Dream Pang
    In Neglect
    The Vantage Point
    Mowing
    Going for Water
    Revelation
    The Trial by Existence
    In Equal Sacrifice
    The Tuft of Flowers

Spoils of the Dead
Pan With Us
The Demiurge's Laugh
Now Close the Windows
A Line-Storm Song
October
My Butterfly
Reluctance

3 North of Boston.   London: David Nutt, 1914; New York:
Holt, 1915.
The Pasture
Mending Wall
The Death of the Hired Man
The Mountain
A Hundred Collars
Home Burial
The Black Cottage
Blueberries
A Servant to Servants
After Apple-Picking
The Code
The Generations of Men
The Housekeeper
The Fear
The Self-Seeker
The Wood-Pile
Good Hours

4 Mountain Interval.   New York: Holt, 1916.
The Road Not Taken
Christmas Trees
An Old Man's Winter Night
A Patch of Old Snow
In the Home Stretch
The Telephone
Meeting and Passing
Hyla Brook
The Oven Bird
Bond and Free
Birches
Pea Brush
Putting in the Seed
A Time to Talk
The Cow in Apple Time
An Encounter
Range-Finding
The Hill Wife
    I.   Loneliness

To Earthward
Good-By and Keep Cold
Two Look at Two
Not to Keep
A Brook in the City
The Kitchen Chimney
Looking for a Sunset Bird in Winter
A Boundless Moment
Evening in a Sugar Orchard
Gathering Leaves
The Valley's Singing Day
Misgiving
A Hillside Thaw
Plowmen
On a Tree Fallen Across the Road
Our Singing Strength
The Lockless Door
The Need of Being Versed in Country Things

6   Selected Poems.   New York: Holt, 1923; London: William
Heinemann, 1923.
The Pasture
The Cow in Apple Time
The Runaway
An Old Man's Winter Night
Home Burial
The Death of the Hired Man
A Servant to Servants
The Self-Seeker
The Hill Wife
"Out, Out--"
Putting in the Seed
Going for Water
Mowing
After Apple-Picking
Birches
The Gum-Gatherer
The Mountain
The Tuft of Flowers
Mending Wall
An Encounter
The Wood Pile
Snow
In the Home Stretch
The Road Not Taken
The Oven Bird
A Vantage Point
The Sound of Trees

Hyla Brook
My November Guest
Range-Finding
October
To the Thawing Wind
A Time to Talk
The Code
A Hundred Collars
Blueberries
Brown's Descent
Revelation
Storm Fear
Bond and Free
Flower-Gathering
Reluctance
Into My Own

7 West-Running Brook.   New York: Holt, 1928.
        I.   Spring Pools
Spring Pools
The Freedom of the Moon
The Rose Family
Fireflies in the Garden
Atmosphere
Devotion
On Going Unnoticed
The Cocoon
A Passing Glimpse
A Peck of Gold
Acceptance
        II.   Fiat Nox
Once by the Pacific
Lodged
A Minor Bird
Bereft
Tree at My Window
The Peaceful Shepherd
The Thatch
A Winter Eden
The Flood
Acquainted With the Night
        III.   West-Running Brook
West-Running Brook
        IV.   Sand Dunes
Sand Dunes
Canis Major
A Soldier
Immigrants

Hannibal
The Flower Boat
    V.   Over Back
The Times Table
The Investment
The Last Mowing
The Birthplace
    VI.   My Native Simile
The Door in the Dark
Dust in the Eyes
Sitting by a Bush in Broad Sunlight
The Armful
Riders
On Looking Up by Chance at the Constellations
The Bear

8   <u>Selected Poems</u>.   New York: Holt, 1928.
        The Pasture
The Cow in Apple-Time
The Runaway
To Earthward
Nothing Gold Can Stay
Stopping by Woods on a Snowy Evening
Fire and Ice
Fragmentary Blue
Dust of Snow
An Old Man's Winter Night
Home Burial
The Death of the Hired Man
A Servant to Servants
The Self-Seeker
The Hill Wife
"Out, Out--"
Putting in the Seed
Going for Water
Mowing
The Need of Being Versed in Country Things
Two Look at Two
After Apple-Picking
Birches
The Gum-Gatherer
The Mountain
The Tuft of Flowers
Mending Wall
Good-Bye and Keep Cold
The Grindstone
An Encounter
A Hillside Thaw

The Wood-Pile
Snow
In the Home Stretch
The Black Cottage
The Axe-Helve
The Road Not Taken
The Oven Bird
The Vantage Point
The Sound of the Trees
Hyla Brook
My November Guest
The Onset
Range-Finding
October
To the Thawing Wind
A Time to Talk
The Code
A Hundred Collars
Blueberries
Brown's Descent
Revelation
Storm-Fear
Bond and Free
Flower-Gathering
Reluctance
Into My Own

9   Collected Poems.   New York: Holt, 1930; London: Long-
mans, Green & Co. , 1930.

> A Boy's Will (excluding Asking for Roses, In Equal
> Sacrifice, and Spoils of the Dead; including In
> Hardwood Groves, a poem which was not in A
> Boy's Will of 1913).

> North of Boston

> Mountain Interval (including two additional poems,
> Locked Out, and The Last Word of a Bluebird).

> New Hampshire

> West-Running Brook (including three additional poems,
> The Lovely Shall Be Choosers, What Fifty Said,
> and The Egg and the Machine).

10   The Augustan Books of Poetry: Robert Frost.   London:
Ernest Benn Ltd. , 1932.
The Runaway
The Onset
Storm Fear
Stopping by Woods on a Snowy Evening

An Old Man's Winter Night
Dust of Snow
The Need of Being Versed in Country Things
The Tuft of Flowers
Mending Wall
Two Look at Two
Birches
The Death of the Hired Man
The Road Not Taken
My November Guest
To Earthward
Reluctance
Nothing Gold Can Stay
Tree at My Window
Acquainted with the Night
Once by the Pacific
The Peaceful Shepherd
A Soldier
Fireflies in the Garden
Spring Pools

11   Selected Poems.   New York: Holt,   1934.
The Pasture
The Cow in Apple-Time
The Runaway
To Earthward
Nothing Gold Can Stay
Stopping by Woods on a Snowy Evening
Fire and Ice
Spring Pools
Fragmentary Blue
Dust of Snow
Acquainted With the Night
Once by the Pacific
Bereft
Tree at My Window
The Soldier
An Old Man's Winter Night
Home Burial
The Death of the Hired Man
A Servant to Servants
The Self-Seeker
The Hill Wife
"Out, Out--"
Putting in the Seed
Going for Water
Mowing
The Need of Being Versed in Country Things

Two Look at Two
After Apple Picking
Birches
The Gum-Gatherer
The Mountain
The Tuft of Flowers
Mending Wall
Good-Bye and Keep Cold
The Grindstone
The Bear
An Encounter
A Hillside Thaw
The Wood Pile
The Armful
A Brook in the City
A Peck of Gold
On Looking Up by Chance at the Constellations
Sitting by a Bush in Broad Sunlight
Canis Major
Snow
In the Home Stretch
The Black Cottage
The Axe-Helve
West-Running Brook
The Road Not Taken
The Over Bird
[A] Vantage Point
The Birthplace
The Sound of the Trees
Hyla Brook
My November Guest
Range-Finding
October
To the Thawing Wind
A Time to Talk
The Code
A Hundred Collars
The Witch of Coös
Blueberries
Brown's Descent
Revelation
Storm-Fear
Bond and Free
Flower-Gathering
Reluctance
Into My Own

12 A Further Range. New York: Holt, 1936; London:

Jonathan Cape, 1937.

Taken Doubly

A Lone Striker or, Without Prejudice to Industry
Two Tramps in Mud Time or, A Full-Time Interest
The White-Tailed Hornet or, The Revision of Theories
A Blue Ribbon at Amesbury or, Small Plans Grate-
    fully Heard Of
A Drumlin Woodchuck or, Be Sure to Locate
The Gold Hesperidee or, How to Take a Loss
In Time of Cloudburst or, The Long View
A Roadside Stand or, On Being Put Out of Our Mis-
    ery
Departmental or, The End of My Ant Jerry
The Old Barn at the Bottom of the Fogs or, Class
    Prejudice Afoot
On the Heart's Beginning to Cloud the Mind or,
    From Sight to Insight
The Figure in the Doorway or, On Being Looked at
    in a Train
At Woodward's Gardens or, Resourcefulness Is More
    than Understanding
A Record Stride or, The United States Stated

Taken Singly

Lost in Heaven
Desert Places
Leaves Compared with Flowers
A Leaf-Treader
On Taking from the Top to Broaden the Base
They Were Welcome to Their Belief
The Strong Are Saying Nothing
The Master Speed
Moon Compasses
Neither Out Far Nor In Deep
Voice Ways
Design
On a Bird Singing in Its Sleep
Afterflakes
Clear and Colder
Unharvested
There Are Roughly Zones
A Trial Run
Not Quite Social
Provide, Provide

Ten Mills

I.   Precaution
II.   The Span of Life
III. The Wrights' Biplane

     IV.   Assertive
     V.   Evil Tendencies Cancel
     VI.   Pertinax
     VII. Waspish
     VIII. One Guess
     IX.   The Hardship of Accounting
     X.   Not All There
     XI.   In Divés' Dive
           The Outlands
        The Vindictives
        The Bearer of Evil Tidings
        Iris by Night
           Build Soil
        Build Soil
        To a Thinker
           Afterthought
        A Missive Missle

13   Selected Poems. London: Jonathan Cape, 1936.   Chosen
     by the author; with introductory essays by W. H. Auden,
     C. Day Lewis, Paul Engle, and Edwin Muir.
           I.
        The Pasture
        The Cow in Apple-Time
        The Runaway
           II.
        To Earthward
        Stopping by Woods on a Snowy Evening
        Fire and Ice
        Spring Pools
        Dust of Snow
           III.
        Acquainted with the Night
        Once by the Pacific
        Tree at My Window
        A Soldier
           IV.
        An Old Man's Winter Night
        Home Burial
        The Death of the Hired Man
        A Servant to Servants
        The Self-Seeker
        The Hill Wife
        "Out, Out--"
           V.
        Putting in the Seed
        Going for Water

Mowing
The Need of Being Versed in Country Things
    VI.
Two Look at Two
After Apple-Picking
Birches
The Gum-Gatherer
The Mountain
The Tuft of Flowers
Mending Wall
Good-Bye and Keep Cold
The Grindstone
The Bear
The Wood-Pile
    VII.
The Armful
A Brook in the City
A Peck of Gold
On Looking up by Chance at the Constellations
Canis Major
    VIII.
Snow
The Black Cottage
The Axe-Helve
West-Running Brook
    IX.
The Road Not Taken
The Oven Bird
Hyla Brook
My November Guest
The Onset
Range-Finding
October
To the Thawing Wind
    X.
A Time to Talk
The Code
A Hundred Collars
The Witch of Coös
Blueberries
Brown's Descent
Revelation
Storm-Fear
Flower-Gathering
Reluctance
Into My Own

14   Collected Poems of Robert Frost, 1939.   New York:
     Holt, 1939.
         The Pasture (introductory poem)

         A Boy's Will (as it was represented in Collected
            Poems of 1930).

         North of Boston

         Mountain Interval (as it was represented in Collected
            Poems of 1930).

         New Hampshire

         West-Running Brook (as it was represented in Col-
            lected Poems of 1930).

         A Further Range

15   A Witness Tree.   New York: Holt, 1942; London: Jona-
     than Cape, 1943.
         Beech
         Sycamore
            One or Two
         The Silken Tent
         All Revelation
         Happiness Makes Up in Height for What It Lacks in
            Length
         Come In
         I Could Give All to Time
         Carpe Diem
         The Wind and the Rain
         The Most of It
         Never Again Would Birds' Song Be the Same
         The Subverted Flower
         Willful Homing
         A Cloud Shadow
         The Quest of the Purple-Fringed
         The Discovery of the Madeiras
            Two or More
         The Gift Outright
         Triple Bronze
         Our Hold on the Planet
         To a Young Wretch (Boethian)
         The Lesson for Today
            Time Out
         Time Out

To a Moth Seen in Winter
A Considerable Speck (Microscopic)
The Lost Follower
November
The Rabbit Hunter
A Loose Mountain (Telescopic)
It Is Almost the Year Two Thousand
    Quantula
In a Poem
On Our Sympathy with the Under Dog
A Question
Boethian
The Secret Sits
An Equalizer
A Semi-Revolution
Assurance
An Answer
    Over Back
Trespass
A Nature Note
Of the Stones of the Place
Not of School Age
A Serious Step Lightly Taken
The Literate Farmer and the Planet Venus

16 Come In and Other Poems. New York: Holt, 1943;
    London: Jonathan Cape, 1944. Selected, with introduc-
    tion and commentary by Louis Untermeyer.
        I.   An Invitation
    The Pasture
        II.   The Code and Other Stories
    The Tuft of Flowers
    Blueberries
    Home Burial
    The Witch of Coös
    Paul's Wife
    Ghost House
    At Woodward's Gardens
    The Vindictives
    Wild Grapes
    The Code
        III.   The Hired Man and Other People
    Birches
    Mowing
    Mending Wall
    The Mountain
    Brown's Descent, or The Willy-Nilly Slide

The Sound of the Trees
In Hardwood Groves
Nothing Gold Can Stay
After Apple-Picking
The Grindstone
The Kitchen Chimney
Gathering Leaves
A Leaf Treader
A Hillside Thaw
On a Tree Fallen Across the Road
A Passing Glimpse
Dust of Snow
Fire and Ice
Riders
The Master Speed
The Gift Outright
A Considerable Speck
The Silken Tent
Good-bye and Keep Cold
A Prayer in Spring
Into My Own
Come In
   VII.   Afterword
Choose Something Like a Star

17 A Masque of Reason.   New York: Holt, 1945.

18 The Poems of Robert Frost.   New York: Modern Library, 1946.   With an introductory essay, "The Constant Symbol" (with poem, "To the Right Person"), by the author.

A Boy's Will (excluding "A Late Walk, " "Wind and Window Flower, " "In a Vale, " "A Dream Pang, " "The Trial by Existence, " "Pan With Us, " "Now Close the Windows, " "In Hardwood Groves, " "My Butterfly, " "Asking for Roses, " "In Equal Sacrifice, " "Spoils of the Dead")

North of Boston (excluding "The Self-Seeker")

Mountain Interval (excluding "The Exposed Nest, " "A Patch of Old Snow, " "In the Home Stretch, " "Meeting and Passing, " "A Girl's Garden, " "Locked Out")

New Hampshire (excluding "Maple, " "Place for a Third, " "The Pauper Witch of Grafton, " "A

Fountain, A Bottle, A Donkey's Ears, and Some
Books, " "I Will Sing You One-O, " "In a Disused
Graveyard, " "A Boundless Moment, " "Evening in
a Sugar Orchard, " "The Valley's Singing Day, "
"A Hillside Thaw, " "The Lockless Door")

West-Running Brook (excluding "The Rose Family, "
"The Cocoon, " "The Thatch, " "The Door in the
Dark, " "The Armful")

A Further Range (excluding "The Old Barn at the
Bottom of the Fogs, " "On Taking from the Top to
Broaden the Base, " "Afterflakes, " "Clear and
Colder, " "To a Thinker, " "Assertive")

A Witness Tree (excluding "The Subverted Flower, "
"The Discovery of the Madeiras, " "In a Poem, "
"An Equalizer, " "Not of School Age")

19 A Pocket Book of Robert Frost's Poems.   New York:
Pocket Books, 1946.   With introduction and commentary
by Louis Untermeyer.
(Same as contents of Come In and Other Poems--
item 16)

20 A Masque of Mercy.   New York: Holt, 1947.

21 Steeple Bush.   New York: Holt, 1947.
A Young Birch
Something for Hope
One Step Backward Taken
Directive
Too Anxious for Rivers
An Unstamped Letter in Our Rural Letter Box
To an Ancient
Five Nocturnes
I.   The Night Light
II.   Were I in Trouble
III.   Bravado
IV.   On Making Certain Anything Has Happened
V.   In the Long Night
A Spire and Belfry
A Mood Apart
The Fear of God
The Fear of Man
A Steeple on the House
Innate Helium

The Courage to Be New
Iota Subscript
   Out and Away
The Middleness of the Road
Astrometaphysical
Skeptic
Two Leading Lights
A Rogers Group
On Being Idolized
A Wish to Comply
A Cliff Dwelling
It Bids Pretty Fair
Beyond Words
A Case for Jefferson
Lucretius versus the Lake Poets
   Editorials
Haec Fabula Docet
Etherealizing
Why Wait for Science
Any Size We Please
An Importer
The Planners
No Holy Wars for Them
Bursting Rapture
U.S. 1946 King's X
The Ingenuities of Debt
The Broken Drought
To the Right Person

21a A Masque of Reason: Containing A Masque of Reason,
    A Masque of Mercy (Two New England Biblicals), to-
    gether with Steeple Bush and other poems.   London:
    Jonathan Cape, 1948.   With an introductory essay, "A
    Romantic Chasm, " by the author.
        A Masque of Reason

        A Masque of Mercy

        Steeple Bush

22 Complete Poems of Robert Frost, 1949.   New York:
    Holt, 1949.
        (Volumes, wherein contents alterations were made,
        follow contents as established by Collected Poems of
        1930 and Collected Poems of 1939).

        A Boy's Will

North of Boston

Mountain Interval

New Hampshire

West-Running Brook

A Further Range

A Witness Tree

Steeple Bush

"An Afterword" (consisting of three poems: Choose
Something Like a Star, Closed for Good, and
From Plane to Plane)

A Masque of Reason

A Masque of Mercy

23   The Road Not Taken: An Introduction to Robert Frost.
New York: Holt, Rinehart and Winston, 1951. With
preface and commentary by Louis Untermeyer.
        The Poet's Invitation
            The Pasture
            1.
        The Tuft of Flowers
        Blueberries
        Home Burial
        The Witch of Coös
        Paul's Wife
        Ghost House
        At Woodward's Gardens
        The Vindictives
        Wild Grapes
        The Code
        The Bearer of Evil Tidings
        The Fear
        Snow
            2.
        The Housekeeper
        A Hundred Collars
        The Star-Splitter
        The Hill Wife
            Loneliness

House Fear
The Smile
The Oft-Repeated Dream
The Impulse
The Telephone
Revelation
Going for Water
A Line-Storm Song
Willful Homing
Birches
Mowing
Mending Wall
The Mountain
Brown's Descent
The Vanishing Red
To the Thawing Wind
A Lone Striker
Two Tramps in Mud Time
Love and a Question
An Old Man's Winter Night
The Gum-Gatherer
The Investment
The Figure in the Doorway
To a Young Wretch
The Wood-Pile
The Death of the Hired Man
    3.
On Going Unnoticed
West-running Brook
A Patch of Old Snow
A Time to Talk
A Boundless Moment
Bereft
A Winter Eden
Hyla Brook
The Flower Boat
The Census-Taker
A Brook in the City
Evening in a Sugar Orchard
The Onset
Spring Pools
In a Disused Graveyard
Sand Dunes
The Birthplace
For Once, Then, Something
A Serious Step Lightly Taken
Tree at My Window

My Butterfly
The Need of Being Versed in Country Things
The Sound of the Trees
In Hardwood Groves
Nothing Gold Can Stay
After Apple-Picking
The Grindstone
The Kitchen Chimney
Gathering Leaves
A Leaf Treader
A Hillside Thaw
On a Tree Fallen Across the Road
A Passing Glimpse
Dust of Snow
Putting in the Seed
The Line-Gang
Fire and Ice
Riders
The Master Speed
The Gift Outright
A Considerable Speck
The Silken Tent
Good-Bye and Keep Cold
A Prayer in Spring
Into My Own
Come In
The Road Not Taken

24 Aforesaid. New York: Holt, Rinehart and Winston,
    1954. With a preface, "The Prerequisites, " by the au-
    thor.
    The Silken Tent
    My November Guest
    The Tuft of Flowers
    Reluctance
    Desert Places
    To Earthward
    Once by the Pacific
    A Soldier
    The Gift Outright
    The Death of the Hired Man
    The Mountain
    The Wood-Pile
    Birches
    The Witch of Coös
    Home Burial
    An Old Man's Winter Night

Hyla Brook
The Oven Bird
Stopping by Woods on a Snowy Evening
The Onset
Love and a Question
Looking for a Sunset Bird in Winter
For Once, Then, Something
Spring Pools
Tree at My Window
Acquainted with the Night
Directive
The Lovely Shall be Choosers
West-running Brook
Paul's Wife
Two Tramps in Mud Time
The White-Tailed Hornet
The Investment
Provide, Provide
A Drumlin Woodchuck
In Time of Cloudburst
On Looking Up by Chance at the Constellations
Sitting by a Bush in Broad Sunlight
Design
The Secret Sits
Precaution
Bravado
The Hardship of Accounting
Departmental
A Considerable Speck
Etherealizing
Why Wait for Science
All Revelation
Happiness Makes Up in Height for What It Lacks in
     Length
Come In
Never Again Would Birds' Song Be the Same
Carpe Diem
A Young Birch
The Last Word of a Bluebird
The Night Light
A Mood Apart
Iota Subscript
The Courage to Be New
The Lost Follower
The Most of It
The Road Not Taken
Dust of Snow

A Winter Eden
Choose Something Like a Star
Closed for Good
The Need of Being Versed in Country Things

25 Robert Frost: Selected Poems.   Middlesex: Penguin,
    1955.   With an introductory essay by C. Day Lewis.
        A Boy's Will (excluding "A Late Walk, " "Stars, "
            "Wind and Window Flower, " "Flower-Gathering, "
            "Rose Pogonias, " "Asking for Roses, " "Waiting--
            Afield at Dusk, " "In a Vale, " "A Dream Pang, "
            "The Vantage Point, " "Going for Water, " "In
            Equal Sacrifice, " "Spoils of the Dead, " "Pan with
            Us, " "Now Close the Windows, " "In Hardwood
            Groves, " "My Butterfly")

        North of Boston (excluding "The Generations of Men, "
            "The Housekeeper, " "The Self-Seeker, " "Good
            Hours")

        Mountain Interval (excluding "Christmas Trees, "
            "The Exposed Nest, " "A Patch of Old Snow, " "In
            the Home Stretch, " "Meeting and Passing, " "Bond
            and Free, " "Pea Brush, " "An Encounter, " "The
            Bonfire, " "A Girl's Garden, " "Locked Out, "
            "Brown's Descent, " "The Vanishing Red")

        New Hampshire (excluding "The Census-Taker, "
            "Maple, " "Wild Grapes, " "Place for a Third, "
            "The Pauper Witch of Grafton, " "A Fountain, a
            Bottle, A Donkey's Ears, and Some Books, " "In
            a Disused Graveyard, " "Blue-Butterfly Day, "
            "Not to Keep, " "A Brook in the City, " "The
            Kitchen Chimney, " "A Boundless Moment, " "Even-
            ing in a Sugar Orchard, " "Gathering Leaves, "
            "The Valley's Singing Day, " "A Hillside Thaw, "
            "Plowmen, " "Our Singing Strength, " "The Lock-
            less Door")

        West-Running Brook (excluding "The Freedom of the
            Moon, " "The Rose Family, " "Atmosphere, " "De-
            votion, " "The Cocoon, " "Acceptance, " "The
            Thatch, " "Canis Major, " "The Flower Boat, "
            "The Times Table, " "The Last Mowing, " "The
            Door in the Dark, " "Dust in the Eyes, " "The
            Armful, " "What Fifty Said")

A Further Range (excluding "The Gold Hesperidee, "
"A Roadside Stand, " "The Old Barn at the Bottom
of the Fogs, " "Lost in Heaven, " "On Taking from
the Top to Broaden the Base, " "They Were Welcome to Their Belief, " "The Master Speed, "
"Moon Compasses, " "Afterflakes, " "Clear and
Colder, " "Unharvested, " "To a Thinker")

A Witness Tree (excluding "Beech, " "Sycamore, "
"I Could Give All to Time, " "The Wind and the
Rain, " "A Cloud Shadow, " "The Quest of the
Purple-Fringed, " "The Discovery of the Madeiras, "
"To a Young Wretch, " "Time Out, " "To a Moth
Seen in Winter, " "November, " "The Rabbit-Hunt-
er, " "In a Poem, " "On Our Sympathy with the
Under Dog, " "A Question, " "An Equalizer, " "A
Semi-Revolution, " "Trespass, " "A Nature Note, "
"Of the Stones of the Place, " "Not of School Age, "
"The Literate Farmer and the Planet Venus")

Steeple Bush (excluding "Too Anxious for Rivers, "
"An Unstamped Letter in Our Rural Letter Box, "
"Were I in Trouble, " "In the Long Night, " "The
Fear of God, " "The Fear of Man, " "Innate He-
lium, " "Astrometaphysical, " "Skeptic, " "Two
Leading Lights, " "A Rogers Group, " "A Wish to
Comply, " "A Cliff Dwelling, " "Lucretius versus
the Lake Poets, " "Any Size We Please, " "Burst-
ing Rapture, " "U.S. 1946 King's X, " "The Inge-
nuities of Debt")

"Afterword" (From Complete Poems: "Choose Something Like a Star" and "Closed for Good")

26 You Come Too.   New York: Holt, Rinehart and Winston,
1959.   A collection for young readers.
The Pasture
Good Hours
Going for Water
Blueberries
Looking for a Sunset Bird in Winter
Acquainted with the Night
A Hillside Thaw
Good-Bye and Keep Cold
Stopping by Woods on a Snowy Evening
Christmas Trees
Birches

A Young Birch
A Passing Glimpse
The Last Mowing
Pea Brush
The Telephone
The Rose Family
One Guess
Fireflies in the Garden
Blue-Butterfly Day
A Drumlin Woodchuck
The Runaway
The Cow in Apple Time
The Exposed Nest
The Oven Bird
A Nature Note
A Minor Bird
A Peck of Gold
The Last Word of a Bluebird
Not of School Age
The Birthplace
A Girl's Garden
The Tuft of Flowers
Mending Wall
A Time to Talk
Brown's Descent
The Death of the Hired Man
Fire and Ice
Hyla Brook
Tree at My Window
Dust of Snow
The Freedom of the Moon
The Kitchen Chimney
The Road Not Taken
Gathering Leaves
A Record Stride
After Apple-Picking
Two Tramps in Mud Time

27   In the Clearing.   New York: Holt, Rinehart and Winston,
     1962; London: Jonathan Cape, 1962.
          Frontispiece But God's Own Descent (excerpted from
             "Kitty Hawk")
          Pod of the Milkweed
          Away!
          A Cabin in the Clearing
          Closed for Good
          America is Hard to See

One More Brevity
Escapist--Never
For John F. Kennedy His Inauguration
    Cluster of Faith
Accidentally on Purpose
A Never Naught Song
Version
A Concept Self-Conceived
Forgive, O Lord
Kitty Hawk
Auspex
The Draft Horse
Ends
Peril of Hope
Questioning Faces
Does No One at All Ever Feel This Way in the
    Least?
The Bad Island--Easter
Our Doom to Bloom
The Objection to Being Stepped On
A-Wishing Well
How Hard It Is to Keep from Being King When It's
    in You and in the Situation
Lines Written in Dejection on the Eve of Great
    Success
The Milky Way Is a Cowpath
Some Science Fiction
    Quandary
Quandary
A Reflex
In a Glass of Cider
From Iron
Four-Room Shack Aspiring High
But Outer Space
On Being Chosen Poet of Vermont
We Vainly Wrestle with the Blind Belief
It Takes All Sorts of In and Outdoor Schooling
In Winter in the Woods Alone

28 Selected Poems of Robert Frost. New York: Holt,
    Rinehart and Winston, 1963. Poems selected by the
    author, with an introduction by Robert Graves, and an
    essay, "The Figure a Poem Makes," by the author.
        (with the addition of poems from In the Clearing, the
            contents are the same as those of Complete Poems
            1949--item 22--with the following exclusions:)
        A Boy's Will (excluding Stars, Wind and Window

Flower, Flower Gathering, In a Vale, A Dream
Pang, Going for Water, Pan With Us, Now Close
the Windows, In Hardwood Groves, A Line-Storm
Song, and My Butterfly.)

North of Boston (excluding A Servant to Servants,
The Housekeeper, The Self-Seeker, and Good
Hours.)

Mountain Interval (excluding The Exposed Nest, A
Patch of Old Snow, In the Home Stretch, Meeting
and Passing, Hyla Brook, Pea Brush, The Cow
in Apple Time, Locked Out, The Last Word of a
Bluebird, Brown's Descent and Snow.)

New Hampshire (excluding Maple, The Axe-Helve,
Place for a Third, A Fountain, A Bottle, A
Donkey's Ears, and Some Books, I Will Sing You
One-O, To E. T. , Two Look at Two, Not to
Keep, A Brook in the City, A Boundless Moment,
Evening in a Sugar Orchard, The Valley's Singing
Day, A Hillside Thaw, and Plowmen.)

West-Running Brook (excluding The Freedom of the
Moon, The Rose Family, Atmosphere, The Cocoon, The Thatch, The Flower Boat, The Door
in the Dark, and The Egg and the Machine.)

A Further Range (excluding The Gold Hesperidee, A
Roadside Stand, The Old Barn at the Bottom of
the Fogs, The Figure in the Doorway, Leaves
Compared with Flowers, A Leaf Treader, On
Taking from the Top to Broaden the Base, Moon
Compasses, Afterflakes, Clear and Colder, A
Trial Run, The Bearer of Evil Tidings, To a
Thinker, and A Missive Missile.)

A Witness Tree (excluding The Wind and the Rain,
The Discovery of the Madeiras, The Gift Outright
[position here changed to follow For John F. Ken-
nedy His Inauguration], A Loose Mountain, An
Equalizer, Assurance, A Nature Note, Not of
School Age, and The Literate Farmer and the
Planet Venus.)

Steeple Bush (excluding Too Anxious for Rivers, An
Unstamped Letter in Our Rural Letter Box, Innate

Helium, Astrometaphysical, Two Leading Lights,
A Wish to Comply, Beyond Words, Lucretius
versus the Lake Poets, Haec Fabula Docet, Any
Size We Please, An Importer, Bursting Rapture,
and The Broken Drought.)

"An Afterword" (consisting of Take Something Like a
Star and Closed for Good.)

A Masque of Reason

In the Clearing (excluding One More Brevity,
Escapist--Never, Accidentally on Purpose, Ver-
sion, Auspex, The Draft Horse, Does No One at
All Ever Feel This Way in the Least?, The Bad
Island--Easter, The Objection to Being Stepped On,
A-Wishing Well, How Hard It Is to Keep from
Being King When It's in You and in the Situation,
The Milky Way Is a Cowpath, Some Science Fic-
tion, Quandary, A Reflex, In a Glass of Cider,
But Outer Space, and We Vainly Wrestle with the
Blind Belief.)

29 The Poetry of Robert Frost. New York: Holt, Rinehart
and Winston, 1969.   Edited by Edward Connery Lathem.
Appended is a section of notes which includes bibliographical history of poems and their variants.   [It should be
noted that this volume is considered the definitive edition
of RF's poems].
      Contents: (same as Complete Poems of 1949 with the
      addition of In the Clearing and all later revisions
      or variants.)

30 Robert Frost: Poetry and Prose. New York: Holt,
Rinehart and Winston, 1972.   Edited by Edward Connery
Lathem and Lawrence Thompson.
      I.   Poetry: Selections from Eleven Books

[from] A Boy's Will

Into My Own
Ghost House
My November Guest
Love and a Question
Storm Fear
To the Thawing Wind
A Prayer in Spring

Flower-Gathering
A Dream Pang
In Neglect
Mowing
Revelation
The Trial by Existence
The Tuft of Flowers
The Demiurge's Laugh
October
Reluctance

[from] <u>North of Boston</u>

The Pasture
Mending Wall
The Death of the Hired Man
The Mountain
Home Burial
A Servant to Servants
After Apple-Picking
The Code
The Housekeeper
The Fear
The Wood-Pile

[from] <u>Mountain Interval</u>

The Road Not Taken
An Old Man's Winter Night
The Telephone
Hyla Brook
The Oven Bird
Birches
The Cow in Apple Time
The Hill Wife
"Out, Out--"
The Sound of Trees

[from] <u>New Hampshire</u>

New Hampshire
A Star in a Stoneboat
The Star-Splitter
Wild Grapes
The Witch of Coös
An Empty Threat
I Will Sing You One-O

Fire and Ice
Dust of Snow
Nothing Gold Can Stay
The Runaway
The Aim Was Song
Stopping by Woods on a Snowy Evening
For Once, Then, Something
The Onset
To Earthward
Not to Keep
The Lockless Door
The Need of Being Versed in Country Things

[from] West-Running Brook

Spring Pools
Devotion
On Going Unnoticed
A Passing Glimpse
Once by the Pacific
Lodged
A Minor Bird
Tree at My Window
The Peaceful Shepherd
The Thatch
A Winter Eden
Acquainted with the Night
The Lovely Shall Be Choosers
West-running Brook
Sand Dunes
A Soldier
The Door in the Dark
Sitting by a Bush in Broad Sunlight
Riders
On Looking Up by Chance at the Constellations
The Bear

[from] A Further Range

Two Tramps in Mud Time
The White-Tailed Hornet
A Blue Ribbon at Amesbury
A Drumlin Woodchuck
In Time of Cloudburst
Departmental
Desert Places
They Were Welcome to Their Belief

Neither Out Far Nor in Deep
Design
On a Bird Singing in Its Sleep
Afterflakes
Not Quite Social
Provide, Provide
Precaution
The Span of Life
The Hardship of Accounting
Not All There
Build Soil

[from] A Witness Tree

Beech
The Silken Tent
All Revelation
Happiness Makes Up in Height for What It Lacks
    in Length
Come In
Carpe Diem
The Most of It
The Subverted Flower
Willful Homing
The Discovery of the Madeiras
The Gift Outright
Our Hold on the Planet
The Lesson for Today
A Considerable Speck
November
The Rabbit-Hunter
It Is Almost the Year Two Thousand
In a Poem
A Question
Boeotian
The Secret Sits
An Answer
A Serious Step Lightly Taken

[from] Steeple Bush

A Young Birch
Directive
The Night Light
Bravado
A Mood Apart
The Fear of God

        Iota Subscript
        It Bids Pretty Fair
        A Case for Jefferson
        Why Wait for Science
        An Importer
        No Holy Wars for Them
        Take Something Like a Star

[from] In the Clearing

        Frontpiece (lines excerpted from "Kitty Hawk")
        Away!
        A Cabin in the Clearing
        Closed for Good
        One More Brevity
        Escapist--Never
        Accidentally on Purpose
        A Never Naught Song
        [Forgive, O Lord ...]
        The Draft Horse
        Ends
        Peril of Hope
        Lines Written in Dejection on the Eve of Great
            Success
        In a Glass of Cider
        From Iron
        [Four-Room Shack ...]
        [It Takes All Sorts ...]
        [In Winter in the Woods ...]

[excerpts from] A Masque of Reason

[excerpts from] A Masque of Mercy

II.   Other Samplings: Of Various Periods and Kinds

        Childhood Letters
        Early Verse ["La Noche Triste, " "Song of the
            Wave, " "A Dream of Julius Caesar, " "Caesar's
            Lost Transport Ships, " "The Traitor, " "Clear
            and Colder--Boston Common, " and "Warning"]
        High School Prose ["Petra and Its Surroundings, "
            "(Editorial), " and "A Monument to After-Thought
            Unveiled"]
        My Butterfly ["... the text as submitted for publi-
            cation. "]
        Letters About "My Butterfly"

Stories for His Children
Among the Poems He Left Behind: Group One
   ["When the Speed Comes, " 'Despair, " 'My
   Giving"]
Stories for Chicken Farmers
Letters About A Boy's Will and About Writing
Getting the Sound of Sense: An Interview
Early Letters to Untermeyer
A Way Out: A One-Act Play
Among the Poems He Left Behind: Group Two
   ["The Parlor Joke, " "A Correction, " "The
   Middletown Murder"]
We Seem to Lack the Courage to Be Ourselves:
   An Interview
Some Observations on Style
Education by Presence: An Interview
Six Rhymed Letters
Coaching a Younger Writer
Education by Poetry: A Meditative Monologue
Among the Poems He Left Behind: Group Three
   ["To Prayer I Think I Go, " and "The Offer"]
A Letter to The Amherst Student
Introduction to Robinson's King Jasper
Ten of His Favorite Books
On Crudities and Opposites: Two Letters
Among the Poems He Left Behind: Group Four
   ["Good Relief, " and "Winter Ownership"]
Poverty and Poetry: A Talk
The Poet's Next of Kin in a College: A Talk
This is My Best: A Choice of Sixteen Poems
A Selection of Couplets
What Became of New England: A Commencement
   Address
On a Passage in Paradise Lost: A Letter
The Figure a Poem Makes: An Introduction
The Doctrine of Excursions: A Preface
The Constant Symbol: An Introduction
Speaking of Loyalty: A Talk
Poetry and School: Remarks from His Notebooks
The Prerequisites: A Preface
Don't Get Converted. Stay: Excerpts from an
   Address
Aphoristic Lines of Poetry
Letters to an Incipient Biographer
Among the Poems He Left Behind: Group Five
   ["For Travelers Going Sidereal, " 'Pride of
   Ancestry"]

Observations and Declarations of a Poet-Statesman
On Extravagance: A Talk
Last Poem ["The Prophets Really Prophecy as
   Mystics The Commentators Merely by Statis-
   tics"]
Last Letter

2. ARTICLES

31   "Physical Culture. " High School Bulletin 13 (Lawrence,
      Mass.) (Dec 1891) p. 2.

32   "M. Bonner, Deceased. " High School Bulletin 13
      (Lawrence, Mass.) (Dec 1891) p. 3.

33   "Petra and Its Surroundings. " High School Bulletin
      (Lawrence, Mass.) (Dec 1891) pp. 1-2.

34   [Editorial]. High School Bulletin (Lawrence, Mass.)
      (May 1892).

35   "A Monument to After-Thought Unveiled. " High School
      Bulletin (June 1892) p. 10.

36   [Letter to the Editor]. The Independent (March 28, 1894).

37   "The American About and Abroad. " Lawrence Daily
      American (Feb 2, 1895).

38   "A Just Judge. " The Eastern Poultryman (March 1903).

39   "Old Welch Goes to the Show. " Farm-Poultry (Aug 15,
      1903) pp. 334-335.

40   "Dalkins' Little Indulgence. " Farm-Poultry (Dec 15,
      1905).

41   Preface to Memoirs of the Notorious Stephen Burroughs
      of New Hampshire. (New York: Dial Press,
      1924) pp. v-viii.

42   "Vocal Imagination. " Lewiston (Maine) Evening Journal
      (May 5, 1925) p. 3.

43 "The Poetry of Amy Lowell. " Christian Science Monitor
     (May 16, 1925) p. 8.

44 Introduction to The Arts Anthology: Dartmouth Verse
     1925.   (Portland, Me. : Mosher Press, 1925) pp.
     vii-ix.

45 [How a Poet Teaches]. New Student 5 (Jan 6, 1926) 1-3.

46 [The Manumitted Student]. New Student 6 (Jan 12, 1927)
     5-7.

47 Preface to A Way Out: A One Act Play.   (New York:
     Harbor Press, 1929).

48 "Education by Poetry: A Meditative Monologue. " Am-
     herst Graduates' Quarterly 20 (Feb 1931) 75-85.

49 Two Letters Written on His Undergraduate Days at Dart-
     mouth College in 1892.   (Hanover, N. H. : Printer's
     Devil Press, 1931).

50 [Comment on "Birches"]. Fifty Poets: An American
     Auto-Anthology, ed. William Rose Benét.   (New York:
     Duffield, 1930) p. 30.

51 A Letter to The Amherst Student.   The Amherst Student
     (March 25, 1935) pp. 1-2.

52 Introduction to King Jasper by Edwin Arlington Robinson.
     (New York: Macmillan, 1935) pp. v-xv.

53 "Reading of His Poems. " Proceedings of the American
     Academy of Arts and Letters and the National Insti-
     tute of Arts and Letters 2 (1936) 67-70.

54 [Ten Favorite Books]. Books We Like (Boston: Massa-
     chusetts Library Association, 1936) pp. 140-142.

55 Introduction to Threescore by Sarah N. Cleghorn.   (New
     York: Smith and Hass, 1936) pp. ix-xii.

56 "What Became of New England?" Oberlin Alumni Maga-
     zine (May 1938).

57 "Poverty and Poetry. " Biblia (Princeton University Li-
     brary) 9 (Feb 1938).

58   "The Poet's Next of Kin in College." Biblia (Princeton
      University Library) 9 (Feb 1938).

59   "The Doctrine of Excursions: A Preface." Bread Loaf
      Anthology (Middlebury: Middlebury College Press,
      1939) pp. xix-xx.

60   "Remarks Accepting the Gold Medal of the National In-
      stitute of Arts and Letters." National Institute of
      Arts and Letters News Bulletin 5 (1939) 1, 12.

61   "The Figure a Poem Makes." Introduction to Collected
      Poems of Robert Frost. (New York: Holt, 1939).

62   "The Constant Symbol." Atlantic Monthly 178 (Oct 1946)
      50-52.

63   "Speaking of Loyalty." Amherst Graduates' Quarterly 37
      (Aug 1948) 271-276.

64   "A Romantic Chasm." Preface to A Masque of Reason,
      Containing A Masque of Reason, A Masque of Mercy
      (Two New England Biblicals) Together with Steeple
      Bush and Other Poems. (London: Jonathan Cape,
      1948).

65   "Poetry and School." Atlantic Monthly 187 (June 1951)
      30-31.

66   "The Hear-Say Ballad." Introduction to Ballads Migrant
      in New England by Helen Hartness Flanders and
      Marguerite Olney. (New York: Farrar, Straus and
      Young, 1953) pp. xii-xiii.

67   "The Prerequisites." New York Times Book Review
      (March 21, 1954).

68   "The Commencement Address." Dartmouth Alumni Maga-
      zine 47 (July 1955) 14-16.

69   "'Perfect Day--A Day of Prowess'." Sports Illustrated
      (July 23, 1956) pp. 51-53.

70   A Talk for Students. (New York: Fund for the Republic,
      1956).

71   Introduction to A Swinger of Birches: A Portrait of

Robert Frost by Sidney Cox.   (New York: New York
University Press, 1957) pp. vii-viii.

72   "Maturity No Object. "   New Poets of England and America ed.   Donald Hall,   Robert Pack and Louis Simpson.
(New York: Meridian Books, 1957) pp. 10-12.

73   "It Takes a Hero to Make a Poem, " [with C. Day Lewis].
Claremont Quarterly 5 (Sp 1958) 27-34.

74   "On Emerson. "   Daedalus (Cambridge, Mass.) 88 (Fall
1959) 712-718.

75   "I Want Poets Declared Equal To.... "   New York Times
Magazine (May 15, 1960) 23,   105-106.

76   "Remarks on the Occasion of the Tagore Centenary. "
Poetry 99 (Nov 1961) 106-119.

77   "Between Prose and Verse. "   Atlantic Monthly 209 (Jan
1962) 51-54.

78   "Playful Talk. "   Proceedings of the American Academy
of Arts and Letters and the National Institute of Arts
and Letters 12 (1962) 180-189.

79   "On Extravagance. "   Dartmouth Alumni Magazine 55
(March 1963) 21-24.

80   Robert Frost: Farm-Poultryman, eds. Edward Connery
Lathem and Lawrence Thompson.   (Hanover: Dartmouth Publications, 1963).

81   "Before the Beginning and After the End of a Poem. "
Carrell 6 (1965) 135-141.

82   Robert Frost and the Lawrence, Massachusetts High
School Bulletin: The Beginnings of a Literary Career,
eds.   Edward Connery Lathem and Lawrence Thompson.   (New York: Grolier Club, 1966).

83   Selected Prose of Robert Frost, eds. Hyde Cox and Edward Connery Lathem.   (New York: Holt, Rinehart
and Winston, 1966).

84   "A Trip to Currituck, Elizabeth City, and Kitty Hawk
(1894). "   North Carolina Folklore 16 (1968) 3-8.

85 Robert Frost on Writing, ed. Elaine Barry.   (New Bruns-
        wick: Rutgers University Press, 1973).

3. PLAYS

86 A Way Out: A One Act Play.   New York: Harbor Press,
        1929.

87 The Cow's in the Corn, A One-Act Irish Play in Rhyme.
        Gaylordsville: The Slide Mountain Press, 1929.

88 The Guardeen.   Los Angeles: Ward Ritchie Press, 1943.

B. ROBERT FROST ON RECORDS AND FILMS

89 Robert Frost Reads His Poetry. Decca: 79033E.

90 Robert Frost Reads from His Own Works. Decca: 9172.

91 Robert Frost Reads His Poetry. Caedman: 1060.

92 Twentieth-Century Poetry in English: Robert Frost
   Reading His Own Poems. The Library of Congress
   Recording Laboratory: PL6.

93 Derry Down Derry: Readings by Lesley Frost. Folk:
   9733.

94 Robert Frost. Black & White: 30 minutes. Films, Inc.

95 Robert Frost. Color: 25 minutes. Unites States Information Service; National Audio-Visual Center.

96 Robert Frost: A Lover's Quarrel with the World. Black
   & White: 40 minutes. WGBH-TV; Holt, Rinehart and
   Winston.

C.   LETTERS AND INTERVIEWS

97   Anderson, Margaret B. Robert Frost and John Bartlett: The Record of a Friendship. New York: Holt, Rinehart and Winston, 1963.

98   The Letters of Robert Frost to Louis Untermeyer, ed. Louis Untermeyer. New York: Holt, Rinehart and Winston, 1963.

99   Selected Letters of Robert Frost, ed. Lawrence Thompson. New York: Holt, Rinehart and Winston, 1964.

100   Interviews with Robert Frost, ed. Edward Connery Latham. New York: Holt, Rinehart and Winston, 1966.

101   Family Letters of Robert and Elinor Frost, ed. Arnold Grade. Albany: State University of New York Press, 1972.

D. LIBRARIES WITH SIGNIFICANT MANUSCRIPT HOLDINGS

102 Agnes Scott College Library
     Decatur, Georgia

103 Beinecke Rare Book Room and Manuscript Library
     Yale University
     New Haven, Connecticut

104 Clifton Waller Barrett Library
     University of Virginia
     Charlottesville, Virginia

105 Dartmouth College Library
     Hanover, New Hampshire

106 Frost Room in the Julian Willis Abernathy Library of
         American Literature
     Middlebury College
     Middlebury, Vermont

107 Henry E. Huntington Library
     San Marino, California

108 Houghton Library
     Harvard University
     Cambridge, Massachusetts

109 Jones (Public) Library
     Amherst, Massachusetts

110 Library of Congress
     Washington, D. C.

111 Lockwood Memorial Library
     State University of New York
     Buffalo, New York

112 Mertins Collection

University of California, Berkeley Library
Berkeley, California

113   New York City Public Library
New York, New York

114   Olin Library
Wesleyan University
Middletown, Connecticut

115   Princeton University Library
Princeton, New Jersey

116   Robert Frost Library
Amherst College
Amherst, Massachusetts

117   Tufts University Library
Medford, Massachusetts

118   University of Chicago Library
Chicago, Illinois

119   University of Michigan Library
Ann Arbor, Michigan

120   University of Pittsburgh Library
Pittsburgh, Pennsylvania

121   University of Texas Library
Austin, Texas

122   Wellesley College Library
Wellesley, Massachusetts

PART TWO: SECONDARY MATERIAL

E. REVIEWS OF PRIMARY MATERIAL

123 A Boy's Will (1913)

Abercrombie, Lascelles. Nation (London) 15 (July 13, 1914) 423-424.

Academy 85 (Sept 20, 1913) 360.

Athenaeum 1 (April 5, 1913) 379.

Douglas, Norman. English Review 14 (June 1913) 505.

Firkins, O. W. Nation 101 (Aug 19, 1915) 228.

Flint, F. S. Poetry and Drama 1 (June 1913) 250.

Nation (London) 13 (Sept 20, 1913) 924.

New York Times Book Review (Aug 8, 1915) p. 288.

New York Times Book Review (Nov 21, 1915) p. 453.

Payne, William Morton. Dial 55 (Sept 16, 1913) 211-212.

Pound, Ezra. Poetry 2 (May 1913) 72-74.

Times Literary Supplement (London) (April 10, 1913) p. 155.

Times Literary Supplement (London) (July 2, 1914) p. 316.

Tynan, Katherine. Bookman 44 (June 1913) 129-130.

124 North of Boston (1914)

Akins, Zoe.   Reedy's Mirror 24 (May 7, 1915) 6-7.

Alden, Raymond M.   The Dial 59 (Sept 30, 1915) 274.

Aldington, Richard.   The Egoist 1 (July 1, 1914)
    247-248.

American Review of Reviews 51 (April 1915) 503.

Baxter, Sylvester.   American Review of Reviews 51
    (April 1915) 432-434.

Bradley, William Aspenwall.   The Bookman 41 (April
    1915) 191-192.

Braithwaite, William S.   Boston Evening Transcript
    (April 28, 1915) pt. 3, p. 4.

Brooklyn Daily Eagle (April 24, 1915) sec. 2, p. 5.

Brown, Alice.   Seminarian 11 (June 1915) 4-8.

Comer, Cornelia A. P.   Atlantic Monthly 117 (April
    1916) 496.

Current Opinion 58 (Jan 1915) 54-55.

Current Opinion 58 (June 1915) 427-428.

D., P. D.   Globe and Commercial Advertiser (April
    17, 1915) p. 8.

English Review 18 (Aug 1914) 142-143.

Garnett, Edward.   Atlantic Monthly 116 (Aug 1915)
    214-224.

Gibson, Wilfred Wilson.   Bookman 46 (July 1914) 183.

Henderson, Alice Corbin.   Dial 57 (Oct 1, 1914) 254.

Hueffer, Ford Maddox.   Outlook (London) 33 (June 27,
    1914) 879-880.

Independent 82 (May 31, 1915) 368.

Lowell, Amy.   New Republic 2 (Feb 20, 1915) 81-82.

Literary Digest 50 (May 15, 1915) 1165-1166.

Munro, Harold. Poetry and Drama 2 (Sept 1914) 310-313.

Pound, Ezra. Poetry 5 (Dec 1914) 127-130.

Rittenhouse, Jessie B. New York Times Book Review (May 16, 1915) p. 189.

Times Literary Supplement (London) (May 28, 1914) p. 263.

Untermeyer, Louis. Chicago Evening Post (April 23, 1915) p. 11.

125 Mountain Interval (1916)

American Review of Reviews 54 (Dec 1916) 674.

Bradley, William Aspenwall. Dial 61 (Dec 14, 1916) 530.

Braithwaite, William S. Bookman 45 (June 1917) 430-431.

_____. Boston Evening Transcript (Dec 2, 1916) pt. 3, p. 7.

Colum, Padraic. New Republic 9 (Dec 23, 1916) 219+.

Erskine, John. Yale Review 6 (Jan 1917) 379-395.

Firkins, O. W. Atlantic Monthly 120 (Oct 1917) 502.

Johonnot, Rodney F. Lewiston Evening Journal (Feb 11, 1917) Magazine sec., p. 12.

Literary Digest 52 (April 1, 1916) 908.

New York Times Book Review (Jan 7, 1917) p. 2.

Smith, Geddes. Independent 88 (Dec 25, 1916) 533-538.

Untermeyer, Louis. Seven Arts 1 (April 1917) 668-671.

126   New Hampshire (1923)

>Colum, Padraic.   Measure 35 (Jan 1924) 13-15.

>Dudley, Dorothy.   Poetry 23 (March 1924) 328-335.

>Farrar, John.   Literary Digest International Book Review 1 (Nov 1923) 25-26.

>Fletcher, John Gould.   Freeman 8 (Feb 27, 1924) 593-594.

>Howe, M. A. DeWolfe.   Atlantic Monthly 133 (Jan 1924) 10-12.

>Morton, David.   Outlook 135 (Dec 19, 1923) 688-689.

>Nicholl, Louise Townsend.   American Review 2 (Nov-Dec 1924) 679-683.

>Rankin, Thomas Ernest.   Michigan Education Journal 1 (April 1924) 363-364.

>Sackville-West, V.   Nation and Athenaeum 35 (July 12, 1924) 484.

>Springfield Republican (Nov 25, 1923) p. 7A.

>Squire, J. C.   London Mercury 10 (July 1924) 317-318.

>Times Literary Supplement (London) (July 24, 1924) p. 460.

>Untermeyer, Louis.   Bookman 58 (Jan 1924) 578-580.

127   Selected Poems (1923)

>Outlook 134 (Aug 1, 1923) 521.

>Snow, Wilbert.   Book Review (March 1925) pp. 11-12.

>Times Literary Supplement (London) (March 29, 1923) p. 213.

128   West Running Brook (1928)

Catholic World 129 (June 1929) 377.

Cleghorn, Sarah N.   World Tomorrow 12 (March
1929) 135.

Dial 86 (May 1929) 436.

Hutchinson, Percy.   New York Times Book Review
(Nov 18, 1928) p. 2.

Kilmer, Aline.   Commonweal 9 (Feb 20, 1929) 461.

Monroe, Harriet.   Poetry 33 (March 1929) 333-336.

Morrison, Theodore.   Atlantic Monthly 153 (Feb
1929) Bookshelf, 24.

O'Neill, G.   Outlook 151 (Jan 16, 1929) 110+.

Pierce, Frederick E.   Yale Review 18 (Dec 1928)
365-366.

Root, E. M.   Christian Century 46 (Jan 3, 1929) 18-
20.

Spencer, Theodore.   New Republic 58 (Feb 20, 1929)
24-25.

Untermeyer, Louis.   Saturday Review of Literature 5
(Dec 22, 1928) 533-536.

Van Doren, Mark.   Nation 128 (Jan 23, 1929) 110.

Whipple, Leon.   Survey 61 (Nov 1, 1928) 168-169.

129 Selected Poems (1928)

The Dial 86 (May 1929) 436.

Monroe, Harriet.   Poetry 33 (March 1929) 333-336.

Springfield Republican (Dec 30, 1928) p. 7E.

130 Collected Poems (1930)

Carpenter, Frederick I.   New England Quarterly 5
(Jan 1932) 159-160.

<u>Christian Century</u> 48 (Feb 18, 1931) 242.

Church, Richard.   <u>Spectator</u> 146 (Feb 21, 1931) 277.

Hicks, Granville.   <u>New Republic</u> 65 (Dec 3, 1930) 77-78.

Hillyer, Robert S. <u>Harvard Alumni Bulletin</u> 33 (March 19, 1931) 752-754.

_____.   <u>New England Quarterly</u> 5 (April 1932) 402-404.

<u>Milwaukee Journal</u> (May 5, 1931) sec. 2, p. 6.

Moore, Virginia.   <u>Yale Review</u> 20 (March 1931) 627-629.

<u>New Statesman</u> 36 (Dec 27, 1930) 365.

Nicholl, Louise Townsend.   <u>Outlook</u> 156 (Dec 10, 1930) 590.

Schneider, Isidor.   <u>Nation</u> 132 (Jan 28, 1931) 101-102.

Strong, L. A.   <u>Nation and Athenaeum</u> 48 (Jan 10, 1931) 486.

Taggard, Genevieve.   <u>New York Herald Tribune</u> (Dec 21, 1930) pp. 1, 6.

<u>Times Literary Supplement</u> (London) (Jan 29, 1931) p. 75.

Twitchett, E. G.   <u>London Mercury</u> 23 (March 1931) 496-498.

Untermeyer, Louis.   <u>Saturday Review of Literature</u> 7 (Jan 17, 1931) 529-530.

Warren, C. Henry.   <u>Bookman</u> 79 (Jan 1931) 242-244.

_____.   <u>Fortnightly</u> 135 (Feb 1931) 282-284.

White, Newman L.   <u>South Atlantic Quarterly</u> 30 (Oct 1931) 439-440.

Wilson, James Southall.   Virginia Quarterly Review
7 (April 1931) 316-320.

131 A Further Range (1936)

Benét, William Rose.   Saturday Review of Literature
14 (May 30, 1936) 6.

Blackmur, R. P.   Nation 142 (June 24, 1936) 817-819.

Brickell, Herschel.   New York Post (May 29, 1936)
p. 7.

Colum, Padraic.   Book-of-the-Month Club News
(May 1936)

Fitts, D.   New England Quarterly 9 (Sept 1936) 519-
520.

Gannett, Lewis.   New York Herald Tribune (May 30,
1936) 9.

Gregory, H.   New Republic 87 (June 24, 1936) 214.

Hall, J. N.   Atlantic Monthly 158 (Sept 1936) 388,
390.

Holmes, John.   Boston Evening Transcript (May 29,
1936) Book sec., 3.

Knowlton, Edgar C.   South Atlantic Quarterly 35 (Oct
1936) 460-462.

McBride, James.   Yale Review 25 (June 1936) 826-
827.

Moore, Merrill.   Sewanee Review 45 (Oct-Dec 1937)
507-509.

Morley, Christopher.   Book-of-the-Month Club News
(May 1936).

Nethercot, Arthur H.   Evanston Daily News Index
(June 4, 1936) p. 5.

Newdick, Robert S.   Columbus Sunday Dispatch (June
14, 1936) Passing Show sec., p. 5.

Payne, L. W. Dallas News (May 31, 1936) sec. 3,
p. 10.

Pritchett, V. S. Christian Science Monitor (June 17,
1936) Weekly magazine sec., p. 14.

Root, E. M. Christian Century 53 (Oct 7, 1936)
1329-1330.

St. Clair, G. New Mexico Quarterly 7 (Feb 1937)
63-67.

Strobel, Marion. Chicago Daily Tribune (June 6,
1936) p. 10.

Thompson, Ralph. New York Times (June 3, 1936)
p. 19.

Time 27 (June 8, 1936) 83.

Times Literary Supplement (London) (March 27, 1937)
p. 237.

Untermeyer, Louis. American Mercury 39 (Sept
1936) 123-125.

Walton, Eda Lou. New York Times Book Review
(May 31, 1936) pp. 1, 14.

Wheelwright, John. Poetry 49 (Oct 1936) 45-48.

Whicher, Harriet Fox. Amherst Graduates' Quarterly 25 (Aug 1936) 407-409.

132 Selected Poems (1936)

Newdick, Robert S. New England Quarterly 10 (Dec
1937) 817-818.

Times Literary Supplement (London) (Dec 12, 1936)
p. 1030.

Walton, G. Scrutiny 5 (March 1937) 443-444.

133 Selected Poems (1938)

Times Literary Supplement (London) (July 29, 1938)
p. 422.

134   Collected Poems (1939)

> Books (May 14, 1939) p. 17.
>
> Brooks, Cleanth.   Kenyon Review 1 (Sum 1939) 325-327.
>
> Forum 101 (April 1939) 240.
>
> Jones, H. M.   Boston Evening Transcript (March 4, 1939) p. 1.
>
> Orton, Vrest.   New England Quarterly 12 (Sept 1939) 563-567.
>
> Ritchey, John.   Christian Science Monitor (July 22, 1939) p. 10.
>
> Rukeyser, Muriel.   Poetry 54 (July 1939) 218-224.
>
> Springfield Republican (March 26, 1929) p. 7e.
>
> Times Literary Supplement (London) (Nov 18, 1939) p. 6.
>
> Tinker, E. L.   New York Times (April 2, 1939) p. 24.
>
> Wilson, J. S.   Virginia Quarterly Review 15 (Sp 1939) 303-305.

135   A Witness Tree (1942)

> Benét, S. V.   Saturday Review of Literature 25 (April 25, 1942) 7.
>
> Bookmark 3 (May 1942) 9.
>
> Brégy, Katherine.   Catholic World 155 (Aug 1942) 626.
>
> Colum, M. M.   New York Times (May 3, 1942) p. 5.
>
> Cleveland Open Shelf (May 1942) p. 12.
>
> Hillyer, Robert.   Atlantic Monthly 169 (June 1942) Bookshelf, 1.

Margashes, Adam.   Current History 2 (June 1942)
302.

Meredith, William.   New Republic 106 (June 1, 1942)
772.

New Yorker 18 (May 9, 1942) 79.

Porter, Kenneth.   New England Quarterly 15 (Sept
1942) 548.

Pratt Institute Quarterly (Dec 1942) p. 16.

Scott, Winfield Townley.   Poetry 60 (June 1942) 146-
149.

Snow, Wilbert.   Books (May 10, 1942) p. 5.

Time 39 (May 18, 1942) 91.

Whicher, George F.   Yale Review 31 (Sum 1942) 808.

Wisconsin Library Bulletin 38 (June 1942) 95.

136   "Come In" and Other Poems (1943)

Bishop, Ferman J.   Book Week (April 18, 1943) p. 8.

Bookmark 4 (March 1943) 10.

Collins, T. L.   New York Times (Aug 11, 1943) p.
12.

Jakeman, A. M.   Springfield Republican (April 4,
1943) p. 7e.

Maynard, Theodore.   Catholic World 157 (Aug 1943)
552.

Sloan, F. B.   Christian Science Monitor (Aug 26,
1943) p. 4.

Strachan, Pearl.   Christian Science Monitor (May 1,
1943) p. 10.

Time 41 (April 12, 1943) 100.

Whicher, George F. New York Herald Tribune Weekly Book Review. (April 4, 1943) p. 4.

Wisconsin Library Bulletin 39 (May 1943) 71.

137 A Masque of Reason (1945)

Aiken, Conrad. New Republic 112 (April 16, 1945) 514.

Bacon, Leonard. Saturday Review of Literature 28 (March 24, 1945) 24.

Bogan, L. New Yorker 21 (April 7, 1945) 83-84+.

Boston Globe (March 28, 1945) p. 17.

Brégy, Katherine. Catholic World 161 (Sept 1945) 522.

Christian Science Monitor (April 21, 1945) p. 12.

Cleveland Open Shelf (May 1945) p. 11.

Dupee, F. W. Nation 160 (April 21, 1945) 464-465.

Forgotson, E. S. Poetry 66 (June 1945) 156-159.

Fremantle, Ann. Commonweal 41 (March 30, 1945) 592.

Kennedy, Leo. Book Week (March 25, 1945) p. 3.

Kirkus 13 (Feb 1, 1945) 47.

Library Journal 70 (March 1, 1945) 219.

Newsweek 25 (April 2, 1945) 100-102.

Opie, T. F. Churchman 159 (July 1945) 19.

Schorer, Mark. Atlantic Monthly 175 (March 1945) 133.

Springfield Republican (March 25, 1945) p. 4d.

Theatre Arts 29 (Oct 1945) 607.

Thompson, Lawrance. New York Times (March 25, 1945) p. 3.

Time 45 (May 7, 1945) 99-100.

Van Doren, Mark. New York Herald Tribune Weekly Book Review (March 25, 1945) p. 1.

Whicher, George F. Yale Review 34 (Sp 1945) 549-551.

Wisconsin Library Bulletin 41 (May 1945) 52.

138 Steeple Bush (1947)

Bacon, Leonard. Saturday Review of Literature 30 (May 31, 1947) 15.

Bates, E. W. Christian Science Monitor (June 16, 1947) p. 16.

Brégy, Katherine. Catholic World 166 (Dec 1947) 279.

Campbell, Gladys. Poetry 71 (Dec 1947) 145.

Jarrell, Randall. Nation 165 (Nov 29, 1947) 589-592.

_____. New York Times (June 1, 1947) p. 4.

McDonald, George. Library Journal 72 (June 1, 1947) 889.

New Yorker 23 (June 7, 1947) 128.

Ross, Malcolm. Canadian Forum 27 (Nov 1947) 191.

Snell, George. San Francisco Chronicle (July 13, 1947) p. 20.

Stauffer, Donald A. Atlantic Monthly 180 (Oct 1947) 115-116.

Time 49 (June 16, 1947) 102.

Whicher, George F. New York Herald Tribune Weekly Book Review (July 6, 1947) p. 2.

Untermeyer, Louis. Yale Review 37 (Fall, 1947) 138.

139 A Masque of Mercy (1947)

Cleveland Open Shelf (Nov 1947) p. 21.

Cox, Sidney. New York Times (Nov 9, 1947) p. 6.

Hillyer, Robert. Saturday Review of Literature 30
(Dec 6, 1947) 54-56.

Kay, Alfred. San Francisco Chronicle (Oct 26, 1947)
p. 16.

Kirkus 15 (Aug 15, 1947) 461.

Jarrell, Randall. Nation 165 (Nov 29, 1947) 589-592.

McMillen, Lawrence. Hudson Review 1 (Sp 1948) 105-
107.

Olsen, Lawrence. Furioso (Carlton College, Minn.)
3 (Sp 1948) 47.

New Yorker 23 (Nov 1, 1947) 115.

Williams, William Carlos. Poetry 72 (April 1948)
38-41.

Wisconsin Library Bulletin 43 (Nov 1947) 150.

140 Complete Poems (1949)

Bookmark 9 (Oct 1949) 4.

Cleveland Open Shelf (July 1949) p. 15.

Daiches, David. New York Times Book Review (May
29, 1949) p. 1, 13.

Fitzgerald, Robert. New Republic 121 (Aug 8, 1949)
18.

Holmes, John. Saturday Review of Literature 32
(July 16, 1949) 9-10.

Humphries, R. Nation 169 (July 23, 1949) 92-93.

Johnston, J. H.   Commonweal 50 (July 8, 1949) 324.

Kennedy, Leo.   Chicago Sunday Times (June 20, 1949).

Kirkus 17 (June 15, 1949) 321.

Library Journal 74 (Sept 15, 1949) 1327.

New Yorker 25 (Oct 15, 1949) 139.

Time 53 (June 27, 1949) 94.

Times Literary Supplement (London) (March 9, 1951) p. 148.

Van Doren, Mark.   New York Herald Tribune Weekly Book Review (May 29, 1949) p. 1.

Viereck, Peter.   Atlantic Monthly 184 (Oct 1949) 67-70.

141   In the Clearing (1962)

Bogan, Louise.   New Yorker 38 (Nov 17, 1962) 242, 244.

Bookmark 21 (June 1962) 256.

Booth, Philip.   New York Times Book Review (March 25, 1962) p. 1.

Deen, Rosemary.   Commonweal 76 (May 4, 1962) 155.

Enright, D. J.   New Statesman 64 (Oct 19, 1962) 530.

Harding, Walter.   Chicago Sunday Tribune (March 25, 1962) p. 1.

Holmes, John.   Christian Science Monitor (March 29, 1962) p. 11.

Kell, Richard.   Guardian (Oct 19, 1962) p. 6.

Meredith, William.   Poetry 101 (Dec 1962) 200.

Montague, John. Spectator 210 (Sept 28, 1962) 445.

O'Donnell, William G. Massachusetts Review 4 (Fall 1962) 213-218.

Robie, B. A. Library Journal 87 (April 15, 1962) 1616.

Rosenthal, M. L. Reporter 26 (April 12, 1962) 50-52.

San Francisco Chronicle (March 25, 1962) p. 30.

Springfield Republican (March 25, 1962) p. 4d.

Times Literary Supplement (London) (Dec 21, 1962) p. 987.

Wilbur, Richard. New York Herald Tribune Books (March 25, 1962) p. 3.

Wisconsin Library Bulletin 58 (July 1962) 240.

142 Robert Frost, Farm-Poultryman (1963)

Engle, Paul. New York Times Book Review (Feb 23, 1964) p. 12.

Gohdes, Clarence. American Literature 36 (Nov 1964) 50.

Morse, S. F. Poetry 104 (July 1964) 253-257.

143 The Letters of Robert Frost to Louis Untermeyer (1963)

Anthony, Mother Mary. Best Sellers 23 (Oct 15, 1963) 248.

Brower, Reuben. New York Times Book Review (Sept 15, 1963) p. 6.

Carruth, Hayden. Nation 197 (Dec 14, 1963) 418.

Cox, James M. Saturday Review 46 (Oct 5, 1963) 43-44.

Critic 22 (Feb 1963) 91.

de Bellis, Jack. Sewanee Review 73 (Win 65) 166-
170.

Jackson, K. G. Harper's 227 (Nov 1963) 135.

Mann, C. W. Library Journal 88 (Oct 1, 1963)
3619-3620.

Meixner, John. Southern Review n. s., 2 (Oct 1966)
862-877.

Morse, S. F. Poetry 104 (July 1964) 253-257.

New Yorker 39 (Oct 26, 1963) 219.

Nordell, Roderick. Christian Science Monitor (Sept
12, 1963) p. 11.

Poirier, Richard. Book Week 1 (Sept 29, 1963) 5.

_____. Christian Century 80 (Oct 2, 1963) 1215.

Time 82 (Sept 20, 1963) 102.

Virginia Quarterly Review 40 (Win 1964) 26.

144   The Selected Letters of Robert Frost (1964)

Adams, Phoebe. Atlantic Monthly 214 (Sept 1964)
118.

Bemis, R. National Review 16 (Sept 22, 1964) 835.

Berger, Harry. Yale Review 54 (Dec 1964) 277.

Carruth, Hayden. Poetry 107 (Dec 1965) 192-195.

Chapin, K. G. New Republic 152 (Jan 2, 1965) 16.

Daiches, David. New York Times Book Review
(Sept 20, 1964) p. 5.

Deen, Rosemary F. Commonweal 81 (Oct 2, 1964)
53-55.

Edel, Leon. Saturday Review 42 (Sept 5, 1964) 23.

Fadiman, Clifton. Holiday 37 (March 1965) 34.

Flint, R. W. New York Review of Books 3 (Sept 10, 1964) 6.

Heath, Gary E. Vermont History n. s. , 32 (Oct 1964) 227-228.

Jarrell, Randall. Book Week (Aug 30, 1964) p. 1.

Kazin, Alfred. Commentary 38 (Dec 1964) 49.

Lynen, John F. Modern Age 9 (Win 1964-1965) 103-104.

Meixner, John. Southern Review n. s. , 2 (Oct 1966) 862-877.

Meredith, William. American Scholar 34 (Win 1964-1965) 130.

Newsweek 64 (Aug 31, 1964) 75-76.

New Yorker 40 (Sept 12, 1964) 208.

Nordell, Roderick. Christian Science Monitor (Sept 3, 1964) p. 7.

Pearce, Roy Harvey. Kenyon Review 27 (Win 1965) 167-171.

Schlueter, Paul. Christian Century 81 (Sept 30, 1964) 1216.

Thomas, W. B. NEA Journal 54 (March 1965) 69.

Tillinghast, Richard. Sewanee Review 74 (Sp 1966) 554-565.

Time 84 (Dec 11, 1964) 127.

Virginia Quarterly Review 41 (Win 1965) 16.

145   The Selected Prose of Robert Frost (1966)

Choice 3 (Dec 1966) 901.

Christian Science Monitor (Sept 8, 1966) p. 11.

Craig, G. Armour.   New York Times (July 24, 1966)
    p. 4.

Emerson, E. H.   Southern Review n. s. , 6 (April
    1970) 555-560.

Hicks, Granville.   Saturday Review 49 (July 1966) 23.

Mann, C. W.   Library Journal 91 (Sept 15, 1966)
    4116.

Perrine, Laurence.   Southwest Review 51 (Fall 1966)
    411-412.

Thompson, John.   New York Review of Books 7 (Jan
    26, 1967) 5.

146   The Poetry of Robert Frost (1969)

Bidart, F.   Partisan Review 38 (Nov 1971) 350-353.

Burns, G.   Southwest Review 56 (Sum 1971) 295-298.

Light, J. F.   Nation 210 (Jan 12, 1970) 26-28.

Miller, L. H.   Massachusetts Review 11 (Sum 1970)
    602-604.

Pritchard, W. H.   Atlantic Monthly 226 (Oct 1970)
    130+.

_____.   Hudson Review 23 (Win 1970-1971) 747-748.

F. BOOKS ON ROBERT FROST
(with a selection of reviews of some works)

147 Adams, Frederick B. To Russia with Frost. Boston:
     Club of Odd Volumes, 1963.

148 Anderson, Margaret Bartlett. Robert Frost and John
     Bartlett: The Record of a Friendship. New York:
     Holt, Rinehart & Winston, 1963.
     Meixner, John. Southern Review n. s. , 2 (Oct
          1966) 862-877.
     Morse, Samuel F. Poetry 104 (July 1964) 253-
          257.
     Tillinghast, Richard. Sewanee Review 74 (Sp 1966)
          554-565.

149 Ando, Ichiro. Robert Frost. Tokyo: 1958.

150 Anzai, Shichinosuke. Robert Frost no Shi. Tokyo:
     Tiagnshobo, 1972.

151 Barry, Elaine. Robert Frost. New York: Frederick
     Ungar, 1973.

152 Brower, Reuben. The Poetry of Robert Frost: Con-
     stellations of Intention. New York: Oxford Univer-
     sity Press, 1963.
     Allott, K. Modern Language Review 59 (Jan 1964)
          131-133.
     Cleophas, Sister M. Thought 38 (Win 1963) 613-
          615.
     DeMott, Benjamin. Harper's 226-227 (July 1963)
          91-92.
     Fiscalini, Janet. Commonweal 78 (May 17, 1963)
          228-229.
     Fuchs, Daniel. Chicago Review 16 (#4 1964) 193-
          200.
     Fussell, Paul. Saturday Review 46 (June 15,
          1963) 27, 43.

Lane, M. Travis. Fiddlehead [Fredericton, New Brunswick] (Fall 1964) 20.

MacNeice, Louis. New Statesman 66 (July 12, 1963) 46.

Meredith, William. Massachusetts Review 5 (Fall 1963) 177-180.

Moore, Marianne. Modern Philology 62 (Aug 1964) 88.

Morse, Samuel F. Poetry 104 (July 1964) 253-257.

Mulder, William. American Literature 36 (May 1964) 242-243.

Napier, John. Voices (Sept 1963) 45.

Nims, J. F. College English 25 (Dec 1963) 239-240.

Perrine, Laurence. Southwest Review 48 (Sum 1963) 301.

Tanner, Tony. Spectator 211 (Oct 18, 1963) 498.

Times Literary Supplement (London) (Aug 20, 1964) 746.

Thompson, Lawrence. New York Times Book Review (June 23, 1963) 6.

Tomlinson, C. Critical Quarterly (London) 8 (Sp 1966) 90.

153   Clemens, Cyril. A Chat with Robert Frost. Webster Groves, Mo. : International Mark Twain Society, 1940.

154   Coffin, Robert P. Tristram. New Poetry of New England: Frost and Robinson. Baltimore: Johns Hopkins, 1938.

Saturday Review of Literature 19 (Oct 19, 1938) 20.

Times Literary Supplement (London) (Jan 7, 1939) 14.

Walton, E. L. Books (Jan 1, 1939) 12.

155   Cook, Reginald L. The Dimensions of Robert Frost. New York: Rinehart, 1958.

Brown, Calvin S. American Oxonian 46 (1958) 88-90.

Cox, James M. Kenyon Review 21 (Win 1959) 149-154.

Frankenberg, Lloyd. New York Times Book Review (July 6, 1958) 4.

McDonnell, Thomas P. Catholic World 187 (1958)

396-397.

New York Herald Tribune Books (July 6, 1958) 4.

Parrish, W. M.   Quarterly Journal of Speech 44
(Oct 1958) 335-336.

156   Cox, James M. , ed.   Robert Frost: A Collection of
Critical Essays.   Englewood Cliffs, N. J. :   Prentice-
Hall, 1962.

157   Cox, Sidney.   Robert Frost: Original 'Ordinary' Man.
New York: Holt, 1929.
New York Evening Post (March 23, 1929) 11m.
New York World (April 7, 1929) 11m.

158   _____.   A Swinger of Birches: A Portrait of Robert
Frost.   New York: New York University, 1957.
Craig, G. Armour.   American Scholar 26 (Sum
1957) 385.
Edwards, John.   Books Abroad 31 (Fall 1957)
419-420.
Jarrell, Randall.   New York Times (March 10,
1957) 5.
Scott, W. T.   Saturday Review 40 (May 4, 1957)
26.
Wilson, Garff B.   Quarterly Journal of Speech 43
(Dec 1957) 440-441.

159   Doyle, John R. , Jr.   The Poetry of Robert Frost: An
Analysis.   Johannesburg: W. T. Watersrand Univer-
sity Press, 1962.
Allott, K.   Modern Language Review 59 (Jan 1964)
131-133.
Fiscalini, Janet.   Commonweal 78 (May 17, 1963)
228-229.
Haresnape, G.   Books Abroad 37 (Sp 1964) 185.
Lynch, M. C.   Spirit 30 (July 1963) 84.
Lyons, C.   American Literature 35 (March 1964)
105.
Tillinghast, Richard.   Sewanee Review 74 (Sp
1966) 554-565.
Times Literary Supplement (London) (Feb 1, 1963)
76.

160   Faber, Doris.   Robert Frost: American Poet.   Englewood Cliffs, N. J. :   Prentice-Hall, 1964 (For grades
4-7).

161   Ford, Caroline.   The Less Traveled Road: A Study of
        Robert Frost.   Cambridge: Harvard University Press,
        1935.
            Holmes, John.   Boston Evening Transcript (Feb 8,
            1936) Book sec. , 2.
            Williams, S. T.   New England Quarterly 8 (Dec
            1935) 624.

162   Francis, Robert.   Frost: A Time to Talk.   Amherst:
        University of Massachusetts Press, 1972.

163   Frost, Lesley.   New Hampshire's Child: The Derry
        Journals of Lesley Frost.   Albany: State University
        of New York Press, 1969.

164   Frost: Centennial Essays.   Compiled by the Committee
        on the Frost Centennial of the University of Southern
        Mississippi.   Jackson: University Press of Mississip-
        pi, 1974.

165   Gerber, Philip L.   Robert Frost (Twayne United States
        Authors Series, 107) New York: Twayne, 1966.

166   Gould, Jean.   Robert Frost: The Aim Was Song.   New
        York: Dodd, Mead & Co. , 1964.
            Daiches, David.   New York Times Book Review
            (Sept 20, 1964) 5.
            Mann, C. W.   Library Journal 89 (May 1, 1964)
            1953.

167   Grant, Douglas.   Robert Frost and His Reputation (pam-
        phlet).   Parkville, Australia: Melbourne University
        Press, 1965.

168   Greenberg, Robert and James G. Hepburn, eds.   Robert
        Frost: An Introduction.   New York: Holt, Rinehart
        and Winston, 1961.

169   Greiner, Donald J.   A Guide to Robert Frost.   Colum-
        bus: Charles E. Merrill, 1969.   [pamphlet].

170   Hillyer, Robert.   A Letter to Robert Frost and Others.
        New York and London: A. A. Knopf, 1937.
            American Literature 9 (Nov 1937) 397.
            Boie, M.   Atlantic Monthly 160 (Nov 1937) Book-
            shelf.
            Brunini, J. G.   Commonweal 27 (Dec 3, 1937) 164.

Lazare, C. Nation 145 (Nov 23, 1937) 538-539.
Millspaugh, C. A. Poetry 51 (Feb 1938) 267-270.
Untermeyer, Louis. Saturday Review of Litera-
ture 41 (Sept 18, 1937) 4-5.
Walton, E. L. New York Times Book Review
(Sept 19, 1937) 9.

171   Isaacs, Elizabeth. An Introduction to Robert Frost.
Denver: Alan Swallow, 1962.
Barron, L. College English 25 (Jan 1964) 306.
Cox, James M. American Literature 35 (Nov
1963) 391.
Tillinghast, Richard. Sewanee Review 74 (Sp
1966) 554-565.
Willingham, J. R. Library Journal 87 (March 1,
1963) 1015.

172   Jennings, Elizabeth. Frost. New York: Barnes &
Noble, 1966.

173   Kataoka, Jintaro. Robert Frost Kenkyu. Tokyo:
Hokuseido, 1973.

174   Lathem, Edward C. A Concordance to the Poetry of
Robert Frost. New York: Holt Information Systems,
1971.

175   Longo, Lucas. Robert Frost: Twentieth Century Modern American Poet Laureate. Charlotteville, N. Y. :
Samttar Press, 1972 (for young Readers).

176   Lynen, John F. The Pastoral Art of Robert Frost
(Yale Studies in English, 147) New Haven: Yale
University Press, 1960.
Allott, Kenneth. Modern Language Review 57
(April 1962) 256-257.
Anderson, Charles R. Modern Language Notes 76
(Dec 1961) 910-913.
Brower, Reuben A. New England Quarterly 34
(June 1961) 243-252.
Cox, James M. Virginia Quarterly Review 36
(Sum 1960) 469-473.
Ganz, Robert Norton. Journal of English and
Germanic Philology 60 (Jan 1961) 188-191.
Nitchie, George W. American Literature 33 (No.
1, 1961) 94-96.
Pinto, V. de S. Critical Quarterly 3 (Sp 1961)

93-94.
Thompson, Lawrence.   Saturday Review 43 (July
2, 1960) 22-23.

177   Mertins, Louis.   Robert Frost, Life and Talks-Walking.
Norman: University of Oklahoma Press, 1965.

178   Morrison, Kathleen.   Robert Frost: A Pictorial Chronicle.   New York: Holt, Rinehart and Winston, 1974.

179   Munson, Gorham B.   Robert Frost: A Study in Sensi-
bility and Good Sense.   New York: Doran, 1927.
The Dial 84 (Jan 1928) 72.
Fenn, W. W.   New England Quarterly 1 (April
1928) 246-249.
Mansfield, Margery.   Poetry 31 (Feb 1928) 292.
Mumford, Lewis.   New York Herald Tribune (Nov
6, 1927) 1+.
Nation 126 (Feb 1, 1928) 129.
New York Times (May 13, 1928) 15.
New York World (Feb 26, 1928) 11m.
Pittsburgh Monthly Bulletin 33 (Feb 28, 1928) 115.
Warren, Robert Penn.   New Republic 54 (May 16,
1928) 399-401.

180   Nitchie, George W.   Human Values in the Poetry of
Robert Frost: A Study of a Poet's Convictions.
Durham: Duke University Press, 1960.
Anderson, Charles R.   Modern Language Notes 76
(Dec 1961) 913-916.
Brower, Reuben A.   New England Quarterly 34
(June 1961) 243-252.
Cox, James M.   Virginia Quarterly Review 36
(Sum. 1960) 469-473.
Ganz, Robert Norton.   Journal of English and
Germanic Philology 60 (Jan 1961) 188-191.
Mulder, William.   American Literature 33 (no. 1,
1967) 96-97.
Thompson, Lawrence.   Saturday Review 43 (July
2, 1960) 22-23.

181   Orton, Vrest.   Vermont Afternoons with Robert Frost.
Rutland, Vermont: Charles E. Tuttle, 1971.

182   Reeve, F. D.   Robert Frost in Russia.   Boston: Little,
Brown & Co., 1964.

183   Richards, Norman. Robert Frost. Chicago: Children's
         Press, 1968 (for young Readers).

184   Sergeant, Elizabeth S. Robert Frost: The Trial by
         Existence. New York: Holt, Rinehart and Winston,
         1960.
         Aquin, Sister Mary. America 103 (July 2, 1960)
            420.
         Bogan, Louise. New Yorker 36 (Oct 8, 1960) 197.
         Booth, Philip. Christian Science Monitor (June
            16, 1960) 11.
         Brower, Reuben. New England Quarterly 34 (June
            1961) 243-252.
         Christian Century 77 (Sept 14, 1960) 1060.
         Cox, James M. Virginia Quarterly Review 36
            (Sum 1961) 469-473.
         Finnegan, Sister Mary Jeremy. Catholic World
            192 (Sept 1960) 383.
         Kriecht, Edward W. Chicago Sunday Tribune
            (June 19, 1960) 5.
         Lynen, John F. Journal of English and Germanic
            Philology 60 (Jan 1961) 111-119.
         Miller, Perry. New York Herald Tribune Books
            (June 19, 1960) 1, 12.
         Nitchie, George W. American Literature 33 (no.
            1, 1961) 94-96.
         Robie, B. A. Library Journal 85 (May 15, 1960)
            1898.
         Scott, W. T. New York Times Book Review
            (June 19, 1966) 1.
         Springfield Republican (July 17, 1960) 40.
         Thompson, Lawrence. Saturday Review 43 (July
            2, 1960) 22-23.
         Townley, Winfield. New York Times Book Review
            (June 19, 1960) 1.
         Weeks, Edward. Atlantic Monthly 206 (Aug 1960)
            95.

185   Simpson, Lewis P. The Merrill Profile of Robert
         Frost. Columbus: Charles E. Merrill, 1971.

186   Smythe, Daniel. Robert Frost Speaks. New York:
         Twayne, 1964.

187   Sohn, David A. and Richard Tyre. Frost: The Poet
         and His Poetry. New York: Holt, Rinehart and
         Winston, 1967.

188   Squires, Radcliffe. The Major Themes of Robert Frost.
      Ann Arbor: University of Michigan Press, 1963.
            Anderson, Charles R. American Literature 36
            (May 1964) 243-244.
            Fiscalini, Janet. Commonweal 78 (May 17, 1963)
            228-229.
            Fuchs, Daniel. Chicago Review 16 (#4 1964) 193-
            200.
            Gibbons, K. G. Books Abroad 37 (Fall 1963) 451.
            Morse, Samuel F. Poetry 104 (July 1964) 253-
            257.
            Perrine, Laurence. Southwest Review 48 (Sum
            1963) 301.
            Robie, Burton A. Library Journal 88 (Oct 1,
            1963) 3622.
            Rogers, David M. Cross-Currents 13 (Fall 1963)
            512.
            Tanner, Tony. Spectator 211 (Oct 18, 1963) 498-
            499.
            Tillinghast, R. Sewanee Review 74 (Sp 1966)
            554-565.
            Times Literary Supplement (London) (Aug 20,
            1964) 746.

189   Tatham, David. A Poet Recognized: Notes About Rob-
      ert Frost's First Trip to England and Where He
      Lived. Syracuse, N. Y. , 1970.

190   Thompson, Lawrence. Emerson and Frost: Critics of
      Their Times. Philadelphia: Philo-Biblon Club, 1940.

191   _____ . Fire and Ice: The Art and Thought of Rob-
      ert Frost. New York: Holt, 1942.
            Atlantic 170 (Oct. 1942) 142.
            Coffin, Robert P. Tristram. American Literature
            14 (Jan 1943) 435-440.
            Library Journal 67 (Aug 1942) 682.
            New Republic 107 (Oct 5, 1942) 422.
            Survey 31 (Dec 1942) 602.
            Wisconsin Library Bulletin 38 (Nov 1942) 159.

192   _____ . Robert Frost (University of Minnesota Pam-
      phlets on American Writers, 2). Minneapolis:
      Minnesota University Press, 1960.

193   _____ . Robert Frost: The Early Years, 1874-1915.
      New York: Holt, Rinehart and Winston, 1966.

Anderson, Quentin. Nation 204 (Feb 6, 1967) 182-184.

Bogan, Louise. New Yorker 43 (March 4, 1967) 162.

Brower, Reuben A. Partisan Review 34 (Win 1967) 116-124.

Cox, James M. Virginia Quarterly Review 43 (April 1967) 318-322.

DeMott, Benjamin. Book Week 4 (Nov 13, 1966) 5.

Early, James. Southwest Review 52 (Sp 1967) 199.

Howes, Barbara. Poetry 110 (Sept 1967) 425-426.

Lask, Thomas. New York Times (Nov 1, 1966) 39.

Maddocks, Melvin. Christian Science Monitor (Nov 31, 1966) B13.

Maloff, Saul. Newsweek 68 (Oct 31, 1966) 112-113.

Mann, C. W. Library Journal 91 (Nov 1, 1966) 5389.

McAleer, J. J. Thought 42 (Sp 1967) 125-126.

Morgan, H. Wayne. Journal of American History 53 (March 1967) 838.

Poirier, Richard. New York Times Book Review (Nov 6, 1966) 4.

Sampley, A. M. South Atlantic Quarterly 66 (Sp 1967) 269-270.

Spencer, B. T. American Literature 39 (Nov 1967) 419-421.

Thompson, John. New York Review of Books (Jan 26, 1967) 5.

Time 88 (Oct 28, 1966) 114+.

Times Literary Supplement (London) (Dec 14, 1967) 1201.

Untermeyer, Louis. Saturday Review 49 (Nov 5, 1966) 32-33.

194 _____. Robert Frost: The Years of Triumph, 1915-1938. New York: Holt, Rinehart and Winston, 1970.

Aldridge, J. W. Saturday Review 53 (Aug 15, 1970) 21-23.

Duffy, M. Time 96 (Aug 31, 1970) 720.

Epstein, J. Book World 4 (Sept 13, 1970) 3, 6.

French, R. W. Nation 211 (Sept 7, 1970) 185-186.

Jacobson, D. Commentary 52 (July 1971) 90-94.

Jerome, J. Writer's Digest 51 (Feb 1971) 43-47.

Lask, Thomas. New York Times (Aug 11, 1970)

35.
Pritchard, W. H. Hudson Review 23 (Fall 1970)
    577.
Spencer, B. T. American Literature 43 (March
    1971) 139-142.
Stanford, D. E. Southern Review 7 (Fall 1971)
    17-21.
Times Literary Supplement (London) (April 16,
    1971) 433-434.
Tyler, D. Michigan Quarterly Review 11 (Sp 1972)
    135-136.
Vendler, Helen. New York Times Book Review
    (Aug 9, 1970) 1.
Wolff, G. Newsweek 76 (Aug 24, 1970) 66-68.

195 Thornton, Richard, ed. Recognition of Robert Frost.
    New York: Holt, 1937.
        American Literature 10 (March 1938) 113-114.
        DeVoto, Bernard. Saturday Review of Literature
            17 (Jan 1, 1938) 3-4+.
        Morrison, Theodore. New England Quarterly 11
            (June 1938) 430.
        Walton, E. L. New York Times Book Review
            (Jan 30, 1938) 9.

196 Untermeyer, Louis. Robert Frost: A Backward Look.
    Washington: Library of Congress, 1964. [Lecture].

197 Wilson, Ellen. Robert Frost: A Boy with Promises to
    Keep. Indianapolis: Bobbs-Merrill, 1967 (for young
    Readers).

G. PARTS OF BOOKS ON ROBERT FROST

198 Aldridge, J. W. "The Other Frost" in The Devil in
the Fire: Retrospective Essays on American Literature and Culture 1951-1971. New York: Harper's
Magazine Press, 1972, pp. 134-141.

199 Angoff, Charles. "Robert Frost" in The Tone of the
Twenties and Other Essays. South Brunswick, N.
J. : A. S. Barnes, 1966, pp. 62-68.

200 Auden, W. H. "Robert Frost" in The Dyer's Hand and
Other Essays. New York: Random House, 1962, pp.
337-353.

201 Blankenship, Russell. American Literature as an Expression of the National Mind. New York: Holt,
Rinehart and Winston, 1931, pp. 588-594.

202 Bogan, Louise. "Robert Frost" in Achievement in
American Poetry. Chicago: Henry Regnery, 1951,
pp. 44-48.

203 Boynton, Percy H. "Robert Frost" in Some Contemporary Americans. Chicago: University of Chicago
Press, 1924, pp. 33-49.

204 Breit, H. "Robert Frost" in Writer Observed. Cleveland: World Publishing, 1956, pp. 95-97.

205 Brenner, Rica. "Robert Frost" in Ten Modern Poets.
New York: Harcourt-Brace, 1930, pp. 1-28.

206 Brooks, Cleanth. "Frost, MacLeish and Auden" in
Modern Poetry and the Tradition. Chapel Hill: University of North Carolina Press, 1939, pp. 110-135.

207 Brower, Reuben A. "The Americanness and Un-Ameri-
canness of Robert Frost. " 1967 Proceedings of [the]

Conference of College Teachers of English of Texas,
ed. Martin Shockley.   Lubbock: Texas Tech. College,
1967, pp. 6-10.

208   Burnshaw, S. A.   [Review of New Hampshire].   Modern
Essays of Various Types, ed. Charles A. Cockayne.
New York: Merrill, 1927, pp. 291-292.

209   Calverton, Victor F.   The Liberation of American Literature.   New York: Octagon Books, 1973, pp. 414-
418.

210   Canby, H. S.   "Homespun Philosophers" in Seven Years'
Harvest.   London: W. Heinemann, 1934, pp. 49-53.

211   Celli, Aldo.   "Il Momento Simbolico nella Poesia di
Robert Frost."   Il Simbolismo nella Literatura Nord-
Americana, ed. Mario Praz.   Florence: La Nuova
Italia, 1965, pp. 207-257.

212   Church, R.   "Robert Frost: A Prophet in His Own
Country" in Eight for Immortality.   London: J. M.
Dent & Sons, 1941, pp. 27-40.

213   Ciardi, John.   Dialogue with an Audience.   Philadelphia:
Lippincott, 1963, pp. 147-195.

214   Cook, Howard W.   "Robert Frost" in Our Poets of Today.   New York: Moffat, 1918, pp. 30-34.

215   Cooke, Alistair.   "Robert Frost" in Talk About America.
New York: Knopf, 1968, pp. 202-208.

216   Cowley, Malcolm.   "The Case Against Mr. Frost."
Robert Frost: A Collection of Critical Essays, ed.
James M. Cox.   Englewood Cliffs, N. J. :   Prentice-
Hall, 1962, pp. 36-45.

217   _____.   "Robert Frost: A Dissenting Opinion."   A
Many-Windowed House, ed. Henry Dan Piper.   Car-
bondale: Southern Illinois University Press, 1970,
pp. 201-212.

218   Cox, James M.   "Introduction."   Robert Frost: A Collection of Critical Essays.   Englewood Cliffs, N. J. :
Prentice-Hall, 1962, pp. 1-15.

219 Cunliffe, Marcus. The Literature of the United States.
     London: Penguin, 1954, pp. 251-253.

220 Dabney, Lewis M. "Mortality and Nature: A Cycle of
     Frost's Lyrics" in Private Dealings: Eight Modern
     American Writers. Stockholm: Almquist & Wiksell,
     1970, pp. 11-31.

221 Deutsch, Babette. "The Glove of a Neighborhood" in
     Poetry in Our Time. New York: Holt, 1952, pp.
     59-84.

222 _____. This Modern Poetry. New York: W. W.
     Norton, 1935, pp. 39-45, 162-164.

223 DeVoto, Bernard A. "Waste Land" in The Literary
     Fallacy. Boston: Little, Brown & Co. , 1944, pp.
     95-123.

224 Donoghue, Denis. "Robert Frost" in Connoisseurs of
     Chaos. New York: Macmillan, 1965, pp. 160-189.

225 Drinkwater, John, Henry Sirdel and William Rose Benét,
     eds. Twentieth Century Poetry. Boston: Houghton,
     1929, pp. 326-338.

226 Elliott, G. R. "The Neighborly Humour of Robert
     Frost" in The Cycle of Modern Poetry: A Series of
     Essays Toward Clearing Our Present Poetic Dilemma.
     Princeton: Princeton University Press, 1929, pp.
     112-134.

227 Elmen, P. "Robert Frost: The Design of Darkness. "
     Four Ways of Modern Poetry, ed. Nathan A. Scott.
     Richmond: John Knox Press, 1965, pp. 33-50.

228 Erskine, John. "Robert Frost" in The Kinds of Poetry
     and Other Essays. New York: Duffield, 1920, pp.
     123-126.

229 Fairchild, Hoxie N. "Realists" in Religious Trends in
     English Poetry 9. New York: Columbia University
     Press, 1939, 234-238.

230 Farrar, John. "New Hampshire, by Robert Frost. "
     Modern Essays of Various Types, ed. Charles A.
     Cockayne. New York: Merrill, 1927, pp. 283-291.

231 Fisher, Dorothy C. "Robert Frost. " Vermonters, ed.
     Walter H. Crockett. Brattleboro, Vt. : Stephen
     Daye, 1931, pp. 102-105.

232 Foster, C. H. "Robert Frost and the New England
     Tradition" in Elizabethan Studies and Other Essays
     [in honor of George F. Reynolds]. Boulder: Studies
     in Humanities, 1942, pp. 370-381.

233 Freeman, J. [Robert Frost]. Contemporary American
     Authors, ed. J. C. Squire, et. al. New York: Holt,
     1928, pp. 15-42.

234 Garnett, Edward. "Robert Frost's North of Boston" in
     Literary Criticisms and Appreciations. London:
     Jonathan Cape, 1922, pp. 221-242.

235 Gordon, J. B. "Robert Frost's Circle of Enchantment. "
     Modern American Poetry: Essays in Criticism, ed.
     J. Mazzaro. New York: David McKay, 1970, pp.
     60-92.

236 Graves, Robert. "Introduction. " Selected Poems [by
     Robert Frost]. New York: Holt, Rinehart and Win-
     ston, 1963, pp. ix-xiv.

237 Gregory H. and M. A. Zaturenska. "The Horatian Se-
     renity of Robert Frost" in The History of American
     Poetry, 1900-1940. New York: Harcourt, Brace,
     1942, pp. 150-162.

238 Gross, Harvey S. "Modern Poetry in the Metrical
     Tradition" in Sound and Form in Modern Poetry.
     Ann Arbor: University of Michigan Press, 1964, pp.
     65-67.

239 Hicks, Granville. "Two Roads" in The Great Tradition:
     An Interpretation of American Literature Since the
     Civil War. New York: International, 1935, pp. 207-
     256.

240 Hillyer, Robert. "A Letter to Robert Frost" in A Let-
     ter to Robert Frost and Others. New York: Knopf,
     1937.

241 Holliday, Robert Cortes. "Small Hours with Robert
     Frost" in Literary Lanes and Other Byways. New

York: Doran, 1925, pp. 27-32.

242 Howe, Irving. "Robert Frost: A Momentary Stay" in
A World More Attractive: A View of Modern Literature and Politics. New York: Horizon Press, 1963,
pp. 144-157.

243 Jarrell, Randall. "Robert Frost's 'Home Burial'" in
The Third Book of Criticism. New York: Farrar,
Straus & Giroux, 1969, pp. 191-231; also in The
Moment of Poetry, ed. D. C. Allen. Baltimore:
Johns Hopkins Press, 1962, pp. 99-132.

244 _____. "To the Laodicians" in Poetry and the Age.
New York: Random House, 1955, pp. 34-62; also in
Robert Frost: A Collection of Critical Essays, ed.
James M. Cox. Englewood Cliffs, N. J.: Prentice-
Hall, 1962, pp. 83-104.

245 _____. "The Other Frost" in Poetry and the Age.
New York: Random House, 1955, pp. 26-33.

246 Jones, Howard Mumford. "The Cosmic Loneliness of
Robert Frost" in Belief and Disbelief in American
Literature. Chicago: University of Chicago Press,
1967, pp. 116-142.

247 Jones, Llewellyn. "Robert Frost" in First Impressions:
Essays on Poetry, Criticism, and Prosody. New
York: Knopf, 1925, pp. 37-52.

248 Kennedy, John F. "The Artist in America." American Culture in the 60s, ed. V. Colby. New York:
H. W. Wilson, 1964, pp. 113-115.

249 Kjørven, Johannes. "Two Studies in Frost." Ameri-
cana-Norvegica: Norwegian Contributions to American Studies 2. Philadelphia: University of Pennsylvania Press, 1968, 191-218.

250 _____. "Robert Frost's Dialogue: Self-discovery in
the Midst of Belief and Unbelief" in Americana-
Norvegica: Norwegian Contributions to American
Studies Dedicated to Sigmund Skard. Oslo: Univer-
sitetsforlaget, 1973, 211-268.

251 Kreymbourg, Alfred. "The Fire and Ice of Robert

Frost" in Our Singing Strength. New York: Coward-
McCann, 1929, pp. 316-322.

252 [Kunitz, Stanley J.] "Robert Frost," by Dilly Tante
     [pseud.] in Living Authors: A Book of Biographies,
     New York: H. W. Wilson, 1931, pp. 135-136.

253 Lewisohn, Ludwig. Expression in America. New York:
     Harper & Brothers, 1932, passim.

254 Loggins, V. "Regional Variations" in I Hear America.
     New York: Biblo & Tanner, 1932, pp. 195-224.

255 Lowell, Amy. "Robert Frost" in Poets and Their Art.
     New York: Macmillan, 1926, pp. 56-62.

256 _____. "Robert Frost." Backgrounds of Book Re-
     viewing, ed. Herbert S. Mallory. Ann Arbor: Uni-
     versity of Michigan Press, 1931, pp. 124-140.

257 _____. Tendencies in Modern American Poetry.
     New York: Macmillan, 1917, pp. 79-136.

258 Lynen, John F. "The Poet's Meaning and the Poem's
     World." Modern Poetry, ed. J. Hollander. New
     York: Oxford University Press, 1968, pp. 485-500.

259 _____. "Frost as Modern Poet." Robert Frost: A
     Collection of Critical Essays, ed. James M. Cox.
     Englewood Cliffs, N. J.: Prentice-Hall, 1962, pp.
     177-197.

260 MacLeish, Archibald. "Robert Frost and John F. Ken-
     nedy" in A Continuing Journey. Boston: Houghton
     Mifflin, 1967, pp. 299-306.

261 Mallory, Herbert S. "November Host: A Footnote by
     the Editor." Backgrounds of Book Reviewing, ed.
     Herbert S. Mallory. Ann Arbor: University of
     Michigan Press, 1931, pp. 141-146.

263 Martin, Jay. Harvests of Change: American Literature,
     1865-1914. Englewood Cliffs, N. J.: Prentice-Hall,
     1967, pp. 159-164.

264 Maynard, Theodore. "Robert Frost: His Frostiness" in
     Our Best Poets: English and American. New York:

Holt, 1922, pp. 169-180.

265 Michaud Regis. Panorama de la Littérature Américaine.
     Paris: 1928, pp. 186-188.

266 Monroe, Harriet. Poets and Their Art. New York:
     Macmillan, 1926, pp. 56-62.

267 Montgomery, M. "Robert Frost and His Use of Barriers:
     Man vs. Nature Toward God. " Robert Frost: A Col-
     lection of Critical Essays, ed. James M. Cox. Engle-
     wood Cliffs, N. J.: Prentice-Hall, 1962, pp. 138-150.

268 Napier, John T. "A Momentary Stay Against Confusion. "
     Robert Frost: A Collection of Critical Essays, ed.
     James M. Cox. Englewood Cliffs, N. J.: Prentice-
     Hall, 1962, pp. 123-137.

269 Newdick, Robert S. "Robert Frost and the Sound of
     Sense. " This America, eds. J. D. Kern and I.
     Griggs. New York: Macmillan, 1942, pp. 569-581.

270 Nitchie, George F. "A Momentary Stay Against Con-
     fusion. " Robert Frost: A Collection of Critical Es-
     says. Englewood Cliffs, N. J.: Prentice-Hall, 1962,
     pp. 159-176.

271 O'Conner, W. V. "Robert Frost: Profane Optimist" in
     The Grotesque: An American Genre and Other Es-
     says. Carbondale: Southern Illinois University Press,
     1962, pp. 137-154.

272 O'Donnell, W. G. "Robert Frost and New England: A
     Revaluation. " Robert Frost: A Collection of Critical
     Essays, ed. James M. Cox. Englewood Cliffs, N. J.:
     Prentice-Hall, 1962, pp. 46-57.

273 Pattee, Fred Lewis. "Robert Frost" in The New Ameri-
     can Literature: 1890-1930. New York: Century,
     1930, pp. 298-302.

274 Payne, Leonidas W. "Robert Frost" in Later American
     Writers: Part Two of Selections from American
     Literature. Chicago: Rand McNally, 1927, pp. 921,
     932-937.

275 Pearce, Roy Harvey. The Continuity of American

Poetry. Princeton: Princeton University Press,
1961, pp. 271-283.

276 Phelps, William Lyon. "Vachel Lindsay and Robert
     Frost" in The Advance of English Poetry in the
     Twentieth Century. New York: Dodd, 1917, pp.
     213-244.

277 Poirier, Richard W. The Performing Self. New York:
     Oxford University Press, 1971, pp. 86-111.

278 _____. "Robert Frost" in The Paris Review: Writ-
     ers at Work. New York: Viking Press, 1963, pp.
     7-34.

279 Pound, Ezra. "Robert Frost" in Literary Essays. New
     York: New Directions, 1954, pp. 382-386.

280 Pritchard, William H. "North of Boston: Frost's Po-
     etry of Dialogue. " In Defense of Reading, eds.
     Reuben Brower and Richard Poirier. New York:
     Dutton, 1962, pp. 38-56.

281 _____. "Wildness of Logic in the Modern Lyric. "
     Forms of Lyric: Selected Papers from the English
     Institute, ed. Reuben Brower. New York: Columbia
     University Press, 1970, pp. 127-150.

282 Rittenhouse, Jessie. "Poetry of New England. " An-
     thology of Magazine Verse for 1926, ed. William S.
     Braithwaite. Boston: Brimmer, 1926, pp. 1-27.

283 Rosenthal, M. L. The Modern Poets: A Critical In-
     troduction. New York: Oxford University Press,
     1960, pp. 110-113.

284 Ryan, Alvan S. "Symbolic Action in the Poetry of
     Robert Frost. " Freie Gesellschaft 29. Heidelberg:
     1963, 295-312.

285 Schulz, Fraz. "A Momentary Stay Against Confusion:
     A Discussion of Robert Frost's Poetry as Seen by
     Four of His Critics. " Literatur und Sprache der
     Vereinigten Staaten. Heidelberg, 1969, 124-134.

286 Sergeant, Elizabeth S. "Robert Frost, Good Greek out
     of New England" in Fire Under the Andes: A Group

of North American Portraits. New York: Knopf,
1927, pp. 283-303.

287   Simpson, C. M.   "Robert Frost and Man's 'Royal
      Role.'" Aspects of American Poetry: Essays Pre-
      sented to Howard Mumford Jones, ed. Richard M.
      Ludwig. Columbus: Ohio State University Press,
      1962, pp. 121-147.

288   Siniavskii, A. D.   "Come Walk with Us" in For Freedom
      of Imagination [translated and with an introduction by
      L. Tikos and M. Peppord]. New York: Holt, Rine-
      hart and Winston, 1971, pp. 63-71.

289   Snow, C. P.   "Robert Frost" in Variety of Men. New
      York: Scribner's, 1967, pp. 130-150.

290   Southworth, J. G.   "Robert Frost" in Some Modern
      American Poets. Freeport, New York: Books for
      Libraries Press, 1968, pp. 42-87.

291   Spender, Stephen.   "Ebbtide in England: Frost and Ed-
      ward Thomas." Love-Hate Relations: English and
      American Sensibilities. New York: Random House,
      1974, pp. 170-177.

292   Spiller, R. E.   Cycle of American Literature. New
      York: Macmillan, 1955, pp. 211-242.

293   Straumann, Heinrich.   American Literature in the
      Twentieth Century. London, New York: Hutchinson's
      University Library Press, 1951, pp. 147-150.

294   Stevenson, Adlai E.   "Why Is Robert Frost Our Bard?"
      in Looking Outward. New York: Harper & Row,
      1963, pp. 277-280.

295   Stovall, Floyd.   "Robinson and Frost" in American
      Idealism. Norman: University of Oklahoma Press,
      1943, pp. 167-186.

296   Taylor, Walter F.   The Story of American Letters.
      Chicago: Henry Regnery, 1956, pp. 313-319.

297   Thompson, Lawrence R.   "Robert Frost." Seven Mod-
      ern American Poets, ed. L. Unger. Minneapolis:
      University of Minnesota Press, 1967, pp. 9-44.

298 _____. "Robert Frost's Theory of Poetry." Robert
        Frost: A Collection of Critical Essays, ed. James
        M. Cox. Englewood Cliffs, N. J.: Prentice-Hall,
        1962, pp. 16-35.

299 Thorp, Willard. American Writing in the Twentieth
        Century. Cambridge: Harvard University Press,
        1960, pp. 42-46.

300 _____. "The New Poetry." Literary History of the
        United States, 2d ed. Robert Spiller. New York:
        Macmillan 1949, 1189-1196.

301 Toliver, Harold E. "Frost's Enclosures and Clearings"
        in Pastoral Forms and Attitudes. Berkeley and Los
        Angeles: University of California Press, 1971, pp.
        334-360.

302 Trilling, Lionel. "A Speech on Robert Frost: A Cul-
        tural Episode." Robert Frost: A Collection of Criti-
        cal Essays, ed. James M. Cox. Englewood Cliffs,
        N. J.: Prentice-Hall, 1962, pp. 151-158.

303 Untermeyer, Louis. American Poetry Since 1900. New
        York: Holt, 1923, pp. 15-41.

304 _____. The New Era in American Poetry. New
        York: Holt, 1919, pp. 15-39.

305 _____. "The Northeast Corner" in From Another
        World: The Autobiography of Louis Untermeyer.
        New York: Harcourt, 1939, pp. 206-228.

306 _____. "Robert Frost" in Makers of the Modern
        World. New York: Simon & Schuster, 1955, pp.
        468-477.

307 _____. "Robert Frost." Facts and Ideas for Stu-
        dents of English Composition, eds. John O. Beaty,
        Ernest Leisy and Mary Lamar. New York: Crofts,
        1930, pp. 207-209.

308 Van Doren, Carl. "The Soil of the Puritans: Robert
        Frost" in Many Minds. New York: Knopf, 1924, pp.
        50-66.

309 _____ and Mark Van Doren. "Robert Frost" in

American and British Literature Since 1890. New
York: Century, 1925, pp. 20-23.

310   Van Doren, Mark.   "The Permanence of Robert Frost"
      in The Private Reader. New York: Holt, 1942, pp.
      87-96.

311   Waggoner, Hyatt H.   American Poets, From the Puri-
      tans to the Present. Boston: Houghton Mifflin, 1968,
      pp. 293-327.

312   _____.   "Robert Frost: The Strategic Retreat" in
      The Heel of Elohim. Norman: University of Okla-
      homa Press, 1950, pp. 41-60.

313   Warren, R. P.   "Themes of Robert Frost." The Writ-
      er and His Craft (Hopwood Lectures, 1932-1952; with
      foreword by Roy W. Cowden). Ann Arbor: Univer-
      sity of Michigan Press, 1954, pp. 218-233.

314   Watts, Harold H.   "Robert Frost and the Interrupted
      Dialogue." Robert Frost: A Collection of Critical
      Essays, ed. James M. Cox. Englewood Cliffs, N.
      J.: Prentice-Hall, 1962, pp. 105-122.

315   Weirick, Bruce.   From Whitman to Sandburg in Ameri-
      can Poetry. New York: Macmillan, 1924, pp. 177-
      184.

316   Wells, Henry W.   The American Way of Poetry. New
      York: Columbia University Press, 1943, pp. 106-
      121.

317   _____.   New Poets from Old. New York: Columbia
      University Press, 1940, pp. 80-84.

318   West, H. F.   "My Robert Frost Collection" in Mind on
      the Wing. New York: Coward-McCann, 1947, pp.
      51-72.

319   Weygandt, Cornelius.   The White Hills. New York:
      Holt, 1934, pp. 231-254.

320   Whicher, George F.   "In the American Grain." Litera-
      ture of the American People, ed. A. H. Quinn. New
      York: Appleton-Century-Crofts, 1951, pp. 903-907.

321 _____. "Out for Stars: A Meditation on Robert
     Frost" in Poetry and Civilization. Ithaca, N. Y.:
     Cornell University Press, 1955, pp. 19-30.

322 Whipple, T. K. Spokesmen: Modern Writers and Ameri-
     can Life. New York: Appleton, 1928, pp. 94-114.

323 Winters, Yvor. "Robert Frost: Or, The Spiritual Drift-
     er as Poet" in The Function of Criticism. Denver:
     Swallow Press, 1957, pp. 157-188.
          Also in Literary Opinion in America, ed. M. D.
          Zabel. New York: Harper & Row, 1962, pp.
          417-439.
          Also in Robert Frost: A Collection of Critical
          Essays, ed. James M. Cox. Englewood Cliffs,
          N. J.: Prentice-Hall, 1962, pp. 58-82.

324 Wood, Clement. "Robert Frost: The Twilight of New
     England" in Poets of America. New York: Dutton,
     1925, pp. 142-162.

H. SCHOLARLY ARTICLES

1913-1919

325 Hedges, M. H. "Creative Teaching. " School and Society 7 (Jan 27, 1918) 117-118.

326 Jepson, Edgar. "Recent United States Poetry. " English Review 26 (May 1918) 419-428.

327 Monroe, Harriet. "Frost and Masters. " Poetry 9 (Jan 1917) 202-207.

1920-1929

328 Aykroyed, George O. "The Classical in Robert Frost. " Poet Lore 40 (Dec 1929) 610-614.

329 Boynton, Percy H. [Robert Frost]. English Journal 11 (Oct 1922) 455-462.

330 Elliott, George R. "An Undiscovered America in Frost's Poetry. " Virginia Quarterly Review 1 (July 1925) 205-215.

331 Farrar, John. "Robert Frost and Other Green Mountain Writers. " English Journal 16 (Oct 1927) 581-587.

332 Jones, Llewellyn. "Robert Frost. " American Review 2 (March-April 1924) 165-171.

333 Monroe, Harriet. "Robert Frost. " Poetry 25 (Dec 1924) 146-153.

1930-1939

334 Bond, Marjorie N. "Robert Frost. " Twentieth

Century American Literature (University of North
Carolina Extension Bulletin) 13 (July 1933) 29-31.

335 Colophon 3 (Sum 1937) 470-477. 'Revisions in the Collected Poems. "

336 Cox, Sidney H. 'New England and Robert Frost. "
New Mexico Quarterly Review 4 (May 1934) 89-94.

337 Croff, Grace. "A Side-Light on Robert Frost. " Christmas Books (Hunter College) (Dec 1937) 29-30.

338 Dabbs, J. McBride. 'Robert Frost and the Dark Woods. "
Yale Review 23 (March 1934) 514-520.

339 _____ . 'Robert Frost, Poet of Action. " English
Journal 25 (June 1936) 443-451.

340 Eisenhard, John. 'Robert Frost: Peasant Poet. "
Scholastic 24 (April 28, 1934) 28-29.

341 Emerson, Dorothy. 'Robert Frost. " Scholastic 29
(Sept 19, 1936) 6-7.

342 Engle, Paul. "About Robert Frost. " American Prefaces 3 (April 1939) 100.

343 Fair, Jessie Frances. 'Robert Frost Visits the Demon-
stration Class. " English Journal 20 (Feb 1931) 124-
128.

344 Mitchell, Stewart. 'Notes on Nightingales. " New England Quarterly 5 (April 1932) 404-407.

345 Newdick, Robert S. "Children in the Poems of Robert
Frost. " Ohio Schools 15 (Sept 1937) 286-287, 313.

346 _____ . 'Design in the Books of Robert Frost. "
Reading and Collecting 1 (Sept 1937) 5-6, 15.

347 _____ . 'The Early Verse of Robert Frost and Some
of His Revisions. " American Literature 7 (May
1935) 181-187.

348 _____ . 'Robert Frost and the American College. "
Journal of Higher Education 7 (May 1936) 237-243.

349 _____ . ''Robert Frost and the Dramatic. '' New England Quarterly 10 (June 1937) 262-269.

350 _____ . ''Robert Frost Looks at War. '' South Atlantic Quarterly 38 (Jan 1939) 52-59.

351 _____ . ''Robert Frost and the Sound of Sense. '' American Literature 9 (Nov 1937) 289-300.

352 _____ . ''Robert Frost Speaks Out. '' Sewanee Review 45 (April-June 1937) 239-241.

353 _____ . ''Robert Frost as Teacher of Literature and Composition. '' English Journal 25 (Oct 1936) 632-637.

354 _____ . ''Some Notes on Robert Frost and Shakespeare. '' Shakespeare Association Bulletin 12 (July 1937) 187-189.

355 _____ . ''Three Poems by Robert Frost. '' American Literature 7 (Nov 1935) 329.

356 Payne, L. W. ''Scholarship and the Creative Writer. '' Texas Outlook 22 (Jan 1938) 40.

357 Romig, Edna Davis. ''To Robert Frost. '' English Journal 21 (Sept 1932) 537.

358 Scholastic 34 (Feb 4, 1939) 25. ''Gold Medal Poet. ''

359 Thomas, C. W. ''Double Wisdom. '' Wisconsin State Journal (June 21, 1936) 4.

360 Van Doren, Mark. ''The Permanence of Robert Frost. '' American Scholar 5 (Sp 1936) 190-198.

1940-1949

361 Berkelman, R. G. ''Robert Frost and the Middle Way. '' College English 3 (Jan 1942) 347-353.

362 Campbell, H. M. ''Frost's 'Sitting by a Bush in Broad Sunlight. '" Explicator 5 (Dec 1946) 18.

363 Cook, Reginald L. ''Frost as Parablist. '' Accent 10 (Aug 1949) 33-41.

364 _____. "Poet in the Mountains. " Western Review
         11 (Sp 1947) 175-181.

365 _____. "Robert Frost's Asides on His Poetry. "
         American Literature 19 (Jan 1948) 351-359.

366 _____. "Robert Frost as Teacher. " College English
         8 (Feb 1947) 251-255.

367 _____. "Robert Frost: A Time to Listen. " College
         English 7 (Nov 1945) 66-71.

368 Corbin, H. H. , Jr. and C. H. Hendricks. "Frost's
         'Neither Out Far Nor in Deep. '" Explicator 1 (May
         1943) 58.

369 Cox, Sidney H. "Mischief in Robert Frost's Ways of
         Teaching. " Educational Forum 13 (Jan 1949) 171-
         177.

370 _____. "Robert Frost and Poetic Fashion. " Ameri-
         can Scholar 18 (Win 1948-49) 78-86.

371 Davis, M. H. and E. L. Rose. "Robert Frost's
         'Mending Wall': A Lesson in Human Understanding. "
         High School Journal 26 (March 1943) 69-72.

372 Eckert, R. P. "Robert Frost in England. " Mark
         Twain Quarterly 3 (Sp 1940) 14-16.

373 Fletcher, John G. "Robert Frost the Outlander. "
         Mark Twain Quarterly 3 (Sp 1940) 5-8.

374 Foster, C. H. "Robert Frost and the New England
         Tradition. " University of Colorado Studies 2, series
         B (Oct 1945) 370-381.

375 Francis, R. "Shared Solitude of Robert Frost. "
         Forum 108 (Oct 1947) 193-197.

376 Hatfield, H. C. "Frost's 'The Masque of Reason. '"
         Explicator 4 (Nov 1945) 9.

377 Hayford, J. H. and Granville Hicks. "Literary Philos-
         ophy for 1942 on Criticism of Robert Frost. " Col-
         lege English 4 (Nov 1942) 133-135.

378 Horton, R. W. and Lawrance Thompson. "Frost."
     CEA Critic 11 (Feb 1949) 45.

379 Long, W. S. "Frost." CEA Critic 10 (Nov 1948) 4.

380 McGiffert, John. "Something in Robert Frost." English Journal 34 (Nov 1945) 469-471.

381 Mathias, Roland. "Robert Frost: An Appreciation."
     Poetry Review 38 (March-April 1947) 102-106.

382 Morse, Stearns. "The Wholeness of Robert Frost."
     Virginia Quarterly Review 19 (Sum 1943) 412-416.

383 Newdick, Robert S. "Robert Frost and the Classics."
     Classical Journal 35 (April 1940) 403-416.

384 _____. "Robert Frost's Other Harmony." Sewanee
     Review 48 (July 1940) 409-418.

385 O'Donnell, William G. "Parable in Poetry." Virginia
     Quarterly Review 25 (Sp 1949) 269-282.

386 _____. "Robert Frost and New England: A Revaluation." Yale Review 37 (Sum 1948) 698-712.

387 Perrine, Laurence. "Frost's 'Neither Far Out Nor in
     Deep.'" Explicator 7 (April 1949) 46.

388 Ryan, Alvan S. "Frost's A Witness Tree." Explicator
     7 (March 1949) 39.

389 Saul, G. B. "Brief Observations on Frost and Stevens."
     News Letter of the College English Association 4
     (Oct 1942) 6.

390 Spitz, Leon. "Robert Frost's Job Drama." American
     Hebrew 157 (Sept 12, 1947) 13, 89.

391 Waggoner, H. H. "Frost's 'A Masque of Reason.'"
     Explicator 4 (March 1946) 32.

392 _____. "The Humanistic Idealism of Robert Frost."
     American Literature 13 (Nov 1941) 207-223.

393 Walcutt, Charles C. "Frost's 'Death of a Hired Man.'"
     Explicator 3 (Oct 1944) 7.

394   Whicher, George F.   "Frost at Seventy. " American
        Scholar 14 (Aug 1945) 412-414.

395   Winters, Yvor.   "Robert Frost: Or, the Spiritual
        Drifter as Poet. " Sewanee Review 56 (Aug 1948)
        564-596.

                              1950-1959

396   Archibald, R. O.   "The Year of Frost's Birth. " Notes
        and Queries 199 (Jan 1954) 40.

397   Baker, Carlos.   "Frost on the Pumpkin. " Georgia Re-
        view 11 (Sum 1957) 117-131.

398   Beach, Joseph W.   "Robert Frost. " Yale Review 43
        (Dec 1953) 204-217.

399   Bowra, C. M.   "Reassessments: Robert Frost. "
        Adelphi 27 (Nov 1950) 46-64.

400   Broderick, John.   "Frost's 'Mending Wall. '" Explica-
        tor 14 (Jan 1956) 24.

401   Chatman, Seymour.   "Robert Frost's 'Mowing': An In-
        quiry into Prosodic Structure. " Kenyon Review 18
        (Sum 1956) 421-438.

402   Cook, Reginald L.   "Emerson and Frost: A Parallel
        of Seers. " New England Quarterly 31 (June 1958)
        200-217.

403   _____ .   "Frost on Analytic Criticism. " College
        English 17 (May 1956) 434-438.

404   _____ .   "Frost on Frost: The Making of Poems. "
        American Literature 28 (March 1956) 62-73.

405   _____ .   "Notes on Frost the Lecturer. " Quarterly
        Journal of Speech 42 (April 1956) 127-132.

406   _____ .   "The Stand of Robert Frost, Early and Late. "
        English Journal 48 (May 1959) 233-241, 261.

407   Cox, James M.   "Robert Frost and the Edge of the
        Clearing. " Virginia Quarterly Review 35 (Win 1959)
        73-88.

408   Cox, Sidney.   "The Courage to Be New: A Reappraisal
      of Robert Frost. "   Vermont History 22 (April 1954)
      119-126.

409   Donoghue, Denis.   "The Limitations of Robert Frost. "
      Twentieth Century 166 (July 1959) 13-22.

410   Doyle, John R.   "The Poetry of Robert Frost. "   Theoria
      12 (1959) 29-40.

411   _____.   "Some Attitudes and Ideas of Robert Frost. "
      English Studies in Africa 1 (Sept 1958) 164-183.

412   E. ,   C. D.   "Frost's 'The Road Not Taken. '"   Explicator
      17 (May 1959) Q3.

413   English Journal 39 (June 1950) 345.   "On Occasion of
      Robert Frost's 75th Birthday, U. S. Senate Resolu-
      tion. "

414   Fowle, Rosemary.   "The Indwelling Spider: An Aspect
      of the Poetry of Robert Frost. "   Papers of the Mich-
      igan Academy of Science, Arts and Letters 37 (1951)
      437-444.

415   Francis, Robert.   "Robert Frost from his Green Moun-
      tain. "   Dalhousie Review 33 (Sum 1953) 117-127.

416   Gierasch, Walter.   "Frost's 'Brown's Descent. '"   Ex-
      plicator 11 (June 1953) 60.

417   _____.   "Frost's 'The Last Mowing. '"   Explicator 10
      (Feb 1952) 25.

418   Greene, Marc T.   "Robert Frost at Home. "   Poetry
      Review 47-48 (Jan-March 1956) 16-18.

419   Griffith, Ben W.   "Frost's 'The Road Not Taken. '"
      Explicator 12 (June 1954) 55.

420   Hartstock, Mildred E.   "Frost's 'Directive. '"   Explica-
      tor 16 (April 1958) 42.

421   Hill, Archibald A.   "Principles Governing Semantic
      Parallels. "   Texas Studies in Literature and Language
      1 (Fall 1959) 356-365.

423   Hoffman, Daniel G.   "Frost's 'For Once, Then, Some-
        thing.'"   Explicator 9 (Nov 1950) 17.

424   _____.   "Robert Frost's Paul Bunyan: A Frontier
        Hero in New England Exile."   Midwest Folklore 1
        (April 1951) 13-18.

425   Hopkins, Bess Cooper.   "A Study of 'The Death of a
        Hired Man.'"   English Journal 43 (April 1954) 175-
        176, 186.

426   Jarrell, Randall.   "To the Laodiceans."   Kenyon Re-
        view 14 (Fall 1952) 535-561.

427   Kaplan, Charles.   "Frost's 'Two Tramps in Mud
        Time.'"   Explicator 12 (June 1954) 51.

428   Langbaum, Robert.   "The New Nature Poetry."   Amer-
        ican Scholar 28 (Sum 1959) 323-340.

429   Larson, Mildred R.   "No False Curves: Robert Frost
        on Education."   School and Society 72 (Sept 16,
        1950) 177-180.

430   _____.   "Robert Frost as Teacher."   Journal of
        Higher Education 22 (April 1951) 197-201.

431   Lasser, Michael L.   "The Loneliness of Robert Frost."
        Literary Review 3 (Win 1959-1960) 287-297.

432   Lewis, Arthur O.   "Frost's 'Departmental.'"   Explica-
        tor 10 (Oct 1951) 7.

433   Lord, Richard D.   "Frost and Cyclism."   Renascence
        10 (Fall 1957) 19-25, 31.

434   McLaughlin, Charles A.   "Two Voices of Poetic Unity."
        University of Kansas City Review 22 (Sum 1956)
        309-316.

435   Montgomery, Marion.   "Robert Frost and His Use of
        Barriers."   South Atlantic Quarterly 57 (Sum 1958)
        339-353.

436   Moynihan, William T.   "Fall and Winter in Frost."
        Modern Language Notes 73 (May 1958) 348-350.

437   Mulder, William.   "Freedom and Form: Robert

Frost's Double Discipline. " South Atlantic Quarterly 54 (July 1955) 386-393.

438 Munford, Howard. "Frost's 'The Subverted Flower. '"
     Explicator 17 (Jan 1959) 31.

439 Napier, John T. "A Momentary Stay Against Confu-
     sion. " Virginia Quarterly Review 33 (Sum 1957)
     378-394.

440 Nitchie, E. and M. L. Werner. "Frost's 'The Lovely
     Shall Be Choosers. '" Explicator 13 (April 1955) 37.

441 Ogilvie, John T. "From Woods to Stars: A Pattern
     of Imagery in Robert Frost's Poetry. " South Atlan-
     tic Quarterly 58 (Win 1959) 64-76.

442 Ornstein, Robert. "Frost's 'Come In. '" Explicator 15
     (June 1957) 61.

443 Pearce, Roy Harvey. "The Poet as Person. " Yale
     Review 41 (Sp 1952) 421-440.

444 Perrine, Laurence. "Frost's 'Sand Dunes. '" Explica-
     tor 14 (March 1956) 38.

445 Pierson, George W. "The Moving American. " Yale
     Review 44 (Sept 1954) 99-112.

446 _____. "The Obstinate Concept of New England: A
     Study in Denudation. " New England Quarterly 28
     (March 1955) 3-17.

447 Popkin, H. "Poets as Performers: Revival of Poetry
     Reading. " Theater Arts 36 (Feb 1952) 27+.

448 Rago, Henry. "Why We're Still Here. " Poetry 87
     (March 1956) 360-361.

449 Ryan, Alvan S. "Frost and Emerson: Voice and Vi-
     sion. " Massachusetts Review 1 (Oct 1959) 5-23.

450 Schartz, Edward. "Frost's 'The Lovely Shall Be
     Choosers. '" Explicator 13 (Oct 1954) 3.

451 Scott, Wilbur S. "Frost's 'To Earthward. '" Explica-
     tor 16 (Jan 1958) 23.

452 Sergeant, Howard. "The Poetry of Robert Frost. "
     English 9 (Sp 1952) 13-16.

453 Shalvey, T. J. "Valery and Frost: Two Views of Sub-
     jective Reality. " Renascence 11 (Sum 1959) 185-188.

454 Stallman, R. W. "The Position of Poetry Today. "
     English Journal 46 (May 1957) 241-251.

455 Stauffer, Donald B. "Frost's 'The Subverted Flower. '"
     Explicator 15 (March 1957) 38.

456 Trilling, Lionel. "A Speech on Robert Frost: A Cul-
     tural Episode. " Partisan Review 26 (Sum 1959)
     445-452.

457 Walcutt, Charles C. "Interpreting the Symbol. " Col-
     lege English 14 (May 1953) 446-454.

458 Watts, Harold H. "Robert Frost and the Interrupted
     Dialogue. " American Literature 27 (March 1955)
     69-87.

459 _____. "Three Entities and Robert Frost. " Buck-
     nell Review 5 (Dec 1955) 19-38.

460 Webster, H. T. "Frost's 'West-running Brook. '" Ex-
     plicator 8 (Feb 1950) 32.

461 Yates, Norris. "An Instance of Parallel Imagery in
     Hawthorne, Melville, and Frost. " Philological
     Quarterly 36 (April 1957) 276-280.

                         1960-1969

462 Ahluwalia, Harsharan S. "The 'Conservatism' of
     Robert Frost. " Bulletin of the New York Public
     Library 70 (Oct 1966) 485-494.

463 Allen, Ward. "Robert Frost's 'Iota Subscript. '" Eng-
     lish Language Notes 6 (June 1969) 285-287.

464 Anderson, Charles R. "'Nothing Gold Can Stay. '" Ex-
     plicator 22 (April 1964) 63.

465 _____. "On Robert Frost's 'Stopping by Woods on

a Snowy Evening. '" Kyushu American Literature 10
(1967) 1-10.

466 Anderson, James B.   'Frost and Sandburg: A Theological Criticism. " Renascence 19 (Sum 1967) 171-
183.

467 Angoff, Charles.   'Three Towering Figures: Reflec-
tions Upon the Passing of Robert Frost, Robinson
Jeffers and William Carlos Williams. " Literary
Review 6 (Sum 1963) 423-429.

468 _____.   'Robert Frost. " Forum 4 (Fall 1964) 11-14.

469 Armstrong, James.   'The 'Death Wish' in 'Stopping by
Woods. '" College English 25 (March 1964) 440-445.

470 Barnes, Lewis W.   'Robert Frost: Reconcilement
Through Expectancy, Surprise, and Congruency. "
Xavier University Studies 1 (Sum-Fall 1962) 223-237.

471 Bartlett, Donald.   'Two Recollections of Frost. "
Southern Review n. s. , 2 (Oct 1966) 842-846.

472 Baym, Nina.   "An Approach to Robert Frost's Nature
Poetry. " American Quarterly 17 (Win 1965) 713-
723.

473 Berger, Harry.   'Poetry as Revision: Interpreting
Robert Frost. " Criticism 10 (Oct 1968) 1-22.

474 Bishop, Ferman.   'Frost's 'The Wood-Pile. '" Explicator 18 (June 1960) 58.

475 Blum, Margaret M.   'Robert Frost's 'Directive': A
Theological Reading. " Modern Language Notes 76
(June 1961) 524-525.

476 Boroff, Marie.   'Robert Frost's 'The Most of It. '"
Ventures (Yale) 9 (Fall 1969) 77-82.

477 Bort, Barry D.   'Frost and the Deeper Vision. " Mid-
west Quarterly 5 (Fall 1963) 59-67.

478 Bowen, James K.   'The Persona in Frost's 'Mending
Wall': Mended or Amended? " CEA Critic 31 (Nov
1968) 14.

479   _____.   "Propositional and Emotional Knowledge in
         Robert Frost's 'The Death of a Hired Man,' 'The
         Fear,' and 'Home Burial.'"   CLA Journal 12 (Dec
         1968) 155-160.

480   Briggs, Pearlanna.   "Frost's 'Directive.'"   Explicator
         21 (May 1963) 71.

481   Broderick, John C.   "Not Quite Poetry: An Analysis
         of a Robert Frost Manuscript."   Manuscripts 20 (Sp
         1968) 28-31.

482   Burgess, C. F.   "Frost's 'The Oven Bird.'"   Explica-
         tor 20 (March 1962) 59.

483   Burrell, Paul.   "Frost's 'The Draft Horse.'"   Explica-
         tor 25 (March 1967) 60.

484   Carlson, Eric W.   "Robert Frost on 'Vocal Imagination':
         The Merger of Form and Content."   American Lit-
         erature 33 (Jan 1962) 519-522.

485   Carpenter, T. P.   "Robert Frost and Katherine Blunt:
         A Confrontation."   American Notes & Queries 8
         (Nov 1969) 35-37.

486   Chamberlain, William.   "The Emersonianism of Robert
         Frost."   Emerson Society Quarterly 57 (IV Quarter,
         pt. 2 1969) 61-66.

487   Chickering, Howell D.   "Robert Frost, Romantic Hu-
         morist."   Literature and Psychology 16 (Sum-Fall
         1966) 139-150.

488   Childs, K. W.   "Reality in Some of the Writings of
         Robert Frost and William James."   Proceedings of
         the Utah Academy of Science, Arts and Letters 44
         (1967) 150-158.

489   Cole, Charles W.   "Metaphor and Syllogism."   Massa-
         chusetts Review 4 (Win 1963) 239-242.

490   Combellack, C. R. B.   "Frost's 'The Oven Bird.'"
         Explicator 22 (Nov 1963) 17.

491   Comprone, Joseph J.   "Play and the 'Aesthetic State.'"
         Massachusetts Studies in English 1 (Sp 1967) 22-29.

492   Cook, Raymond A. "Robert Frost: Poetic Astronomer. "
      Emory University Quarterly 16 (Sp 1960) 32-39.

493   Cook, Reginald L. "A Fine Old Eye: The Unconquered
      Flame. " Massachusetts Review 4 (Win 1963) 242-249.

494   _____. "Frost the Diversionist. " New England
      Quarterly 40 (Sept 1967) 323-338.

495   _____. "Robert Frost's Constellated Sky. " Western
      Humanities Review 22 (Sum 1968) 189-198.

496   Corning, H. M. "Robert Frost: The Trial by Market. "
      Voices 184 (May-Aug 1964) 36-38.

497   Coursen, Herbert R.   "A Dramatic Necessity: The
      Poetry of Robert Frost. " Bucknell Review 10 (Dec
      1961) 138-147.

498   _____. "The Ghost of Christmas Past: 'Stopping by
      Woods on a Snowy Evening. '" College English 24
      (Dec 1962) 259-265.

499   Danzig, Allan. "An Unexpected Echo of Beddoes in
      Frost. " Notes & Queries 10 (April 1963) 150-151.

500   Davis, Charles G. "Frost's 'Acquainted with the
      Night. '" Explicator 27 (Nov 1968) 19.

501   DeFalco, Joseph M. "Frost's 'Paul's Wife': The
      Death of an Ideal. " Southern Folklore Quarterly 29
      (Dec 1965) 259-265.

502   Dendinger, Lloyd N. "The Irrational Appeal of Frost's
      Dark, Deep Woods. " Southern Review n. s. , 2 (Oct
      1966) 822-829.

503   _____. "Robert Frost: The Popular and Central
      Poetic Images. " American Quarterly 21 (Win 1969)
      792-804.

504   Donoghue, Denis. "A Mode of Communication: Frost
      and the 'Middle Style. '" Yale Review 52 (Dec 1962)
      205-219.

505   Dougherty, James P. "Robert Frost's 'Directive' to the
      Wilderness. " American Quarterly 18 (Sum 1966)
      209-219.

506 Dowell, Peter. "Counter-Images and Their Function in
     the Poetry of Robert Frost." Tennessee Studies in
     Literature 14 (1969) 15-30.

507 Dowell, Robert. "Revealing Incident as Technique in
     the Poetry of Robert Frost." CEA Critic 31 (Dec
     1968) 12-13.

508 Doyle, John R. "A Reading of Frost's 'Directive.'"
     Georgia Review 22 (Win 1968) 501-508.

509 Dragland, S. L. "Frost's 'Mending Wall.'" Explica-
     tor 25 (Jan 1967) 39.

510 Duvall, S. P. C. "Robert Frost's 'Directive' Out of
     Walden." American Literature 31 (Jan 1960) 482-
     488.

511 Eberhart, Richard. "Robert Frost: His Personality."
     Southern Review n. s. , 2 (Oct 1966) 762-788.

512 Ellis, James. "Frost's 'Desert Places' and Hawthorne. "
     English Record 15 (April 1965) 15-17.

513 Elsbree, Langdon. "Frost and the Isolation of Man. "
     Claremont Quarterly 7 (Sum 1960) 29-40.

514 Faulkner, Virginia. "More Frosting on the Woods. "
     College English 24 (April 1963) 560-561.

515 Ferguson, A. R. "Frost, Sill, and 'A-Wishing Well. '"
     American Literature 33 (Nov 1961) 370-373.

516 Ferguson, J. M. "Frost's 'After Apple Picking. '" Ex-
     plicator 22 (March 1969) 53.

517 Fleissner, Robert F. "Frost and Faust. " Notes and
     Queries n. s. , 12 (Oct 1965) 432.

518 Flint, F. C. "Frost at Dartmouth: Reminiscences. "
     Southern Review n. s. , 2 (Oct 1966) 830-838.

519 Francis, Robert. "Two Pictures. " Massachusetts Re-
     view 4 (Win 1963) 237-239.

520 Garland, H. B. "Robert Frost. " Nostro Tempo 12
     (1963) 16-17.

521   Geode, William.   'The 'Code Hero' in Frost's 'Blue-
         berries. '"   Discourse 11 (Win 1968) 26-31.

522   Gerber, Philip L.   '"My Rising Contemporaries':
         Robert Frost Amid His Peers. "   Western Humanities
         Review 20 (Sp 1966) 135-141.

523   Gibb, Carson.   'Frost's 'Mending Wall. '"   Explicator
         20 (Feb 1962) 48.

524   Grade, Arnold E.   "A Chronicle of Robert Frost's Early
         Reading, 1874-1899. "   Bulletin of the New York
         Public Library 72 (Nov 1968) 611-628.

525   Greenberg, Robert A.   'Frost in England: A Publish-
         ing Incident. "   New England Quarterly 34 (Sept 1961)
         375-379.

526   Greiner, Donald J.   '"A Few Remarks and Acknowledge-
         ments': An Unpublished Note. "   Notes and Queries
         n. s. , 15 (Aug 1968) 294-295.

527   _____ .   "Confusion and Form: Robert Frost as Na-
         ture Poet. "   Discourse 11 (Sum 1968) 390-402.

528   Griffith, Clark.   'Frost and the American View of Na-
         ture. "   American Quarterly 20 (Sp 1968) 21-37.

529   Gwynn, Frederick L.   "Analysis and Synthesis in Frost's
         'The Draft Horse. '"   College English 26 (Dec 1964)
         223-225.

530   _____ .   "Reply. "   to James Hoetker's article on '"The
         Draft Horse"   College English 26 (March 1965) 486.

531   Haight, Gordon S.   'Robert Frost at Yale. "   Yale Uni-
         versity Library Gazette 40 (July 1965) 12-17.

532   Hands, C. E.   'The Hidden Terror of Robert Frost. "
         English Journal 58 (Nov 1969) 1162-1168.

533   Hartstock, Mildred E.   'Robert Frost: Poet of Risk. "
         Personalist 45 (April 1964) 157-175.

534   Haugh, R. F.   'Intention and Achievement in Frost's
         Poetry. "   Voices 184 (May-Aug 1964) 41-42.

535 Heflin, Wilson.   "A Note on Frost's 'Love and a Ques-
     tion. '" Notes and Queries 16 (July 1969) 262.

536 Hepburn, James G.   "Robert Frost and His Critics. "
     New England Quarterly 35 (Sept 1962) 367-376.

537 Hoetker, James.   "Frost's 'The Draft Horse. '" College
     English 26 (March 1965) 485.

538 Hoffman, Daniel G.   "Thoreau's 'Old Settler' and Frost's
     'Paul Bunyan. '" Journal of American Folklore 73
     (July-Sept 1960) 236-238.

539 Hopkins, Vivian C.   "Robert Frost: Out Far and In
     Deep. " Western Humanities Review 14 (Sum 1960)
     247-263.

540 Howarth, Herbert.   "Frost in a Period Setting. "
     Southern Review n. s. , 2 (Oct 1966) 789-799.

541 Hunting, Robert.   "Who Needs Mending?" Western Hu-
     manities Review 17 (Win 1963) 88-89.

542 Huston, J. Dennis.   "'The Wonder of Unexpected Supply':
     Robert Frost and a Poetry beyond Confusion. " Cen-
     tennial Review 13 (Sum 1969) 317-29.

543 Irving, Jerome M.   "A Parting Visit with Robert Frost. "
     Hudson Review 16 (Sp 1963) 54-60.

544 Irwin, W. R.   "Robert Frost and the Comic Spirit. "
     American Literature 35 (Nov 1963) 299-310.

545 _____.   "The Unity of Frost's Masques. " American
     Literature 32 (Nov 1960) 302-312.

546 James, Stuart B.   "The Home's Tyranny: Robert
     Frost's 'A Servant to Servants' and Andrew Wyeth's
     'Christina's World. '" South Dakota Review 1 (May
     1964) 3-15.

547 Jensen, Arthur E.   "The Character of Robert Frost. "
     Southern Review n. s. , 2 (Oct 1966) 860-861.

548 Jerome, Judson.   "Robert Frost. " Humanist 23 (Mar-
     April 1963) 67.

549 Jones, Donald.   "Kindred Entanglements in Frost's 'A

Servant to Servants. '" Papers on Language and Literature 2 (Sp 1966) 150-161.

550   Joyce, Hewette E.   "A Few Personal Memories of
      Robert Frost. " Southern Review n. s. , 2 (Oct 1966)
      847-849.

551   Judd, Dorothy.   "Reserve in the Art of Robert Frost. "
      Texas Quarterly 6 (Sum 1963) 60-67.

552   Juhnke, Anna K.   "Religion in Frost's Poetry: The
      Play for Self-Possession. " American Literature 36
      (May 1964) 153-164.

553   Kantak, V. Y.   "How to Read a Frost Poem. " Literary Criterion 3 (Mysore, India) 4 (Sum 1960) 10-18.

554   _____.   "The Structure of a Frost Poem. " Literary
      Criterion 5 (Win 1962) 115-127.

555   Khan, Salamatullah.   "Levels of Meaning in Robert
      Frost's Poetry. " Literary Criterion 5 (Win 1962)
      110-114.

556   Knapp, E. H.   "Frost's 'Dust of Snow. '" Explicator
      28 (Sept 1969) 9.

557   Knox, George.   "A Backward Motion Toward the
      Source. " Personalist 47 (1966) 365-381.

558   Laing, Alexander.   "Robert Frost and Great Issues. "
      Southern Review n. s. , 2 (Oct 1966) 855-859.

559   Laing, Dilys.   "Interview with a Poet. " Southern Review n. s. , 2 (Oct 1966) 850-854.

560   Larson, Mildred R.   "Frost out of Chaos. " English
      Record 17 (April 1967) 2-6.

561   Lepore, D. J.   "Robert Frost--The Middle Ground: An
      Analysis of 'Neither Out Far Nor in Deep. '" English Journal 53 (March 1964) 215-216.

562   _____.   "Setting and/or Statement. " English Journal
      55 (March 1966) 624-626.

563   Leyburn, Ellen D.   "A Note on Robert Frost's A Masque

of Reason. " Modern Drama 4 (Feb 1962) 426-428.

564 Love, Glen A. "Frost's 'The Census-Taker' and de la
     Mare's 'The Listeners. '" Papers on Language and
     Literature 4 (Sp 1968) 198-200.

565 Lynen, John F. "Frost's Works and Days. " Journal
     of English and Germanic Philology 60 (Jan 1961) 111-
     119.

566 _____. "The Poet's Meaning and the Poem's World. "
     Southern Review n. s. , 2 (Oct 1966) 800-816.

567 MacDonald, Dwight. "Masscult and Midcoult. " Parti-
     san Review 27 (Sp 1960) 203-233 and (Fall 1960) 589-
     631.

568 Malbone, R. G. "Frost's 'The Road Not Taken. '" Ex-
     plicator 24 (Nov 1965) 27.

569 Mansell, D. "Frost's 'Range-Finding. '" Explicator 24
     (April 1966) 63.

570 Marinello, L. J. "Robert Frost's Inaugural Dedication:
     The Poet in Public Ceremony. " Today's Speech 9
     (Nov 1961) 22-23.

571 Martin, Wallace. "Frost's 'Acquainted with the Night. '"
     Explicator 26 (April 1968) 64.

572 Meredith, William. "Robert Frost in Book Review and
     Under the Aspect of Eternity. " Poetry 101 (Dec
     1962) 200-203.

573 Miller, Lewis H. "Two Poems of Winter. " College
     English 28 (Jan 1967) 314-317.

574 Monteiro, George. "Birches in Winter: A Note on
     Thoreau and Frost. " CLA Journal 12 (Dec 1968)
     129-133.

575 _____. "Redemption Through Nature: A Recurring
     Theme in Thoreau, Frost and Richard Wilbur. "
     American Quarterly 20 (Win 1968) 795-809.

576 _____. "Robert Frost and the Politics of Self. "
     Bulletin of the New York Public Library 73 (May
     1969) 309-314.

577   Moore, Robert P.   "The Eminently Teachable Mr.
      Frost. " English Journal 54 (Nov 1965) 693-698.

578   Morrow, Patrick.   "The Greek Nexus in Robert Frost's
      'West-Running Brook. " Personalist 49 (Win 1968)
      24-33.

579   Morse, Stearns.   "The Phoenix and the Desert Places. "
      Massachusetts Review 9 (Fall 1968) 773-784.

580   _____. "Something Like a Star. "   Southern Review
      n. s. , 2 (Oct 1966) 839-841.

581   Narveson, Robert.   "On Frost's 'The Wood Pile. '"
      English Journal 57 (Jan 1968) 39-40.

582   Nilakantan, Mangalam.   "Something Beyond Conflict: A
      Study of the Dual Vision of Robert Frost. " Indian
      Journal of American Studies 1 (July 1969) 25-34.

583   Nitchie, George W.   "Frost as Underground Man. "
      Southern Review n. s. , 2 (Oct 1966) 817-821.

584   Osborne, William R.   "Frost's 'The Oven Bird. '"   Ex-
      plicator 26 (Feb 1968) 47.

585   Parsons, Thornton H.   "Thoreau, Frost, and the Ameri-
      can Humanist Tradition. " Emerson Society Quarterly
      33 (IV Quarter 1963) 33-43.

586   Pearce, Roy Harvey.   "Frost's Momentary Stay. " Ken-
      yon Review 23 (Sp 1961) 258-273.

587   Pendleton, Conrad.   "The Classic Dimension of Robert
      Frost. " Prairie Schooner 38 (Sp 1964) 76-87.

588   Perrine, Laurence.   "Frost's 'The Rose Family. '"
      Explicator 26 (Jan 1968) 43.

589   _____ and Elenor M. Sickels.   "Frost's 'The Road
      Not Taken. '"   Explicator 19 (Feb 1961) 28.

590   _____ and Margaret M. Blum.   "Frost's 'The Draft
      Horse. '"   Explicator 24 (May 1966) 79.

591   Peters, Robert.   "The Truth of Frost's 'Directive. '"
      Modern Language Notes 75 (Jan 1960) 29-32.

592 Poirier, Richard. "Robert Frost: The Art of Poetry,
     II. " Paris Review 24 (Sum-Fall 1960) 88-120. [an
     interview collected by E. C. Lathem; see item 100].

593 Poss, Stanley. "Frost, Freud and Delmore Schwartz. "
     CEA Critic 30 (April 1968) 6-7.

594 _____. "Low Skies, Some Clearing, Local Frost. "
     New England Quarterly 14 (Sept 1968) 438-442.

595 Pritchard, William H. "Diminished Nature. " Massa-
     chusetts Review 1 (May 1960) 475-492.

596 Quinn, Sister M. Bernetta. "Symbolic Landscape in
     Frost's 'Nothing Gold Can Stay. '" English Journal
     55 (May 1966) 621-624.

597 Rao, C. Vimala. "The 'Other Mood': A Note on the
     Prose Works of Robert Frost. " Literary Criterion
     8 (Sum 1969) 63-69.

598 Robbins, J. Albert. "America and the Poet: Whitman,
     Hart Crane and Frost. " American Poetry 31 (1965)
     45-67.

599 Robson, W. W. "The Achievement of Robert Frost. "
     Southern Review n. s. , 2 (Oct 1966) 735-762.

600 Rockas, Leo. "I Choose Frost. " English Record 15
     (Feb 1965) 2-13.

601 Rosenberry, Edward H. "Toward Notes for 'Stopping
     by Woods': Some Classical Analogs. " College Eng-
     lish 24 (April 1963) 526-528.

602 Rubenstein, Annette T. "A Stay Against Confusion. "
     Science and Society 33 (Win 1969) 25-41.

603 St. Armand, Barton L. "The Power of Sympathy in the
     Poetry of Robinson and Frost: The 'Inside' vs. the
     'Outside' Narrative. " American Quarterly 19 (Fall
     1967) 564-574.

604 Sampley, Arthur M. "The Tensions of Robert Frost. "
     South Atlantic Quarterly 65 (Fall 1966) 431-437.

605 Saradhi, K. P. "Frost and Browning: The Dramatic

Mode. " Kyushu American Literature 10 (1967) 11-27.

606 Sasso, Laurence J. "Robert Frost: Love's Question. "
New England Quarterly 42 (March 1969) 95-107.

607 Saul, G. B. "A Frost Item. " Bulletin of the New York
Public Library 70 (Oct 1966) 484.

608 Shea, F. X. "'The Hill Wife': A Romance. " English
Record 16 (Feb 1966) 36-37.

609 Sheffey, Ruthe T. "From Delight to Wisdom: Thematic
Progression in the Poetry of Robert Frost. " CLA
Journal 8 (Sept 1964) 51-59.

610 Sinyazsky, A. "On Robert Frost's Poems, " [translated
by L. Tikos and F. C. Ellert]. Massachusetts Review 7 (Sum 1966) 431-441.

611 Slights, Camille and William. "Frost's 'The Witch of
Coos. '" Explicator 27 (Feb 1969) 40.

612 Snow, Wilbert. "The Robert Frost I Knew. " Texas
Quarterly 11 (Fall 1968) 9-48.

613 Stein, W. B. "'After Apple Picking': Echoic Parody. "
University Review 35 (Sum 1969) 301-305.

614 Stock, Ely. "A Masque of Reason and J. B. : Two
Treatments of the Book of Job. " Modern Drama 3
(Feb 1961) 378-386.

615 Stone, Albert E. "Robert Frost. " Emory University
Quarterly 21 (Sp 1965) 59-69.

616 Thornton, Welden. "Frost's 'Out, Out. '" Explicator
25 (May 1967) 71.

617 Todasco, Ruth. "Dramatic Characterization in Frost:
A Masque of Reason. " University of Kansas City
Review 29 (March 1963) 227-230.

618 Toor, D. "Frost's 'Spring Pools. '" Explicator 28 (Nov
1969) 28.

619 Townsend, R. C. "In Defense of Form: A Letter from
Robert Frost to Sylvester Baxter. " New England
Quarterly 36 (June 1963) 241-249.

620   Traschen, Isadore.   "Robert Frost: Some Divisions in
      a Whole Man. "   Yale Review 55 (Oct 1965) 57-70.

621   Vargish, A.   "The Child and Robert Frost. "   Vermont
      History 33 (Oct 1965) 469-475.

622   Walen, Harry L.   "A Man Named Robert Frost. "   Eng-
      lish Journal 55 (Oct 1966) 860-862.

623   Warnke, Frank J.   "Four American Poets: Frost, Jef-
      fers, Roethke and Lowell. "   Mitteilungsblatt des
      Allgemeinen Deutschen Neuphilologenverbandes (Berlin)
      (Jan 1964) 208-217.

624   Weinig, Sister Mary Anthony.   "Frost's 'Tuft of Flow-
      ers. '"   Concerning Poetry 2 (Sp 1969) 79.

625   Whitridge, Arnold.   "Robert Frost and Carl Sandburg:
      Two Elder Statesmen of American Poetry. "   Bulle-
      tin of the New York Public Library 66 (March 1962)
      164-177.

626   Wilcox, Earl.   "Frost's 'Stopping by Woods on a Snowy
      Evening, ' 8. "   Explicator 27 (Sept 1968) 7.

627   Willige, Eckhart.   "Formal Devices in Robert Frost's
      Short Poems. "   Georgia Review 15 (Fall 1961) 324-
      330.

628   Yevish, Irving A.   "Robert Frost: Campus Rebel. "
      Texas Quarterly 11 (Fall 1968) 49-55.

                              1970-1974

629   Abad, Gemino H.   "Stopping by Woods: The Hermeneu-
      tics of a Lyric Poem. "   Diliman Review 20 (1972)
      25-40.

630   Asnani, Shyam M.   "The Dark, Deep and Lovely Woods
      of Robert Frost. "   Banasthali Patrika 14 (1970) 45-
      47.

631   Bache, William B.   "Rationalization in Two Frost
      Poems. "   Ball State University Forum 11 (Win 1970)
      33-35.

632   Bacon, H. H.   "In- and Outdoor-Schooling: Robert

Frost and the Classics. " American Scholar 43 (Fall 1974) 640-649.

633 Ballatine, Lesley Frost. "Somewhat Atavistic. " Ball State University Forum 11 (Win 1970) 3-6.

634 Barnes, Daniel R. "Frost's 'Putting in the Seed. '" Explicator 31 (April 1973) 59.

635 Bass, Eben. "Frost's Poetry of Fear. " American Literature 43 (Jan 1972) 603-615.

636 Boroff, Marie. 'Robert Frost's New Testament: Language and the Poem. " Modern Philology 69 (Aug 1971) 36-56.

637 Bosmajian, Hamida. 'Robert Frost's 'The Gift Outright': Wish and Reality in History and Poetry. " American Quarterly 22 (Sp 1970) 95-108.

638 Bourdette, Robert E. and Michael M. Cohen. "Frost's 'Aim' and the Problem of Interpretation. " English Record 25 (Sp 1974) 53-63.

639 Braverman, Albert and Bernard Einbond. "Frost's 'Two Tramps in Mud Time. '" Explicator 29 (Nov 1970) 25.

640 Cane, Melville. 'Robert Frost: An Intermittant Intimacy. " American Scholar 40 (Win 1970-71) 158-166.

641 Carruth, Hayden. 'New England Traditions. " American Libraries 2 (Oct 1971) 939-948.

642 Clark, David R. "An Excursion upon the Criticism of Robert Frost's 'Directive. '" Costerus: Essays in English and American Language and Literature 8 (1973) 3-56.

643 _____. 'Robert Frost: 'The Thatch' and 'Directive. '" Costerus: Essays in English and American Language and Literature 7 (1973) 47-80.

644 Cohen, E. H. 'Robert Frost in England: An Unpublished Letter. " New England Quarterly 43 (June 1970) 285-287.

645 Combellack, C. R. B. "Frost's 'Spring Pools. '" Explicator 30 (Nov 1971) 27.

646   Cox, Keith. "A Syntactic Comparison of Robert Frost's
      ' ... Snowy Evening' and 'Desert Places.'" <u>Ball</u>
      <u>State University Forum</u> 11 (Win 1970) 25-28.

647   Crane, Joan St. C. "Issues and Binding Variants of
      Robert Frost's <u>A Boy's Will</u> and <u>North of Boston.</u> "
      <u>Serif</u> 8 (Sept 1971) 3-6.

648   D'Avanzo, Mario L. "Frost's 'A Young Birch': A
      Thing of Beauty." <u>Concerning Poetry</u> 3 (Fall 1970)
      69-70.

649   Dendinger, Lloyd N. "The Ghoul-Haunted Woodland of
      Robert Frost." <u>South Atlantic Bulletin</u> 38 (Nov 1973)
      87-94.

650   _____. "Robert Frost in Birmingham." <u>Ball State</u>
      <u>University Forum</u> 14 (Sum 1973) 47-52.

651   Dillingham, Richard. "The Value of Social Conserva-
      tism According to Robert Frost." <u>South Atlantic</u>
      <u>Bulletin</u> 37 (Nov 1972) 61-65.

652   Doxey, W. S. "Frost's 'Out, Out.'" <u>Explicator</u> 29
      (April 1971) 70.

653   Dube, Gunakar. "Autumn in Frost and Keats: A Study
      of Themes and Patterns." <u>Literary Criticism</u> 9
      (1970) 84-88.

654   Elkins, William J. "The Spiritual Crisis in 'Stopping
      by Woods.'" <u>Cresset</u> 35 (Feb 1972) 6-8.

655   Fitzgerald, Gregory and Paul Ferguson. "The Frost
      Tradition: A Conversation with William Meredith."
      <u>Sewanee Review</u> 57 (Sp 1972) 108-117.

656   Fleissner, Robert F. "Frost's 'Not All There.'" <u>Ex-</u>
      <u>plicator</u> 31 (Jan 1973) 33.

657   _____. "Frost's Response to Keats' Risibility."
      <u>Ball State University Forum</u> 11 (Win 1970) 40-43.

658   Foster, Richard. "Leaves Compared with Flowers: A
      Reading in Robert Frost's Poems." <u>New England</u>
      <u>Quarterly</u> 46 (Sept 1973) 403-423.

659   Freedman, W. "Frost's 'The Pasture.'" <u>Explicator</u>

29 (May 1971) 80.

660 Geyer, C. W. "A Poulterer's Pleasure: Robert Frost
     as Prose Humorist. " Studies in Short Fiction 8 (Fall
     1971) 589-599.

661 Gierasch, Walter. "Frost's 'The Silken Tent. '" Expli-
     cator 30 (Sept 1971) 10.

662 Greiner, Donald L. "On Teaching Robert Frost's 'Sen-
     tence Sounds. '" English Record 21 (Oct 1970) 11-14.

663 _____. "The Use of Irony in Robert Frost. " South
     Atlantic Bulletin 38 (May 1973) 52-60.

664 Grieder, J. "Robert Frost or Ezra Pound. " New Eng-
     land Quarterly 44 (June 1971) 301-305.

665 Hall, Dorothy J. "Painterly Qualities in Frost's Lyric
     Poetry. " Ball State University Forum 11 (Win 1970)
     9-13.

666 Haynes, Donald T. "The Narrative Unity of A Boy's
     Will. " PMLA 87 (May 1972) 452-464.

667 Herndon, J. A. "Frost's 'The Oven Bird. '" Explica-
     tor 28 (April 1970) 65.

668 Hiatt, D. "Frost's 'In White' and 'Design. '" Explica-
     tor 28 (Jan 1970) 41.

669 Hiers, John T. "Robert Frost's Quarrel with Science
     and Technology. " Georgia Review 25 (Sum 1971)
     182-205.

670 Holtz, William. "Thermodynamics and the Comic and
     Tragic Modes. " Western Humanities Review 25
     (Sum 1971) 203-216.

671 Jacobson, Dan. "Vurry Amurk'n. " The Review 25 (Sp
     1971) 3-10.

672 Jayne, Edward. "Up Against the 'Mending Wall': The
     Psychoanalysis of a Poem by Frost. " College Eng-
     lish 34 (April 1973) 934-951.

673 Kern, Alexander. "Frost's 'The Wood-Pile. '" Explica-
     tor 28 (Feb 1970) 49.

674   Kittredge, Selwyn.   "'Stopping by the [sic] Woods on a
      Snowy Evening'--Without Tugging at the Reins. "
      English Record 23 (Fall 1972) 37-39.

675   Lambdin, William G.   "Frost's 'The Oven Bird. '"   Ex-
      plicator 31 (Sept 1972) 3.

676   Lentricchia, Frank.   "Experience as Meaning: Robert
      Frost's 'Mending Wall. '"   CEA Critic 34 (May 1972)
      8-12.

677   _____.   "Robert Frost: The Aesthetics of Voice and
      the Theory of Poetry. "   Criticism 15 (Win 1973) 28-
      42.

678   Linder, Carl M.   "Robert Frost: Dark Romantic. "
      Arizona Quarterly 29 (Fall 1973) 235-245.

679   Lycette, Ronald L.   "The Vortex Points of Robert
      Frost. "   Ball State University Forum 14 (Sum 1973)
      54-59.

680   Martin, R. Glenn.   "Two Versions of a Poem by Robert
      Frost. "   Ball State University Forum 11 (Win 1970)
      65-68.

681   Meredith, William.   "In Memory of Robert Frost, " (a
      poem).   Shenendoah 21 (Sp 1970) 105-106.

682   Miller, Lewis H.   "The Poet as Swinger: Fact and
      Fancy in Robert Frost. "   Criticism 16 (Win 1974)
      58-72.

683   Monteiro, George.   "Frost's 'After Apple-Picking. '"
      Explicator 30 (March 1972) 62.

684   _____.   "Good Fences Make Good Neighbors: A
      Proverb and a Poem. "   Revista de Etnografia 16
      (1972) 83-88.

685   _____.   "Robert Frost's Linked Analogies. "   New
      England Quarterly 46 (Sept 1973) 463-468.

686   _____.   "Robert Frost's Solitary Singer. "   New Eng-
      land Quarterly 44 (March 1971) 134-140.

687   Morris, John.   "The Poet as Philosopher: Robert

Frost. " Michigan Quarterly Review 11 (Sp 1972)
127-134.

688   Morrison, Theodore. "Frost: Country Poet and Cos-
mopolitan Poet. " Yale Review 59 (Win 1970) 179-
196.

689   Morse, Stearns. "Lament for a Maker: Reminiscences
of Robert Frost. " Southern Review n. s. , 9 (Jan
1973) 53-68.

690   Parsons, D. S. J. "Night of Dark Intent. " Papers on
Language and Literature 6 (Sp 1970) 205-210.

691   Perrine, Laurence. "The Dilemma in Frost's 'Love
and a Question. '" Concerning Poetry 5 (Feb 1972)
5-8.

692   _____. "Frost's 'Dust of Snow. '" Explicator 29
(March 1971) 61.

693   _____. "Frost's 'An Empty Threat. '" Explicator
30 (April 1972) 63.

694   _____. "Frost's 'Gathering Leaves. '" CEA Critic
34 (Nov 1971) 29.

695   _____. "Frost's 'The Mountain': Concerning Poetry. "
Concerning Poetry 4 (Sp 1971) 5-11.

696   _____. "Frost's 'Two Tramps in Mud Time' and The
Critics. " American Literature 44 (Jan 1973) 671-676.

697   Reed, Kenneth. "Longfellow's 'Sleep' and Frost's 'After
Apple-Picking. '" American Notes and Queries 10
(May 1972) 134-135.

698   Sampley, A. M. "The Myth and the Quest: The Stature
of Robert Frost. " South Atlantic Quarterly 70 (Sum
1971) 287-298.

699   Srivastava, Ramesh. "Barriers and Boundaries: Wall
Imagery in Robert Frost. " Banasthali Patrika 16
(1970) 19-30.

700   Stanlis, Peter J. "Robert Frost: The Individual and
Society. " Intercollegiate Review (Bryn Mawr) 8 (Sum

1973) 211-234.

701 Stillians, Bruce.   "Frost's 'To the Thawing Wind. '"
     Explicator 31 (Dec 1972) 31.

702 Suderman, Elmer F.   "The Frozen Lake in Frost's
     'Stopping by Woods on a Snowy Evening. '"   Ball
     State University Forum 11 (Win 1970) 22.

703 Sutton, William A.   "A Frost-Sandburg Rivalry?"   Ball
     State University Forum 11 (Win 1970) 59-61.

704 Swennes, Robert H.   "Man and Wife: The Dialogue of
     Contraries in Robert Frost's Poetry. "   American
     Literature 42 (Nov 1970) 363-372.

705 Teresa, Sister Catherine.   "New Testament Interpreta-
     tions of Robert Frost's Poems. "   Ball State Univer-
     sity Forum 11 (Win 1970) 50-54.

706 Thornburg, Thomas R.   "Mother's Private Ghost: A
     Note on Frost's 'The Witch of Coös. '"   Ball State
     University Forum 11 (Win 1970) 16-20.

707 Utley, Francis L.   "Robert Frost's Virgilian Monster. "
     English Language Notes 10 (March 1973) 221-223.

708 Vail, Dennis.   "Frost's 'Ghost House. '"   Explicator 30
     (Oct 1971) 11.

709 _____ .   "Tree Imagery in Frost's 'Mending Wall. '"
     Notes on Contemporary Literature 3 (Sept 1973) 9-11.

710 _____ .   "Frost's 'Mowing':   Work and Poetry. "
     Notes on Contemporary Literature 4 (Jan 1974) 4-8.

711 Vander Ven, Thomas.   "Robert Frost's Dramatic Princi-
     ple of Oversound. '"   American Literature 45 (May
     1973) 238-251.

712 Van Dore, Wade.   "In Robert Frost's Rubbers. "
     Michigan Quarterly Review 11 (Sp 1972) 122-126.

713 _____ .   "Robert Frost: A Memoir and a Remon-
     strance. "   Journal of Modern Literature 2 (Nov 1972)
     554-560.

714   Venson, Robert S.   "The Roads of Robert Frost. "
          Connecticut Review 3 (1970) 102-107.

715   Watkins, Floyd C.   "The Poetry of the Unsaid: Robert
          Frost's Narrative and Dramatic Poems. " Texas
          Quarterly 15 (1972) 85-98.

716   Watson, C. N.   'Frost's Wall: The View from the
          Other Side. " New England Quarterly 44 (Dec 1971)
          653-656.

717   Weinstein, Norman.   'Robert Frost's Ideas of Order. "
          Language and Literature 1 (1972) 5-21.

I. POPULAR ARTICLES

1913-1919

718 Boston Evening Transcript (May 6, 1915) 16. "Frost Reads His Poems."

719 Boston Sunday Globe (May 9, 1915) 11. "[Frost] Found Honor in a Far Country."

720 Braithwaite, W. S. "Robert Frost, New American Poet." Boston Evening Transcript (May 8, 1915) pt. 3, 4.

721 Browne, George H. "Robert Frost, A Poet of Speech." Independent 86 (May 22, 1916) 283-284.

722 Cox, Sidney. "The Sincerity of Robert Frost." New Republic 12 (Aug 25, 1917) 109-111.

723 Elliott, G. R. "The Neighborliness of Robert Frost." Nation 109 (Dec 6, 1919) 713-715.

724 Garnett, Edward. "Critical Notes on American Poetry." Atlantic Monthly 120 (Sept 1917) 369-370.

725 Howells, William Dean. Harper's 131 (Sept 1915) 635.

726 New York Times Book Review (Aug 8, 1915). [Editorial].

727 New York Times Book Review (Dec 24, 1916) 568.

728 Phelps, William L. "The Advance of English Poetry in The Twentieth Century." Bookman 47 (April 1918) 125-138.

729 See, Anna Phillips. "The House of Independence, Where a Servant Is Not Necessary." Touchstone 2 (Jan 1918) 423-426.

730   Shanks, Edward. "Literary Affairs in London." Dial
      63 (Dec 20, 1917) 631-633.

731   Tietjens, Eunice. "Thoughts on Robert Frost." Los
      Angeles Graphic (Aug 28, 1915) 5.

732   Tilley, M. P. "Notes from Conversations with Robert
      Frost." Inlander 20 (Feb 1918) 3-8.

733   Wilkinson, Marguerite. "Poets of the People No. V:
      Robert Frost." Touchstone 3 (April 1918) 71-74.

734   Wilmore, Carl. "Finds Famous American Poet in
      White Mountain Village." Boston Post (Feb 14,
      1916) 16. [an interview collected in item 100].

                          1920-1929

735   Abbot, Waldo. "Robert Frost: Professor of English."
      Michigan Alumnus 32 (Dec 12, 1925) 208-209.

736   Amherst Graduates' Quarterly 13 (Aug 1924) 311. "Col-
      lege Notes: The Faculty."

737   Amherst Graduates' Quarterly 15 (Aug 1926) 271-273.
      "Robert Frost Returns to Amherst."

738   Anthony, Joseph. "Robert Frost: The Farmer Poet."
      Farm and Fireside 45 (June 1921) 4.

739   _____. [on Robert Frost]. New York Times Book
      Review (July 4, 1920) 19.

740   Armstrong, Martin. "Bucolic Poetry." Spectator 130
      (April 21, 1923) 671-672.

741   Batal, James A. "Poet Frost Tells of His High School
      Days in Lawrence." Lawrence Telegram (March 28,
      1925) 14.

742   Benjamin, Paul L. "Robert Frost: Poet of Neighborli-
      ness." Survey 45 (Nov 27, 1920) 318-319.

743   Bookman 61 (May 1925) 374. "The Gossip Shop: Two
      American Poets."

744   Bookman 57 (May 1923) 304-308.   "The Literary Spot-
         light: Robert Frost. "

745   Boston Evening Transcript (Nov 4, 1924) 11.   "Robert
         Frost, Poet, Leaves Amherst to Go to Michigan. "

746   Boston Herald (Oct 18, 1923) 6.   "Turns Away from
         Big Boston Hotel, Says Robert Frost, Poet. "

747   Boston Post (Dec 11, 1927) A7.   "Policeman's Advice
         Brought Fame to New England Poet. "

748   Bowen, Stirling.   "A Poet on the Campus of the Univer-
         sity of Michigan. "   Detroit News (Nov 27, 1921) pt.
         7, p. 1.

748a Bowles, Ella S.   "Robert Frost: A Belated Apprecia-
         tion. "   Granite Monthly 57 (July 1925) 267-270.

749   Cardinal 1 (Jan 1926) 29-31.   [Robert Frost Comments
         on College Education].

750   Cestre, Charles.   "Amy Lowell, Robert Frost and Edwin
         Arlington Robinson. "   Johns Hopkins Alumni Magazine
         14 (March 1926) 363-388.

751   Christian Science Monitor (Oct 18, 1920) 3.   "Literature
         and the Colleges. "

752   Christian Science Monitor (May 29, 1925) 5.   "Tribute Is
         Paid [by Robert Frost] to Dr. Burton. "

753   Cowles, Jason.   "An Au Revoir to Robert Frost. "
         Michigan Daily (May 30, 1923) Magazine Section 1.

754   D. , N.   "American and Armenian. "   Christian Science
         Monitor (Feb 15, 1920) 11.

755   Deutsch, Babette.   "Inner Weather. "   New York Herald
         Tribune Books 5 (Nov 18, 1928) 1-2.

756   F. , L. L.   "Legion. "   New Statesman 20 (April 7,
         1923) 780.

757   Feld, Rose C.   "Robert Frost Relieves His Mind. "   New
         York Times Book Review (Oct 21, 1923) 2+. [an in-
         terview collected by E. C. Lathem; see item 100].

758   Fisher, Dorothy C.   "Robert Frost's Hilltop. "   Book-
      man 64 (Dec 1926) 403-405.

759   Forum 5 (June 1921) 590-599.   "University Fellowships
      in Creative Art by Percy MacKaye. "

760   Freeman, John.   "Contemporary American Authors:
      Robert Frost. "   London Mercury 13 (Dec 1925) 176-
      187.

761   Guiterman, Arthur.   "The Poet's Housekeeping. "   Satur-
      day Review of Literature 2 (July 3, 1926) 903.

762   Hurd, John.   "Poets and Writers Flock to Bowdoin for
      the Round Table of Literature. "   Boston Sunday
      Globe (May 10, 1925) Editorial Feature Sec. 12.

763   Jackson, Gardner.   "'I Will Teach Only When I Have
      Something to Tell': Robert Frost, Apostle of 'Take
      It or Leave It' Theory of Education, Wins Professor-
      ship on His Own Terms. "   Boston Sunday Globe (Nov
      23, 1924) Editorial Sec. 3. [an interview collected by
      E. C. Lathem; see item 100].

764   Literary Digest 74 (July 22, 1922) 28-29.   "America's
      Literary Stars. "

765   Literary Digest 79 (Oct 6, 1923) 31-32.   "A Poet Among
      the Hills. "

766   Literary Digest 66 (July 17, 1920) 32-33.   "The 'Poet
      of Frost. '"

767   Littell, Robert.   "Stone Walls and Precious Stones. "
      New Republic 37 (Dec 5, 1923) 24-26.

768   Mabie, Janet.   "Robert Frost, Poet of New England. "
      Dearborn Independent 26 (June 26, 1926) 2, 30-32.

769   _____ .   "Robert Frost Interprets His Teaching
      Method. "   Christian Science Monitor (Dec 24, 1925)
      11+. [an interview collected in item 100].

770   McCord, David.   "Robert Frost. "   Harvard Alumni
      Bulletin 26 (May 29, 1924) 985-987.

771   Melcher, Daniel.   "English Classes Should Not Analyze

Books, Says Poet. " Mountaineer 2 (Jan 13, 1928)
1, 3.

772   Michigan Alumnus 28 (Oct 20, 1921) 43-45.   "Robert
      Frost: Michigan's Guest. "

773   Michigan Alumnus 31 (June 6, 1925) 703-704.   "Robert
      Frost Speaks in Memory of Dr. Burton. "

774   Michigan Alumnus 28 (Dec 1, 1921) 234.   "Some Ob-
      servations by Robert Frost. "

775   Moore, Harold A.   "Robert Frost, New England Poet,
      and the Genesis of His Poetry. " Springfield Sunday
      Republican (Jan 4, 1925) 4A.

776   Moult, Thomas.   "Robert Frost's Poetry. " Bookman
      64 (July 1923) 202.

777   Munson, Gorham B.   "Robert Frost. " Saturday Review
      of Literature 1 (March 28, 1925) 625-626.

778   New York Times Book Review (Nov 18, 1923) 6.   "Bards
      of New England and New York. "

779   New York World (Nov 5, 1924) 19.   "Robert Frost, New
      England Poet, Goes to University of Michigan. "

780   Our World Weekly 2 (Feb 9, 1925) 28.   "The Last of
      the Yankees: Robert Frost, An American Poet Who
      Holds Up a Mirror to One Phase of American Life. "

781   Ridge, Lola.   "Covered Roads. " New Republic 23 (June
      23, 1920) 131-132.

782   Rugg, Harold G.   "Robert Frost. " Dartmouth Bema 12
      (June 1923) 10, 22.

783   Saturday Review of Literature 1 (June 2, 1923) 735-736.
      "A Mixed Company. "

784   Sayler, Oliver M.   "The Return of the Pilgrim. " New
      Republic 27 (Aug 10, 1921) 302-303.

785   Scherer, Ruth van Bach.   "A Welcome Back to Robert
      Frost. " Michigan Chimes 7 (Oct 25, 1925) 1, 3, 7.

786 Sergeant, Elizabeth Shipley. "Robert Frost, a Good
     Greek Out of New England. " New Republic 44 (Sept
     30, 1925) 144-148.

787 Smith, Katherine. "Robert Frost and the Ann Arbor
     Fellowship in Creative Art. " Lyric West 2 (Sept
     1922) 28-29.

788 Spectator no. 4830 (Jan 22, 1921) 114-115. "Poets and
     Poetry: A New England Poet. "

789 Springfield Republican (Nov 29, 1924). "Robert Frost,
     Poet, May Do as He Pleases on His New Job. "

790 Stewart, Bernice. "Robert Frost Comes to Ann Arbor. "
     Detroit Free Press (Oct 16, 1921) Magazine Sec. 5.

791 Tanager (May 1926) 17-20. "Robert Frost: Farmer
     and Poet. "

792 Van Doren, Carl. "The Soil of the Puritans: Robert
     Frost, Quintessence and Subsoil. " Century Magazine
     105 (Feb 1923) 629-636.

793 Van Doren, Mark. "The Power of Reticence. " New
     York Herald Tribune Books 2 (March 22, 1925) 1.

794 _____ and Carl Van Doren. "Robert Frost. " Nation
     117 (Dec 19, 1923) 715-716.

795 Waitt, Paul. "America's Great Poet Revels in Beauties
     of Old Vermont. " Boston Traveler (April 11, 1921)
     6. [an interview collected by E. C. Lathem; see
     item 100].

796 Whipple, T. H. "Robert Frost. " Literary Review of
     the New York Evening Post 4 (March 22, 1924) 605-
     606.

797 Wilson Bulletin 4 (Nov 1929) 100. "Robert Frost, Au-
     thor of West-Running Brook. "

                          1930-1939

798 Amherst Alumni Council News 8 (July 1935) 83-85.
     "Robert Frost, Remarks at Senior Chapel. "

799   Amherst Graduates' Quarterly 25 (Aug 1936) 342.
        [Robert Frost Receives Degree of Doctor of Humane
        Letters from Bates College].

800   Amherst Record 93 (May 29, 1935) 8. "Professor
        Frost Delivers Lectures on Poetry. "

801   Amherst Record 94 (March 25, 1936) 3. "Robert
        Frost's Book Chosen by Book-of-the-Month Club. "

802   Amherst Student 68 (May 27, 1935) 1-2. "Frost's
        Second Talk Stresses Originality. "

803   Amherst Student 67 (March 25, 1935) 1-2. "Robert
        Frost on Sixtieth Birthday Talks of the Joys of Liv-
        ing. "

804   Amherst Student 68 (May 27, 1935) 1-2. "Robert Frost
        Speaks to Large Crowds Here. "

805   Benet, W. R. "Phoenix Nest: Poetry Society of Amer-
        ica Honors Robert Frost. " Saturday Review of Lit-
        erature 15 (April 10, 1937) 16.

806   Boston Evening Transcript (Feb 21, 1931) Magazine sec.,
        3.   "A New England Poet Talks on Education by
        Poetry. "

807   Boston Herald (Jan 21, 1936) 5.   "Pulitzer Prize Poet
        Gets Harvard Post. "

808   Bosworth, Raymond F. "Teacher Affords Intimate
        Glimpse of Robert Frost. " Hartford Daily Courant
        (March 11, 1934) pt. 5, D5.

809   Brooks, Philip. "Notes on Rare Books: Robert Frost
        --A Chronological Survey. " New York Times Book
        Review (June 14, 1936) 20.

810   Burlington (Vermont) Free Press and Times (Aug 19,
        1936) 2+.   "Poet Would Give Young Folks More
        Time to Find Themselves. "[an interview collected
        by E. C. Lathem; see item 100].

811   Canadian Forum 11 (June 1931) 336-337.   "Prefer-
        ences. "

812   Carroll, Gladys Hasty.   "New England Sees It Through. "
      Saturday Review of Literature 13 (Nov 9, 1935) 3-4+.

813   Christian Science Monitor (Feb 16, 1938) 11.   "What
      Critics Have Written in Praise of Robert Frost. "

814   Clymer, Shubrick.   "Robert Frost the Realist. "   Yankee
      1 (Oct 1935) 22-25.

815   Conrad, Lawrence H.   "Robert Frost. "   Landmark 12
      (Oct 1930) 643-646.

816   Daily Hampshire Gazette (March 29, 1935) 10.   "Mr.
      Frost at 60. "

817   Dyer, W. A.   "Overlooking the Common: Milestones
      in the Life of Robert Frost. "   Amherst Record 93
      (March 20, 1935) 2, 6.

818   Gregory, Horace.   "Robert Frost. " New Freeman 3
      (April 1, 1931) 60-62.

819   Haines, J. W.   "The Dymock Poets. " Gloucestershire
      Countryside 1 (Oct 1933) 131-133.

820   _____ .   "Edward Thomas: A Welsh Poet in Glouces-
      tershire. "   Gloucester Journal 213 (Feb 16, 1935)
      19.

821   _____ .   "Mr. Robert Frost: An American Poet in
      Gloucestershire. "   Gloucester Journal 213 (Feb 2,
      1935) 20.

822   Hillyer, Robert.   "A Letter to Robert Frost. " Atlantic
      Monthly 158 (Aug 1936) 158-163.

823   Holden, Raymond.   "Profiles: North of Boston. " New
      Yorker 7 (June 6, 1931) 24-27.

824   Holmes, John.   "Robert Frost Conquers the Poetic
      Realm. " Boston Evening Transcript (Feb 13, 1937)
      Sec. 6, 1-2.

825   _____ .   "Robert Frost as He Talks to Multitudes. "
      Boston Evening Transcript (March 21, 1936) Book
      section, 1.

826   _____. "Robert Frost Wins His Fight to Be an
       Ordinary Man. " Boston Evening Transcript (Feb 8,
       1936) Magazine sec., 4.

827   _____. "Up the Sleeve: A Discussion of the Vari-
       ous Reviews of A Further Range. " Boston Evening
       Transcript (July 11, 1936) Book Section, 6.

828   Hopper, V. F. "Robinson and Frost. " Saturday Re-
       view of Literature 13 (Nov 2, 1935) 9.

829   Janney, F. L. "Robert Frost. " Hollins Alumni Quar-
       terly 9 (Founder's Day issue, 1935) 10-15.

830   Lindley, F. Vinton. "Robert Frost. " Groton School
       Quarterly 7 (Oct 1933) 583-595.

831   Massachusetts Collegian 46 (Nov 21, 1935) 1, 6. "Rob-
       ert Frost Reads Well-Known Works at Social Union. "

832   Massachusetts Collegian 46 (Nov 14, 1935) 1, 6. "Well-
       Known Amherst Poet Appears in First Social Union of
       the Season. "

833   Munson, Gorham B. "Robert Frost and the Humanistic
       Temper. " Bookman 71 (July 1930) 419-422.

834   Newdick, Robert S. "Frostana. " Saturday Review of
       Literature 41 (May 29, 1937) 20.

835   _____. "How a Columbus Mother Helped Her Son to
       Become the Dean of America's Living Poets. "
       Columbus Sunday Dispatch (May 17, 1936) Graphic
       section.

836   _____. "Robert Frost: Impressions and Observa-
       tions. " Ohio Stater 2 (May 1936) 3, 18-19.

837   New Statesman 36 (Dec 27, 1930) 365. "Robert Frost. "

838   New York Herald Tribune (Oct 16, 1932). "Florence
       Reeve Opens Exhibit of Sculpture: Busts of Frost
       and Markham in Morristown Showing. "

839   New York Times (Feb 28, 1936) 20. "Poet in Politics"
       (editorial).

840 New York Times (April 6, 1935) 14. "A Poet's Word to Youth."

841 New York Times (March 26, 1935) 22. 'Robert Frost, 60, Reflects on Era."

842 Publisher's Weekly 119 (May 9, 1931) 2312-13. "The Pulitzer Awards, 1931."

843 Ritchey, J. "Figure a Poet Makes." Christian Science Monitor Magazine (July 22, 1939) 10.

844 Root, Edward Tallmadge. 'New England Honors Her Leading Poet." Christian Century 53 (April 15, 1936) 581.

845 Saturday Review of Literature 13 (Feb 15, 1936) 8. 'Dividends from a Poet."

846 Shippey, Lee. [Robert Frost]. Los Angeles Times (Sept 29, 1932) 4.

847 Smith, Fred. "The Sound of a Yankee Voice." Commonweal 15 (Jan 13, 1932) 297-298.

848 Smith, Mary Gilbert. "Robert Frost." Boston Globe (Sept 5, 1935) 16.

849 Snow, Wilbert. "Cheerful New England Poems." New York Herald Tribune Books (June 7, 1936) 4.

850 Springfield Daily News (Aug 19, 1935) 10. "Frost Poem Now in Pamphlet Form."

851 Springfield Republican (June 21, 1933) 3. "Honorary Degree from Dartmouth to Robert Frost."

852 Springfield Republican (March 26, 1935) 2. 'Robert Frost, 60, Declares His Age Is Not Advanced."

853 Springfield Republican (Feb 18, 1936) 2. "Robert Frost's Status Declared Unchanged."

854 Springfield Union (Feb 29, 1936) 5. "Frost Pictures New Deal Lost in Latest Poem."

855 Springfield Union and Republican (April 9, 1933) 2E,

10E.   "Frost Exhibit on View in Poet's Home Town. "

856   The Sun (Baltimore) (Feb 26, 1936) 24-25.   "Latest
      Poem by Robert Frost Versifies New Deal Is Lost"
      [an interview collected by E. C. Lathem; see item 100].

857   The Sun (Feb 27, 1936) 10.   "Recruit Legislator. "

858   The Sunday Star [Washington D. C.] (Dec 2, 1934) B6.
      "Poetry's Rewards Hard Earned, Says Frost, Here
      for a Reading. "

859   Taggard, Genevieve.   "Robert Frost, Poet. " New York
      Herald Tribune Books 7 (Dec 21, 1930) 1, 6.

859a Time 33 (May 15, 1939) 83-5.   "Muse. "

860   Untermeyer, Louis.   "Play in Poetry. " Saturday Re-
      view of Literature 17 (Feb 26, 1938) 3-4, 14, 16.

861   Van Dore, Wade.   "Poet of the Trees. "   Christian
      Science Monitor Magazine (Dec 23, 1939) 3+.

1940-1949

862   Adams, J. D.   New York Times Book Review (Feb 20,
      1944) 2.

863   Bartlett, Donald.   "A Friend's View of Robert Frost. "
      New Hampshire Troubadour 16 (Nov 1946) 22-25.

864   Breit, Harvey.   "Talk with Robert Frost. " New York
      Times Book Review (Nov 27, 1949) 20 [an interview
      collected by E. C. Lathem; see item 100].

865   Church, R.   "Robert Frost: A Prophet in His Own
      Country. " Fortnightly 153 (n. s. 147) (May 1940)
      539-546.

866   Clark, Sylvia.   "Robert Frost: The Derry Years. "
      New Hampshire Troubadour 16 (Nov 1946) 13-16.

867   Clausen, B. C.   "A Portrait for Peacemakers. "
      Friends' Intellegencer 101 (Jan 29, 1944) 71-72.

868   Cook, Reginald L.   "Frost Country. " Vermont Life 3
      (Sum 1949) 15-17.

869 Cowley, Malcolm. "The Case Against Mr. Frost. "
     New Republic 111 (Sept 18, 1944) 345-347.

870 _____. "Frost: A Dissenting Opinion. " New Re-
     public 111 (Sept 11, 1944) 312-313.

871 Cox, Sidney H.   "Robert Frost at Plymouth. " New
     Hampshire Troubadour 16 (Nov 1946) 18-22.

872 Current Biography 3 (Sept 1942) 18-22.   "Robert (Lee)
     Frost. "

873 DeVoto, Bernard.   "The Maturity of American Litera-
     ture. " Saturday Review of Literature 27 (Aug 5,
     1944) 14-18.

874 Dupee, F. W.   "Frost and Tate. " Nation 160 (April
     21, 1945) 464.

875 Greene, M. T.   "Robert Frost at Home. "   Christian
     Science Monitor 15 (Aug 15, 1949) 14.

876 Hall, J. N.   "Reading and Meditating: Robert Frost's
     Poems. " Atlantic Monthly 174 (Sept 1944) 59.

877 Jarrell, Randall.   "The Other Robert Frost. "   Nation
     165 (Nov 29, 1947) 590-601.

878 Keith, J. J.   "Robert Frost. " Saturday Review of
     Literature 31 (Aug 21, 1948) 13.

879 Lambuth, David.   "The Unforgettable Robert Frost. "
     New Hampshire Troubadour 16 (Nov 1946) 25-29.

880 Mardenborough, Aimee.   "Robert Frost: The Old and
     the New. " Catholic World 168 (Dec 1948) 232-236.

881 Morse, Stearns.   "Robert Frost and New Hampshire. "
     New Hampshire Troubadour 16 (Nov 1946) 6-8.

882 Poetry 71 (Dec 1947) 144b.   "Portrait. "

883 Pollard, Alice.   "The Loose-Enders: Dartmouth's
     Roving Professors, A Unique Teaching Group. "
     Dartmouth Alumni Magazine 38 (Jan 1946) 11-12.

884 Polle, Ernest.   "Robert Frost Was Here. " New

Hampshire Troubadour 16 (Nov 1946) 10-12.

885 Publisher's Weekly 156 (Nov 26, 1949) 2207. "Frost
     Awarded Limited Editions Club Medal. "

886 Publisher's Weekly 147 (March 10, 1945) 1120. "To
     Be Honored on 70th Birthday. "

887 Publisher's Weekly 151 (June 7, 1947) 2847.   "Portrait. "

888 Senior Scholastic 42 (Feb 1, 1943) 20. "Portrait. "

889 Time 53 (June 27, 1949) 94+.   "Intolerable Touch. "

890 Time 39 (May 18, 1942) 91-92. "Poetry. "

891 Vangelder, Robert. "An Interview with Robert Frost. "
     New York Times Book Review (May 24, 1942) 2.

892 Whicher, George F. "Out for Stars: A Meditation on
     Robert Frost. " Atlantic Monthly 171 (May 1943)
     64-67.

893 Wolfe, C. S. [Poetry Corner]. Senior Scholastic 36
     (April 1940) 20.

                        1950-1959

894 Adams, J. Donald. [on Kenyon College conference in
     honor of Robert Frost]. New York Times Book Re-
     view (Oct 22, 1950) 2.

895 _____. "Robert Frost. " New York Times Book
     Review (March 21, 1954) 1-2.

896 _____. "Speaking of Books. " New York Times Book
     Review (April 12, 1959) 2.

897 _____. [Lionel Trilling on Robert Frost].   New York
     Times Book Review (May 3, 1959) 24.

898 Brace, G. W. "Robert Frost's New Hampshire. " New
     Hampshire Profiles (May 1955).

899 Bracker, M. "The Quietly Overwhelming Robert Frost. "
     New York Times Magazine (Nov 30, 1958) 15+.

[an interview collected in item 100].

900   Browning, J. P.   "'The Black Cottage. '"   Wingover 1
      (Fall-Win 1958) 11-12.

901   Burgess, O. N.   'Hugh McCrae and Robert Frost. "
      Southerly 16 (1956) 152-157.

902   Christian Science Monitor 49 (April 25, 1957) 2.   "Ox-
      ford and Cambridge to Honor Frost. "

903   Ciardi, John.   "A Letter to Letter-Writers. "   Saturday
      Review 41 (May 17, 1958) 15+.

904   _____.   'Robert Frost, Master Conversationalist at
      Work. "   Saturday Review 42 (March 21, 1959) 17-20,
      54.

905   _____.   'Robert Frost: The Way to the Poem. "
      Saturday Review 41 (April 12, 1958) 13-15, 65.

906   Cook, Reginald L.   "A Walk with Frost. "   Yankee
      (Nov 1955) 18-26.

907   Coronet 27 (March 1950) 14.   'The Voice of New Eng-
      land. "

908   [No entry]

909   [No entry]

910   Deen, Rosemary F.   'The Voices of Robert Frost. "
      Commonweal 69 (Feb 20, 1959) 542-544.

911   Elsea, G. E.   'Two Poems. "   Wingover 1 (Fall-Win
      1958) 21-22.

912   Engle, Paul.   'Paean for a Poet by a Poet. "   Life 46
      (June 15, 1959) 65-66.

913   Farjeon, Elenor.   "Edward Thomas and Robert Frost. "
      London Magazine 1 (May 1954) 50-61.

914   Finnegan, Sister Mary Jeremy.   'Frost's 'Masque of
      Mercy. '"   Catholic World 186 (Feb 1958) 357-361.

915   Hamburger, P.   'Television: An Interview at the
      Frost Farmhouse. "   New Yorker 28 (Dec 13, 1952)
      167-169.

916 Harvard Alumni Bulletin 57 (Feb 1955) 346-348. "The
     Frost Festival. "

917 Holmes, John. "Close-up of an American Poet at 75. "
     New York Times Magazine (March 26, 1950) 12,
     72, 75-77.

918 Isaacs, J. "Best Loved of American Poets. " Listener
     51 (April 1, 1954) 564-567.

919 Jamieson, Paul F. "Robert Frost: Poet of Mountain
     Land. " Appalachia 25 (Dec 1959) 471-479.

920 Lathem, Edward C. "Freshman Days. " [An Interview]
     Dartmouth Alumni Magazine 51 (March 1959) 17.

921 Life 28 (April 3, 1950) 45. "Hale Hearty Old Folk. "

922 Life 43 (Sept 23, 1957) 109-110+. "A Poet's Pilgrimage. "

923 Life 39 (Nov 28, 1955) 91-92. "A Poet and a Plight. "

924 Look 18 (May 18, 1954) 20. "Portrait. "

925 Mertins, L. "Robert Frost in England. " Manchester
     Guardian Weekly 63 (Aug 17, 1950) 13.

926 Morgan, C. "Back Over the Years with Robert Frost. "
     Christian Science Monitor Magazine (March 25, 1950)
     3.

927 Morrison, C. "A Visit with Robert Frost. " Look 23
     (March 31, 1959) 76-78+.

928 Newsweek 54 (July 27, 1959) 89. "How Terrifying a
     Poet?"

929 Newsweek 43 (April 5, 1954) 46. "A Poet Reflects. "

930 Proctor, P. M. "A Tribute to Robert Frost. " Sky
     and Telescope (Harvard College) 15 (March 1956)
     212.

931 Publisher's Weekly 158 (Oct 14, 1950) 1784. "To
     Honor Robert Frost: 75th Birthday Anniversary. "

932 Publisher's Weekly 157 (May 20, 1950) 2175. "Senate

Honors Frost on His 75th Birthday. "

933 Reader's Digest 58 (Jan 1951) 91-97. "Robert Frost:
      Cracker-barrel Socrates. "

934 Rogin, Richard M. "U. S. Education Needs 'Toning
      Up'--Frost. " Lebanon, New Hampshire Valley News
      (Nov 20, 1958) 1-2.

935 Rosenthal, M. L. "The Robert Frost Controversy. "
      Nation 188 (June 20, 1959) 559-561.

936 Russell, Francis. "Frost in the Evening. " Horizon
      1 (Nov 1958) 34-35.

937 Saturday Evening Post 229 (March 2, 1957) 10. "Poet
      Robert Frost Finds Us the Freest People on Earth. "

938 Senior Scholastic 73 (Nov 7, 1958) 13. "Potato Brushed
      Clean. "

939 Sergeant, Elizabeth S. "Roots of a Writer. " Saturday
      Review 36 (April 11, 1953) 50+.

940 Spender, Stephen. "The Subtle Simplicity of Robert
      Frost. " Sunday Times (London) (May 26, 1957) 6.

941 Stevens, Donald D. "'For Once, Then, Something. '"
      Wingover 1 (Fall-Win 1958) 14-16.

942 Stylites, S. "I Wanted to Go Home. " Christian Cen-
      tury 71 (Aug 4, 1954) 919.

943 Thompson, Lawrance. "A Native to the Grain of the
      American Idiom. " Saturday Review 42 (March 21,
      1959) 21, 55-56.

944 Trilling, Lionel. [reply to article by J. D. Adams].
      New York Times Book Review (Sept 20, 1959) 32.

945 Time 56 (Oct 9, 1950) 76-82. "Pawky Poet. "

946 Time 70 (Dec 9, 1957) 114. "Portrait. "

947 Time 58 (Sept 24, 1951) 112. "Vermont Talk. "

948 Time 69 (June 24, 1957) 62. "Visitor. "

949   Van Doren, Mark.   "Robert Frost's America. " Atlan-
        tic Monthly 187 (June 1951) 32-34.

1960-1969

950   Adams, J. D. [on Poirier and Frost].   New York
        Times Book Review (June 11, 1961) 2.

951   Anderson, Charles.   "Robert Frost, 1874-1963. "
        Saturday Review 46 (Feb 23, 1963) 16-20.

952   Anthony, Mother Mary.   "Birches and Stone Walls:
        Frost and Berrigan. " Catholic Standard and Times
        (Philadelphia) Literary Supplement 46 (Feb 3, 1961)
        1, 4.

953   Bennett, P. A.   "Robert Frost: Best Printed U. S.
        Author and His Printer. " Publisher's Weekly 185
        (March 2, 1964) 82-86.

954   Breit, Harvey.   "Robert Frost Speaks Prose. " Esquire
        64 (Dec 1965) 230, 308.

955   Chapin, K. G.   "Prose He Did Not Write. " New Repub-
        lic 152 (Jan 2, 1965) 16-17.

956   Ciardi, John.   "Robert Frost: American Bard. " Satur-
        day Review 45 (March 24, 1962) 15-17+.

957   _____ .   "Robert Frost: To Earthward. " Saturday
        Review 46 (Feb 23, 1963) 24.

958   Davenport, Guy.   "First National Poetry Festival: A
        Report. " National Review 14 (Jan 15, 1963) 26.

959   Davison, Peter.   "Robert Frost: His Own Tradition. "
        Atlantic Monthly 209 (May 1962) 100-101.

960   Day-Lewis, C.   "Robert Frost: 1874-1963. " Listener
        69 (Feb 7, 1963) 253.

961   Dickey, James.   "Robert Frost: Man and Myth. " At-
        lantic Monthly 218 (Nov 1966) 53-56.

962   Dickey, John S.   "Robert Frost: Teacher at Large. "
        Saturday Review 46 (Feb 23, 1963) 21-22.

963   Donoghue, Denis.   'The Sacred Rage: Three American
       Poets. "   Listener 69 (1963) 965-967.

964   Drew, Fraser B.   "A Teacher Visits Robert Frost. "
       New York State Educator 51 (Dec 1963) 5.

965   Drury, M.   'Robert Frost: His Power and His Glory. "
       McCall's 87 (April 1960) 80-81+.

966   Edel, Leon.   'Spirals of Reason and Fancy. "   Saturday
       Review 47 (Sept 5, 1964) 23-24.

967   Harris, Mark.   'The Pride and Wisdom of Two Great
       Old Poets: Sandburg and Frost. "   Life 51 (Dec 1,
       1961) 103-104+ [an interview-article, part of which
       was collected by E. C. Lathem; see item 100].

968   Hewes, H.   "Broadway Postscript. "   Saturday Review
       48 (Oct 30, 1965) 74.

969   Hicks, Granville.   'Robert Frost Revisited. "   Saturday
       Review 49 (July 9, 1966) 23-24.

970   Howe, Irving.   "A Momentary Stay. "   New Republic 148
       (March 23, 1963) 23-28.

971   Hunt, G. P.   "Our Own Remembrance of Robert Frost. "
       Life 54 (Feb 8, 1963) 3.

972   Jacobson, Josephine.   'Legacy of Three Poets. "   Com-
       monweal 78 (May 10, 1963) 189-192.

973   Jeremy, Sister Mary.   "Contrarieties in Robert Frost. "
       Catholic World 192 (Dec 1960) 164-170.

974   Kahn, Roger.   "A Visit with Robert Frost. "   Saturday
       Evening Post 233 (Nov 16, 1960) 26-27+. [an inter-
       view collected by E. C. Lathem; see item 100].

975   _____ .   'Robert Frost: A Reminiscence. "   Nation
       196 (Feb 9, 1963) 121.

976   Kazin, Alfred.   'The Strength of Robert Frost. "   Com-
       mentary 38 (Dec 1964) 49-52.

977   Kennedy, John F.   "Kennedy Speaks at Frost Library
       Dedication: Summary of Address. "   Wilson Library

Bulletin 38 (Dec 1963) 317.

978 _____.   "Poetry and Power. " Atlantic Monthly 213
    (Feb 1964) 53-54.

979 Kenny, A.   "Robert Frost: RIP. " National Review 14
    (Feb 12, 1963) 100.

980 Kunitz, Stanley.   "Frost, Williams and Company. "
    Harper's 225 (Oct 1962) 100-103+.

981 Life 54 (Feb 8, 1963) 46-47.   "Robert Frost: His Last
    Poem. "

982 Love, Kennett.   "Poet of Love and Understanding. "
    USA 1 (April 1962) 72-73.

983 MacLeish, Archibald.   "Gift Outright. " Atlantic Month-
    ly 213 (Feb 1964) 50-52.

984 Marple, A.   "Off the Cuff. " Writer (Boston) 76 (May
    1963) 5-6+.

985 Maxwell, M. , ed.   "Swinger of Birches: An Interview
    of Leslie Frost. " Senior Scholastic 91 (Oct 19,
    1967) 10-11.

986 Melcher, F. G.   "Memory of Robert Frost and His In-
    fluence. " Publisher's Weekly 183 (Feb 11, 1963) 98.

987 Miller, Vincent.   "The Home of Robert Frost. " Na-
    tional Review 12 (June 5, 1962) 411-412.

988 Morrison, Theodore.   "The Agitated Heart: Adaptation
    of Address. " Atlantic Monthly 220 (July 1967) 72-79.

989 Most, Steve.   "Literary Find. " Saturday Review 44
    (Feb 4, 1961) 25.

990 Munson, Gorham B.   "The Classicism of Robert Frost. "
    Modern Age 8 (Sum 1964) 291-305.

991 Newsweek 61 (Feb 11, 1963) 90-91.   "Frost: Courage
    Is the Virtue That Counts Most. "

992 Newsweek 60 (Sept 10, 1962) 60.   "Poet at Large:
    Robert Frost at Moscow's Airport. "

993 New York Times Magazine (Sept 16, 1962) 34.   "Mend-
      ing the Wall in Moscow. "

994 Nims, John Frederick.   "The Classicism of Robert
      Frost. " Saturday Review 46 (Feb 23, 1963) 22-33+.

995 Oliver, E.   "Off Broadway. " New Yorker 41 (Oct 23,
      1965) 96+.

996 Parke, J. [later poetry of Frost]. New York Times
      Book Review (Aug 21, 1960) 16.

997 Prideaux, T.   "Warm Spell of Frost. " Life 60 (March
      4, 1966) 15.

998 Publisher's Weekly 185 (Jan 20, 1964) 105-106.   "Frost
      Books Donated to New York University Library. "

999 Publisher's Weekly 183 (Feb 11, 1963) 96-97.   "Obituary
      Notes: Some Prices Paid for Mr. Frost's Work in
      Recent Years. "

1000 Publisher's Weekly 181 (April 9, 1962) 30-31.   "Robert
       Frost Honored on 88th Birthday: Exhibit at Library
       of Congress. "

1001 Reeve, F. D.   "Robert Frost Confronts Khrushchev. "
       Atlantic Monthly 212 (Sept 1963) 33, 39.

1002 Reporter 28 (Feb 28, 1963) 20.   "Robert Frost, 1874-
       1963. "

1003 Samuel, Rinna.   "Robert Frost in Israel. " New York
       Times Book Review (April 23, 1961) 42-43.

1004 Scannell, Vernon.   "Content with Discontent. " London
       Magazine 1 (Jan 1962) 44-51.

1005 Schlueter, P.   "Not Unlike Job. " Christian Century 81
       (Sept 30, 1964) 126-127.

1006 Senior Scholastic 82 (Feb 13, 1963) 21.   "Insight into
       the Human Soul. "

1007 Sergeant, Elizabeth S.   "England Discovers Robert
       Frost. " Atlantic Monthly 205 (May 1960) 61-65.

1008   Shapiro, Harvey. "Story of a Poem: 'The Gift Out-
         right. '" New York Times Magazine (Jan 15, 1961)
         6, 86.

1009   Sheed, W. 'Frost as Drama. " Commonweal 83 (Nov
         5, 1965) 147-148.

1010   Stanlis, Peter. 'Robert Frost: Individualistic Demo-
         crat. " ILIFF Review (Denver) (Sept 1965).

1011   Stevenson, Adlai E. "American People Find Their
         Poet. " New Republic 146 (April 9, 1962) 20-21.

1012   Stone, Edward. "The Middle Name Is Lee. " Ohio
         Alumnus 40 (April 1961) 22, 26.

1013   Surkov, A. 'Robert Frost and His Visit to the USSR. "
         Soviet Review 3 (Dec 1962) 59-61. Translated from
         Pravda.

1014   Thompson, Lawrance S. "'Look Out I Don't Spoof
         You. '" Princeton Alumni Weekly 65 (Dec 8, 1964)
         40-42.

1015   _____. 'Robert Frost and Carl Burell. " Dartmouth
         College Library Bulletin 6 (April 1966) 65-73.

1016   _____. 'First Love. " Reader's Digest 91 (Aug
         1967) 55-58.

1017   Time 80 (Sept 14, 1962) 31. "American Abroad. "

1018   Time 82 (May 5, 1963) 102+. "Ever Yours, Robert. "

1019   Time 81 (Feb 8, 1963) 84. 'Lovers' Quarrel with the
         World. "

1020   Time 84 (Dec 11, 1964) 127. 'The Poet and the Pub-
         lic Man. "

1021   Time 79 (March 30, 1962) 84. 'Poet Laureate. "

1022   Times Literary Supplement (London) (Dec 14, 1967)
         1201-1202. 'The Young Frost: A Yank from Yank-
         ville. "

1023   Udall, Stewart L. 'Frost's Unique Gift Outright. "

New York Times Magazine (March 26, 1961) 12, 98.

1024   Updike, John.   "Why Robert Frost Should Receive the
       Nobel Prize. " Audience 7 (Sum 1960) 45-46.

1025   Van Doren, Mark.   "Recollections of Robert Frost. "
       Columbia Library Columns 10-12 (May 1963) 3-6.

1970-1974

1026   Davison, P.   "Self-Realization of Robert Frost, 1911-
       1912. " New Republic 170 (March 30, 1974) 17-20.

1027   Kirk, Russell.   "Robert Frost: No Ideologue. " Na-
       tional Review 25 (Nov 23, 1973) 1302.

1028   Littlejohn, D.   "Frost at 100: Still on Tour. " New
       Republic 171 (Nov 16, 1974) 23-24.

1029   Poirier, Richard.   "The Sound of Love and the Love
       of Sound. " Atlantic 233 (April 1974) 50-55.

1030   Pritchard, W. H.   "Frost Revised. " Atlantic 226
       (Oct 1970) 130+.

1031   Stafford, W.   "Terror in Robert Frost. " New York
       Times Magazine (Aug 18, 1974) 24-26+.

1032   Udall, Stewart L.   "' ... and miles to go before I
       sleep. '" New York Times Magazine (June 11, 1972)
       18-19+.

1033   Van Dore, Wade.   "Robert Frost and Wilderness. "
       Living Wilderness 34 (Sum 1970) 47-49.

J. ARTICLES IN FOREIGN LANGUAGES

1034 Asselineau, Roger. "Robert Frost et Paysan." Informations et Documents 177 (March 1, 1963) 18-22.

1035 Barre, Michel. "Robert Frost en France." Le Bayou 23 (Spring 1959) 289-297.

1036 Bosquet, Alain. "Robert Frost." Nouvelle Revue Française 11 (March 1963) 536-537.

1037 _____. "Robert Frost est Mort." Le Monde (Jan 30, 1963) 11.

1038 Brown, Prado Oswaldo. "Frost y el Renacimiento de la Poesía Norteamericana." Ipna (Lima) 10 (May-Aug 1954) 57-65.

1039 Buchloh, Paul G. "Das Verhältnis des amerikanischen Dichters zum Staat, dargestellt an Robert Frosts 'The Gift Outright' und Randall Jarrells 'The Death of the Ball Turret Gunner.'" Jahrbuch für Amerikastudien 13 (1968) 205-214.

1040 Camillucci, Marcello. "Il Virgilio della Nuova Inghilterra." Persona 4 (no. 2 1963) 18-19.

1041 Castillejo, Jorge. "La Poesía de Robert Frost." Bolívar 46 (1957) 39-43.

1042 Catel, Jean. "La Poésie Américaine d'Aujourd'hui." Mercure de France 138 (Feb-March 1920) 601-627.

1043 _____. Mercure de France 170 (Feb 1924) 261-262 [review of New Hampshire].

1044 Cestre, Charles. Revue Anglo-Américaine 6 (Aug 1925) 558-560 [review of New Hampshire].

1045 _____. Revue Anglo-Américaine 6 (June 20, 1929)
458-460 [review of West-running Brook].

1046 Combecher, Hans. "Versuch einer Interpretation von
zwei Gedichten des Neuenglanders Robert Lee Frost."
Neuren Sprachen (1957) 281-289.

1047 Dony, Françoise. "Poète Bucolique de Nouvelle Angle-
terre." Revue de l'Université de Bruxelles 43 (May-
June-July 1938) 393-403.

1048 Feuillerat, Albert. "Poètes Américains d'Aujourd'hui:
Robert Frost." Revue des Deux Mondes 17 (Sept
1923) 185-210.

1049 _____. "Robert Frost." Figaro (Paris) (March 29,
1929) 5.

1050 Fukuda, Rikutaro. "Frost Shihen Chushaku." Eigo
Seinen (Tokyo) 117, 118 (1972) 642+.

1051 Gorlier, Claudio. "E. A. Robinson e Robert Frost."
Paragone n. s., 17 (Feb 1966) 126-132.

1052 Grobard, H. "The Art of the New American Literature:
Robert Frost." Der Oifkum 2 (Aug 1927) 34-36 [in
Yiddish].

1053 Haas, Rudolf. "'Stopping by Woods on a Snowy Evening': Gedanken zur wissenschaftlichen und unterricht-
lichen Erschiliessung eines Gedichts von Robert
Frost." Praxis des Neusprachlichen Unterrichts
(Jan 11, 1964) 295-302.

1054 Heibe, Carolus. "Robert Frost." Der Lebensweiser
30 (Jan 1963) 7-10.

1055 _____. "Robert Frost." Ein Umriss Lehrerzeitung
17 (Jan 1963) 74-75.

1056 Jäger, Dietrich. "Robert Frost und die Traditionen der
Natürdichtung: Die aussermenschiliche Welt als
Thema deutscher und amerikanischer Lyriker des 20.
Jahrhunderts." Literatur in Wessenshaft und Unter-
nicht 1 (Heft 1 1968) 2-27.

1057 _____. "Das Verhältnis zwischen Wirklichkeit und

menschlicher Ordnung als Thema der Lyrik: Robert
Frost und Wallace Stevens im Vergleich mit euro-
päischen Dichtern. " Neuren Sprachen 7 (1968) 65-83.

1058   Kashkeen, Ivan.   'Robert Frost. " Inostrannaia Literatura 10 (Oct 1962) 195-201 [in Russian].

1059   Komanaura, Toshio.   'Robert Frost's View of Life
and Death: A Development of Fire and Ice. " Studies in English Literature 46 (March 1970) 117-127
[in Japanese].

1060   Kulczynskyj, Wolodymyr.   'The Technique of Story-
Telling in Robert Frost's Poems. " Construtura:
Revista de Lingüística, Lingua, e Literatura (Brazil)
1 (1973) 261-268 [in Portuguese].

1061   Lalli, Biancamaria Tedeschini.   'Il 'Regionalismo' di
Robert Frost. " Studi Americani 4 (1958) 317-341.

1062   Landré, Louis.   'Premières Critiques de Robert
Frost. " Études Anglaises 5 (May 1952) 143-151.

1063   Le Breton, M.   Études Anglaises 14 (July-Sept 1961)
280 [review of Sergeant's A Trial by Existence].

1064   Lehrerzeitung (Berlin) 16 (Jan 1962) 172-173.   'Robert
Frost: Ein Dichter des Alltags. "

1065   LeVot, André.   'La Voix de Robert Frost. " Langues
Modernes 59 (May-June 1965) 349-356.

1066   Mercure de France 126 (April 1918) 726-727 [review of
A Boy's Will, North of Boston and Mountain Interval].

1067   Mohrt, Michel.   'Robert Frost: Un Barde Américaine. "
Nouvelles Littéraires (Feb 7, 1963) 3.

1068   Nabuco, Carolina.   'Frost, Poeta da Terra. " Inter-
American Review of Bibliography 1 (1951) 12-16 [in
Portuguese].

1069   Niczky, Helmut.   'Robert Frost. " Moderne Sprachen
(Vienna) (Jan 13, 1969) 3-4, 19-30 (Jan 14, 1970)
1-2, 5-13.

1070   Oka, Jukichi.   'Animals in Robert Frost's Poems. "

Bulletin of Tokyo Gakugei University 14 (March 1963) 1-5 [in Japanese].

1071 _____. 'The Symbolism of Robert Frost. '' Bulletin of Tokyo Gakugei University 13 (1962) 1-10 [in Japanese].

1072 Ortiz-Vargas, Alfredo. ''Perfiles Angloamericanas. '' Revista Iberoamericana 4 (Feb 1942) 163-176.

1073 Panhuysen, J. ''Robert Frost. '' Boekenschouw (Amsterdam) 31 (Jan 1939) 463-468.

1074 Papajewski, Helmut. ''Grundzuge und Substrat in der Lyrik Robert Frosts. '' Archiv 193 (Oct 1956) 8+.

1075 Parks, E. W. ''Robert Frost. '' Boletin de Instituto Brasil-Estados Unidos (Rio de Janiero) 8 (March 1950) 2.

1076 Paz, Octavio. ''Visite al Poeta Robert Frost. '' Sur 15 (Nov 1945) 33-39.

1077 Pisanti, Tommaso. ''La Natura Nella Poesia Di Robert Frost. '' Ausonia 18 (1963) v-vi, 48-50.

1078 Popescu, Petru. ''Poezia lui Robert Frost. '' Viata Românească (Bucurest) 18 (1965) 152-164.

1079 Prévost. Jean. ''Robert Frost. '' Nouvelle Revue Française 52 (May 1939) 818-840.

1080 Romulus, Dianu. ''Robert Frost, sau Dinastia Poetillos Patriarhali. '' Romania Literara (Oct 2, 1969) 19.

1081 Scheffauer, Herman G. ''Amerikanische Literatur der Gegenwart. '' Deutsche Rundschau 186 (Feb 1921) 216, 222.

1082 Schwarz, Karl. ''Ein Dichter Neu-Englands. '' Hochschule und Ausland 13 (March 1935) 46-50.

1083 Serpici, Alessandro. ''Robert Frost. '' Il Ponte 19 (1963) 162-164.

1084 Villard, Leonie. ''Les Tendances Nouvelles de la Littèrature Américaine. '' Mercure de France 163

(May 1, 1923) 596-606.

1085 Ward, Herman M.   "Skaldskapur Roberts Frost. "
      Andvari 5 (1963) 97-107.

1086 Zverev, A.   "Ispytanie Roberta Frosta. "   Voprosy
      Literatury 13 (1969) 204-212.

K. BIBLIOGRAPHIES AND CHECK-LISTS

1087 Boutell, H. S. "A Bibliography of Robert Frost."
Colophon 1 (May 1930) pt. 2.

1088 Byers, Edna H. Robert Frost at Agnes Scott College.
Decatur, Ga.: McCain Library, 1963.

1089 Clymer, W. B. Shubrick and Charles R. Green. Robert Frost: A Bibliography. Amherst, Mass.: Jones
Library, 1937.

1090 Cook, Reginald L. "Robert Frost." Fifteen Modern
American Authors: A Survey of Research and Criti-
cism, ed. Jackson R. Bryer. Durham, N. C.:
Duke University Press, 1969, pp. 323-365.

1091 Crane, Joan St. C. A Descriptive Catalogue of Books
and Manuscripts in the Clifton Waller Barrett Library, University of Virginia. Charlottesville: University Press of Virginia, 1974.

1092 An Exhibition of the Work of Robert Frost. Meadville,
Pa.: Allegheny College, 1938.

1093 Greiner, Donald J. The Merrill Checklist of Robert
Frost. Columbus: Merrill Pub., 1969.

1094 Manly, John Matthews and Edith Rickert. "Robert
Frost." Contemporary American Literature: Bibliographies and Study Outlines, rev. ed. N. Y.: Harcourt-Brace, 1929, pp. 48-49, 179-181.

1095 Melcher, Frederic S. "Robert Frost and His Books."
Colophon 1 (May 1930) 1-7.

1096 Mertins, Louis and Esther. The Intervals of Robert
Frost: A Critical Bibliography. Berkeley: University of California Press, 1947.

1097   "The Mertins Collection of Robert Frost." Bancrofti-
       ana (Berkeley) 55 (June 1973) 11-12.

1098   Munson, Gorham B.   Robert Frost: A Study in Sensi-
       bility and Good Sense.   N. Y. : Doran, 1927, Appen-
       dix B.

1099   Nash, Roy, ed.   Fifty Years of Robert Frost: A
       Catalogue of the Exhibitions Held in Baker Library in
       the Autumn of 1943.   Hanover, N. H. : Dartmouth Col-
       lege Library, 1944.

1100   _____.   "The Poet and the Pirate." New Colophon
       2 (Feb 1950) 311-321.

1101   Newdick, Robert S.   "Bibliographies and Exhibitions of
       the Work of Robert Frost." Amherst Graduates'
       Quarterly 26 (Nov 1936) 79-80.

1102   _____.   "Foreign Responses to Robert Frost."
       Colophon 2 (Win 1937) 289-290.

1103   _____.   "Robert Frost, Teacher and Educator: An
       Annotated Bibliography." Journal of Higher Educa-
       tion 7 (June 1936) 342-344.

1104   _____.   "Uncollected Poems of Robert Frost."
       Book Collectors Journal 2 (Feb 1937) 1-2.

1105   Parameswaran, Uma.   "Robert Frost: A Bibliography
       of Articles and Books, 1958-1964." Bulletin of Bib-
       liography 25 (Jan-April, May-Aug 1967) 46-48, 58,
       69, 72.

1106   Randall, David A.   New Paths in Book Collecting: Es-
       says by Various Hands: American First Editions,
       1900-1930.   N. Y. : Scribner's, 1934, pp. 198, 209,
       212-213, 216-217, 218.

1107   Reading and Collecting (Sept 1937) 15.   "Robert Frost:
       A Check-List Bibliography."

1108   Robert Frost: His "American Send-off"--1915, ed.
       Edward Connery Lathem.   Lunenburg, Vt. : Stine-
       hour Press, 1963.

1109   Robert Frost, His Poems, Portraits, and Printers,

1913-1963: A Comprehensive Exhibit.   Lake Forest,
Ill. : Lake Forest Academy, 1963.

1110   Robert Frost, 1874-1963: An Exhibition of Books,
Manuscripts and Memorabilia Arranged in Honor of
the Poetry Society of Virginia on the Occasion of
Their Meeting in Charlottesville.   Charlottesville,
Va. : Barrett Library, 1966.

1111   Robert Frost 100, compiled by E. C. Lathem.   Boston:
David R. Godine, 1974.

1112   Schwartz, Jacob.   [Bibliography] in 1100 Observe
Points.   London: Ulysses Bookshop, 1931, pp. 54-
55.

1113   Thompson, Lawrence.   "An Early Frost Broadside. "
New Colophon 1 (Jan 1948) 5-12.

1114   _____.   Robert Frost: A Chronological Survey:
Compiled in Connection with an Exhibit of His Work
at the Olin Memorial Library, Wesleylan University,
April 1936.   Middletown,   Conn. : Olin Memorial Library, 1936.

1115   Untermeyer, Louis, ed. Robert Frost: A Backward
Look.   Washington: Library of Congress, 1964
[with partial primary bibliography].

1116   Wedemeyer, Mary Louise.   [Bibliography of Robert
Frost].   Ann Arbor, 1930.   Unpublished.

L. DISSERTATIONS

1117   Allison, Sister Eileen. "Robert Frost's Poetic Treatment of Human Relationships." University of Notre Dame, 1970.

1118   Atkins, Bruce. "Robert Frost: The Orthodoxy of the Self." University of Wisconsin, 1972.

1119   Butler, David W. "Robert Frost and the Clearing in the Wilderness." University of Wisconsin, 1972.

1120   Chamberlain, William. "Robert Frost, Pragmatic Emersonian." Indiana University, 1969.

1121   Cook, Charles H. "Robert Frost, American Symbolist: An Interpretive Study." Boston University, 1957.

1122   Cook, Marjorie E. "Robert Frost: The Challenge of Conflict." Southern Illinois University, 1972.

1123   Daniel, Charles L. "Imagery in the Poetry of Robert Frost." Florida State University, 1973.

1124   Dendinger, Lloyd N. "Robert Frost: Popular Image of a Poet." Louisiana State University, 1966.

1125   Domina, Lyle D. "Frost and Thoreau: A Study in Affinities." University of Missouri, Columbia, 1968.

1126   Eikel, Elizabeth M. "Robert Frost and the Colloquial Tradition in American Poetry." University of Maryland, 1967.

1127   Ganz, Robert N. "The Pattern of Meaning in Robert Frost's Poetry." Harvard University, 1959.

1128   Geyer, Charles W. "Whose Woods? Postures and Tradition in the Prose and Poetry of Robert Frost."

Auburn University, 1967.

1129   Greiner, Donald J.   "Robert Frost's Theory and Prac-
       tice of Poetry. "   University of Virginia, 1967.

1130   Hall, Dorothy.   "Robert Frost: Contours of Faith: A
       Study of a Poet's Religious Belief. "   Boston Univer-
       sity, 1973.

1131   Hannum, William E.   "The Religious Attitudes of
       Robert Frost. "   University of Virginia, 1972.

1132   Harris, Earle G.   "Bond and Free: Robert Frost's
       Early Poetry, 1913-1923. "   Indiana University, 1972.

1133   Haynes, Donald T.   "The Evolution of Form in the
       Early Poetry of Robert Frost: The Emergence of
       a Poetic Self. "   University of Notre Dame, 1968.

1134   Hiebel, William R.   "The Theme of Skepticism in the
       Works of Robert Frost. "   Northwestern University,
       1966.

1135   Horst, Bernard L. , S. M.   "The Poetry of Robert
       Frost: His Use of Personae. "   Fordham University,
       1973.

1136   Hubel, William R.   "The Skepticism of Robert Frost. "
       Northwestern University.

1137   Isaacs, Emily E.   "Robert Frost: The Man and His
       Art. "   Washington University, 1957.

1138   Jacobskind, Barbara R.   "Nature Images in the Poetry
       of Robert Frost: A Three Part Study (Concordance,
       Dictionary, Analysis). "   Brown University, 1970.

1139   Koh, Byron H.   "Robert Frost as Survivalist. "   Univer-
       sity of Massachusetts, 1972.

1140   Kyle, Carol A.   "Epistemological Dualism in the Poet-
       ry of Robert Frost. "   University of Pennsylvania,
       1968.

1141   Lane, Millicent T.   "Agnosticism as Technique: Rob-
       ert Frost's Poetic Style. "   Cornell University, 1967.

1142 Larson, Mildred R. "Robert Frost as a Teacher. "
      New York University, 1949.

1143 Lord, Russell H. "A Study of Robert Frost's Theory
      of Sentence Tones and Some of Its Early Modifica-
      tions. " Boston University, 1972.

1144 Lyford Roland H. "Grammatical Categories in Rob-
      ert Frost's Blank Verse: A Quantitative Analysis. "
      University of California, Davis, 1968.

1145 Lynen, John F. "Pastoralism in the Poetry of Robert
      Frost. " Yale University, 1954.

1146 McCoy, Donald. "The Reception and Development of
      Robert Frost as a Poet. " University of Illinois,
      1952.

1147 Mastendino, Alfred C. "Dualism in the Poetry of Rob-
      ert Frost. " University of Massachusetts, 1971.

1148 Mersch, Arnold R. G. , F. S. C. "Themes of Lone-
      liness and Isolation in the Poetry of Robert Frost. "
      St. Louis University, 1969.

1149 Moore, Andy J. "Topical Philosophy of Robert Frost:
      Science, Politics, Social Philosophy, Education. "
      University of Texas at Austin, 1973.

1150 Nitchie, George W. "Human Values in the Poetry of
      Robert Frost: A Study of a Poet's Convictions. "
      Columbia University, 1958.

1151 Parsons, Thornton H. "The Humanism of Robert
      Frost: A Study in Parallels. " University of Michi-
      gan, 1959.

1152 Pritchard, William H. "The Uses of Nature: A Study
      of Robert Frost's Poetry. " Harvard University, 1960.

1153 Roberts, Esther L. "The Thought in Robert Frost's
      Poetry. " Boston University, 1947.

1154 Ronninger, Lisbeth. "Die Kunstform der Dichtung
      Robert Frosts. " Vienna, 1939.

1155 Ruesch, Lora A. "Man and Nature in the Poetry of

Robert Frost. " Purdue University, 1972.

1156 Schmidt, Sister Mary A. "Metaphor and Opposition in Frost's Poetry. " St. Louis University, 1970.

1157 Seibt, Irma. "Die Dichtung Robert Frosts. " Graz, 1940.

1158 Shackford, John S. "The Development of the Poetry of Robert Frost. " Indiana University, 1971.

1159 Smith, Mary E. "The Function of Natural Phenomena in the Poetry of Robert Frost. " University of Iowa, 1951.

1160 Smythe, Daniel W. "Robert Frost's Poetry as Self-Clarification. " University of Pennsylvania, 1957.

1161 Stone, Virginia S. "Robert Frost: The Breathless Swing Between Content and Form. " East Texas State, 1969.

1162 Vail, Dennis R. "Robert Frost's Imagery and the Poetic Consciousness. " Cornell University, 1972.

1163 Vander Ven, Thomas R. "Inner and Other Voices of Robert Frost: Dramatic Theory and Practice. " University of Colorado, 1968.

1164 Walz, Sister Vincent. "The Doubleness of Nature in Robert Frost's Poetry of Paradox. " St. Louis University, 1968.

APPENDICES

M. THE POEMS: BIBLIOGRAPHICAL HISTORY (AND INDEX TO SECTION A.1.)

The following alphabetized list of Frost's poems serves both as an index to Part One, section A.1. of this text, and as a condensation of the bibliographical history of the poetry. Below each title the reader will find a) place and date of first periodical publication of poem; b) volume of poetry in which poem first appeared; c) subsequent selected and collected volumes in which poem was included; and d) index, by item number, to this text. For those poems which were not published in a periodical prior to publication in a single volume of Frost's poems, part a has simply been eliminated. Left out of part c are those selected or collected editions which contain the same poems as one of the listed volumes --e.g., the contents of the 1946 edition of A Pocket Book of Robert Frost's Poems are the same of those of Come In; the Pocket Book is not listed in part c, Come In is listed. Note that the first number in part d will refer the user to the single volume in which the poem first appeared (which is given by title in part b); following numbers correspond to volumes listed in part c. In part c of the information given after each title, the following abbreviations have been used (given here chronologically):

SP	1923	Selected Poems (New York, 1923)
SP	1928	Selected Poems (New York, 1928)
CP	1930	Collected Poems (New York, 1930)
AB	1932	Augustan Books (London, 1932)
SP	1934	Selected Poems (New York, 1934)
SP	1936	Selected Poems (London, 1936)
CP	1939	Collected Poems (New York, 1939)
Come In	1943	Come In (New York, 1943)
Poems	1946	The Poems of RF (New York, 1946)
CP	1949	Complete Poems (New York, 1949)
RNT	1951	Road Not Taken (New York, 1951)
Aforesaid	1954	Aforesaid (New York, 1954)
SP	1955	Selected Poems (London, 1955)
YCT	1959	You Come Too (New York, 1959)

149

SP 1963   Selected Poems (New York, 1963)
Poetry of RF 1969   Poetry of RF (New York, 1969)
RF: P and P 1972   RF: Poetry and Prose (New York, 1972)

Acceptance
    b) West-Running Brook
    c) CP 1930, CP 1939, Poems 1946, CP 1949, SP
       1963, Poetry of RF 1969
    d) see items: 7, 9, 14, 18, 22, 28, 29

Accidentally on Purpose
    a) in booklet form as Frost's Christmas poem, 1960
    b) In the Clearing
    c) Poetry of RF 1969, RF: P and P 1972
    d) see items: 27, 29, 30

Acquainted with the Night
    a) in Virginia Quarterly Review, Oct 1928
    b) West-Running Brook
    c) CP 1930, AB 1932, SP 1934, SP 1936, CP 1939,
       Poems 1946, CP 1949, Aforesaid 1954, SP 1955,
       YCT 1959, SP 1963, Poetry of RF 1969, RF: P
       and P 1972
    d) see items: 7, 9, 10, 11, 13, 14, 18, 22, 24,
       25, 26, 28, 29, 30

After Apple-Picking
    b) North of Boston
    c) SP 1923, SP 1928, CP 1930, AB 1932, SP 1936,
       CP 1939, Come In 1943, Poems 1946, CP 1949,
       RNT 1951, SP 1955, YCT 1959, SP 1963, Poetry
       of RF 1969, RF: P and P 1972
    d) see items: 3, 6, 8, 9, 10, 11, 13, 14, 16, 18,
       22, 23, 25, 26, 28, 29, 30

Afterflakes
    a) in The Yale Review, Fall 1934
    b) A Further Range
    c) CP 1939, CP 1949, Poetry of RF 1969, RF: P
       and P 1972
    d) see items: 12, 14, 22, 29, 30

Aim Was Song, The
    a) in The Measure, March 1921
    b) New Hampshire

c) CP 1930, CP 1939, Poems 1946, CP 1949, SP
1955, SP 1963, Poetry of RF 1969, RF: P and
P 1972
d) see items: 5, 9, 14, 18, 22, 25, 28, 29, 30

All Revelation
a) as "Geode" in The Yale Review, Spring 1938
b) A Witness Tree
c) Poems 1946, CP 1949, Aforesaid 1954, SP 1955,
SP 1963, Poetry of RF 1969, RF: P and P 1972
d) see items: 15, 18, 22, 24, 25, 28, 29, 30

America Is Hard to See
a) as "And All We Call American" in The Atlantic
Monthly, June 1951
b) In the Clearing
c) SP 1963, Poetry of RF 1969
d) see items: 27, 28, 29

And All We Call American see America Is Hard to See

An Answer
b) A Witness Tree
c) Poems 1946, CP 1949, SP 1955, SP 1963, Poetry of RF 1969, RF: P and P 1972
d) see items: 15, 18, 22, 25, 28, 29, 30

Any Size We Please
b) Steeple Bush
c) CP 1949, Poetry of RF 1969
d) see items: 21, 22, 29

Armful, The
a) in The Nation, Feb 8, 1928
b) West-Running Brook
c) CP 1930, SP 1934, SP 1936, CP 1939, CP 1949,
SP 1963, Poetry of RF 1969, RF: P and P 1972
d) see items: 7, 9, 11, 13, 14, 22, 28, 29, 30

Assurance
b) A Witness Tree
c) Poems 1946, CP 1949, SP 1955, Poetry of RF
1969
d) see items: 15, 18, 22, 25, 29

Astrometaphysical
a) in Virginia Quarterly Review, Winter 1946

  b) Steeple Bush
  c) CP 1949, Poetry of RF 1969
  d) see items: 21, 22, 29

Astronomer, The see [But Outer Space ...]

At Woodward's Gardens
  a) in Poetry, April 1936
  b) A Further Range
  c) CP 1939, Come In 1943, Poems 1946, CP 1949,
     RNT 1951, SP 1955, SP 1963, Poetry of RF 1969
  d) see items: 12, 14, 16, 18, 22, 23, 25, 28, 29

Atmosphere
  a) as "Inscription for a Garden Wall" in Ladies
     Home Journal, Oct 1928
  b) West-Running Brook
  c) CP 1930, CP 1939, Poems 1946, SP 1949, Poet-
     ry of RF 1969
  d) see items: 7, 9, 14, 18, 22, 29

Auspex
  a) in E. S. Sergeant's Robert Frost: The Trial by
     Existence (item 162)
  b) In the Clearing
  c) Poetry of RF 1969
  d) see items: 27, 29

Away!
  a) in booklet form as RF's Christmas poem, 1958
  b) In the Clearing
  c) SP 1963, Poetry of RF 1969, RF: P and P 1972
  d) see items: 27, 28, 29, 30

A-Wishing Well
  a) in booklet form as RF's Christmas poem, 1959
  b) In the Clearing
  c) Poetry of RF 1969
  d) see items: 27, 29

Ax-Helve, The
  a) in The Atlantic Monthly, Sept 1917
  b) New Hampshire
  c) SP 1928, CP 1930, SP 1934, SP 1936, CP 1939,
     Poems 1946, CP 1949, SP 1955, Poetry of RF
     1969
  d) see items: 5, 8, 9, 11, 13, 14, 18, 22, 25, 29

Bad Island--Easter, The
    a) in Times Literary Supplement, Sept 17, 1954
    b) In the Clearing
    c) Poetry of RF 1969
    d) see items: 27, 29

Bear, The
    a) in The Nation, April 18, 1928
    b) West-Running Brook
    c) CP 1930, SP 1934, SP 1936, CP 1939, Poems
       1946, CP 1949, RNT 1951, SP 1955, SP 1963,
       Poetry of RF 1969, RF: P and P 1972
    d) see items: 7, 9, 11, 13, 14, 18, 22, 23, 25,
       28, 29, 30

Bearer of Evil Tidings, The
    a) in The Yale Review, Winter 1936
    b) A Further Range
    c) CP 1939, Poems 1946, CP 1949, RNT 1951, SP
       1955, Poetry of RF 1969
    d) see items: 12, 14, 18, 22, 23, 25, 29

Beech
    b) A Witness Tree
    c) Poems 1946, CP 1949, SP 1963, Poetry of RF
       1969, RF: P and P 1972
    d) see items: 15, 18, 22, 28, 29, 30

Bereft
    a) in The New Republic, Feb 9, 1927
    b) West-Running Brook
    c) CP 1930, SP 1934, CP 1939, Poems 1946, CP
       1949, RNT 1951, SP 1955, SP 1963, Poetry of
       RF 1969
    d) see items: 7, 9, 11, 14, 18, 22, 23, 25, 28,
       29

Beyond Words
    b) Steeple Bush
    c) CP 1949, SP 1955, Poetry of RF 1969
    d) see items: 21, 22, 25, 29

Birches
    a) in The Atlantic Monthly, Aug 1915
    b) Mountain Interval
    c) SP 1923, SP 1928, CP 1930, AB 1932, SP 1934,
       SP 1936, CP 1939, Come In 1943, Poems 1946,

CP 1949, <u>RNT</u> 1951, <u>Aforesaid</u> 1954, <u>SP</u> 1955,
<u>YCT</u> 1959, <u>SP</u> 1963, <u>Poetry of RF</u> 1969, <u>RF: P</u>
<u>and P</u> 1972
   d) see items: 4, 6, 8, 9, 10, 11, 13, 14, 16, 18,
      22, 23, 24, 25, 26, 28, 29, 30

Birthplace, The
   a) in <u>The Dartmouth Bema</u>, June 1923
   b) <u>West-Running Brook</u>
   c) <u>CP 1930</u>, <u>SP 1934</u>, CP 1939, <u>Come In</u> 1943,
      <u>Poems 1946</u>, <u>CP 1949</u>, <u>RNT 1951</u>, <u>SP</u> 1955, <u>YCT</u>
      <u>1959</u>, <u>SP 1963</u>, <u>Poetry of RF</u> 1969
   d) see items: 7, 9, 11, 14, 16, 18, 22, 23, 25,
      26, 28, 29

Black Cottage, The
   b) <u>North of Boston</u>
   c) <u>SP 1928</u>, <u>CP 1930</u>, <u>SP</u> 1934, <u>SP</u> 1936, <u>CP</u> 1939,
      <u>Poems 1946</u>, <u>CP 1949</u>, <u>SP 1955</u>, <u>SP 1963</u>, <u>Poetry</u>
      <u>of RF</u> 1969
   d) see items: 3, 8, 9, 11, 13, 14, 18, 22, 25, 28,
      29

Blood <u>see</u> Flood, The

Blue Ribbon at Amesbury, A
   a) in <u>The Atlantic Monthly</u>, April 1936
   b) <u>A Further Range</u>
   c) <u>CP 1939</u>, <u>Come In</u> 1943, <u>Poems</u> 1946, <u>CP</u> 1949,
      <u>RNT</u> 1951, <u>SP 1955</u>, <u>SP</u> 1963, <u>Poetry of RF</u>
      1969, <u>RF: P and P</u> 1972
   d) see items: 12, 14, 16, 18, 22, 23, 25, 28, 29,
      30

Blueberries
   b) <u>North of Boston</u>
   c) <u>SP 1923</u>, <u>SP 1928</u>, <u>CP 1930</u>, <u>SP</u> 1934, <u>SP</u> 1936,
      <u>CP</u> 1939, <u>Come In</u> 1943, <u>Poems</u> 1946, <u>CP</u> 1949,
      <u>RNT</u> 1951, <u>SP 1955</u>, <u>YCT 1959</u>, <u>SP</u> 1963, <u>Poetry</u>
      <u>of RF</u> 1969
   d) see items: 3, 6, 8, 9, 11, 13, 14, 16, 18, 22,
      23, 25, 26, 28, 29

Blue-Butterfly Day
   a) in <u>The New Republic</u>, March 16, 1921
   b) <u>New Hampshire</u>
   c) <u>CP 1930</u>, <u>CP</u> 1939, <u>Poems</u> 1946, <u>CP</u> 1949, <u>YCT</u>

1959, SP 1963, Poetry of RF 1969
d) see items: 5, 9, 14, 18, 22, 26, 28, 29

Boeotian
b) A Witness Tree
c) Poems 1946, CP 1949, SP 1955, SP 1963, Poetry
of RF 1969, RF: P and P 1972
d) see items: 15, 18, 22, 25, 28, 29, 30

Bond and Free
b) Mountain Interval
c) SP 1923, SP 1928, CP 1930, SP 1934, CP 1939,
Poems 1946, CP 1949, SP 1963, Poetry of RF
1969
d) see items: 4, 6, 8, 9, 11, 14, 18, 22, 28, 29

Bonfire, The
a) in The Seven Arts, Nov 1916
b) Mountain Interval
c) CP 1930, CP 1939, Poems 1946, CP 1949, SP
1963, Poetry of RF 1969
d) see items: 4, 9, 14, 18, 22, 28, 29

Boundless Moment, A
a) in The New Republic, Oct 24, 1923
b) New Hampshire
c) CP 1930, CP 1939, Poems 1946, CP 1949, RNT
1951, Poetry of RF 1969
d) see items: 5, 9, 14, 18, 22, 23, 29

Bravado
a) as "Bravery" in The Yale Review, Autumn 1946
b) Steeple Bush
c) CP 1949, Aforesaid 1954, SP 1955, SP 1963,
Poetry of RF 1969, RF: P and P 1972
d) see items: 21, 22, 24, 25, 28, 29, 30

Broken Drought, The
a) as "But He Meant It" in The Atlantic Monthly,
April 1947
b) Steeple Bush
c) CP 1949, SP 1955, Poetry of RF 1969
d) see items: 21, 22, 25, 29

Brook in the City, A
a) in The New Republic, March 9, 1921
b) New Hampshire

      c) CP 1930, SP 1934, SP 1936, CP 1939, Come In
        1943, Poems 1946, CP 1949, RNT 1951, Poetry
        of RF 1969
      d) see items: 5, 9, 11, 13, 14, 16, 18, 22, 23,
        29

Brown's Descent
      b) Mountain Interval
      c) SP 1923, SP 1928, CP 1930, SP 1934, SP 1936,
        CP 1939, Come In 1943, Poems 1946, CP 1949,
        RNT 1951, YCT 1959, Poetry of RF 1969
      d) see items: 4, 6, 8, 9, 11, 13, 14, 16, 18, 22,
        23, 26, 29

Build Soil
      b) A Further Range
      c) CP 1939, Poems 1946, CP 1949, SP 1955, SP
        1963, Poetry of RF 1969, RF: P and P 1972
      d) see items: 12, 14, 18, 22, 25, 28, 29, 30

Bursting Rapture
      b) Steeple Bush
      c) CP 1949, Poetry of RF 1969
      d) see items: 21, 22, 29

But He Meant It see Broken Drought, The

[But Outer Space ...]
      a) as "The Astronomer" in RF's A Remembrance
        Collection of New Poems (New York, 1959)
      b) In the Clearing
      c) Poetry of RF 1969
      d) see items: 27, 29

Cabin in the Clearing, A
      a) in booklet form as RF's Christmas poem, 1951
      b) In the Clearing
      c) SP 1963, Poetry of RF 1969, RF: P and P 1972
      d) see items: 27, 28, 29, 30

Canis Major
      a) as "On a Star-Bright Night" in New York Herald
        Tribune Books, March 22, 1925
      b) West-Running Brook
      c) CP 1930, SP 1934, SP 1936, CP 1939, Come In
        1943, Poems 1946, CP 1949, RNT 1951, SP 1963,
        Poetry of RF 1969

d) see items: 7, 9, 11, 13, 14, 16, 18, 22, 23, 28, 29

Carpe Diem
a) in The Atlantic Monthly, Sept 1938
b) A Witness Tree
c) Poems 1946, CP 1949, Aforesaid 1954, SP 1955, SP 1963, Poetry of RF 1969, RF: P and P 1972
d) see items: 15, 18, 22, 24, 25, 28, 29, 30

Case for Jefferson, A
b) Steeple Bush
c) CP 1949, SP 1955, SP 1963, Poetry of RF 1969, RF: P and P 1972
d) see items: 21, 22, 25, 28, 29, 30

Census-Taker, The
a) in The New Republic, April 6, 1921
b) New Hampshire
c) CP 1930, CP 1939, Come In 1943, Poems 1946, CP 1949, RNT 1951, SP 1963, Poetry of RF 1969
d) see items: 5, 9, 14, 16, 18, 22, 28, 29

Christmas Trees
b) Mountain Interval
c) CP 1930, CP 1939, Poems 1946, CP 1949, YCT 1959, SP 1963, Poetry of RF 1969
d) see items: 4, 9, 14, 18, 22, 26, 28, 29

Clear and Colder
a) in Direction, Autumn 1934
b) A Further Range
c) CP 1939, CP 1949, Poetry of RF 1969
d) see items: 12, 14, 22, 29

Cliff Dwelling, A
b) Steeple Bush
c) CP 1949, SP 1963, Poetry of RF 1969
d) see items: 21, 22, 28, 29

Closed for Good
a) in booklet form as RF's Christmas poem, 1948; appeared in "Afterword" section of 1949 Collected Poems prior to its incorporation into the contents of In the Clearing
b) In the Clearing
c) CP 1949, Aforesaid 1954, SP 1955, SP 1963,

Poetry of RF 1969, RF: P and P 1972
d) see items: 22, 24, 25, 27, 28, 29, 30

Cloud Shadow, A
b) A Witness Tree
c) Poems 1946, CP 1949, RNT 1951, SP 1963,
Poetry of RF 1969
d) see items: 15, 18, 22, 28, 29

Cocoon, The
a) in The New Republic, Feb 9, 1927
b) West-Running Brook
c) CP 1930, CP 1939, CP 1949, Poetry of RF 1969
d) see items: 7, 9, 14, 22, 29

Code, The
a) as "The Code-Heroics" in Poetry, Feb 1914
b) North of Boston
c) SP 1923, SP 1928, CP 1930, SP 1934, SP 1936,
CP 1939, Come In 1943, Poems 1946, CP 1949,
RNT 1951, SP 1955, SP 1963, Poetry of RF
1969, RF: P and P 1972
d) see items: 3, 6, 8, 9, 11, 13, 14, 16, 18, 22,
23, 25, 28, 29, 30

Come In
a) in The Atlantic Monthly, Feb 1941
b) A Witness Tree
c) Come In 1943, Poems 1946, CP 1949, RNT 1951,
Aforesaid 1954, SP 1955, SP 1963, Poetry of RF
1969, RF: P and P 1972
d) see items: 15, 16, 18, 22, 23, 24, 25, 28, 29,
30

Common Fate, The see Peck of Gold, A

Concept Self-Conceived, A
b) In the Clearing
c) SP 1963, Poetry of RF 1969
d) see items: 27, 28, 29

Considerable Speck, A
a) in The Atlantic Monthly, July 1939
b) A Witness Tree
c) Come In 1943, Poems 1946, CP 1949, RNT 1951,
Aforesaid 1954, SP 1955, SP 1963, Poetry of RF
1969, RF: P and P 1972

    d) see items: 15, 16, 18, 22, 23, 24, 25, 28, 29, 30

Courage to Be New, The
    a) first two stanzas as "1946" in separate form, as a broadside printed for dedication of Orris C. Manning Memorial Park, Ripton, Vermont, July 28, 1946
    b) Steeple Bush
    c) CP 1949, Aforesaid 1954, SP 1955, SP 1963, Poetry of RF 1969
    d) see items: 21, 22, 24, 25, 28, 29

Cow in Apple Time, The
    a) in Poetry and Drama, Dec 1914
    b) Mountain Interval
    c) SP 1923, SP 1928, CP 1930, SP 1934, SP 1936, CP 1939, Come In 1943, Poems 1946, CP 1949, RNT 1951, SP 1955, YCT 1959, Poetry of RF 1969, RF: P and P 1972
    d) see items: 4, 6, 8, 9, 11, 13, 14, 16, 18, 22, 23, 25, 26, 28, 29

Death of the Hired Man, The
    b) North of Boston
    c) SP 1923, SP 1928, CP 1930, AB 1932, SP 1934, SP 1936, CP 1939, Come In 1943, Poems 1946, CP 1949, RNT 1951, Aforesaid 1954, SP 1955, YCT 1959, SP 1963, Poetry of RF 1969, RF: P and P 1972
    d) see items: 3, 6, 8, 9, 11, 13, 14, 16, 18, 22, 23, 24, 25, 26, 28, 29, 30

Demiurge's Laugh, The
    b) A Boy's Will
    c) CP 1930, CP 1939, Poems 1946, CP 1949, SP 1955, SP 1963, Poetry of RF 1969, RF: P and P 1972
    d) see items: 2, 9, 14, 18, 22, 25, 28, 29, 30

Departmental
    a) in The Yale Review, Winter 1936
    b) A Further Range
    c) CP 1939, Come In 1943, Poems 1946, CP 1949, RNT 1951, Aforesaid 1954, SP 1955, SP 1963, Poetry of RF 1969, RF: P and P 1972
    d) see items: 12, 14, 16, 18, 22, 23, 24, 25, 28, 29, 30

Desert Places
  a) in The American Mercury, April 1934
  b) A Further Range
  c) CP 1939, Poems 1946, CP 1949, Aforesaid 1954,
     SP 1955, SP 1963, Poetry of RF 1969, RF: P and
     P 1972
  d) see items: 12, 14, 18, 22, 24, 25, 28, 29, 30

Design
  a) in American Poetry 1922: A Miscellany (New
     York, 1922)
  b) A Further Range
  c) CP 1939, Come In 1943, Poems 1946, CP 1949,
     RNT 1951, Aforesaid 1954, SP 1955, SP 1963,
     Poetry of RF 1969, RF: P and P 1972
  d) see items: 12, 14, 16, 18, 22, 23, 24, 25, 28,
     29, 30

Devotion
  b) West-Running Brook
  c) CP 1930, CP 1939, Poems 1946, CP 1949, SP
     1963, Poetry of RF 1969, RF: P and P 1972
  d) see items: 7, 9, 14, 18, 22, 28, 29, 30

Directive
  a) in The Virginia Quarterly Review, Winter 1946
  b) Steeple Bush
  c) CP 1949, Aforesaid 1954, SP 1955, SP 1963,
     Poetry of RF 1969, RF: P and P 1972
  d) see items: 21, 22, 24, 25, 28, 29, 30

Discovery of the Madeiras, The
  b) A Witness Tree
  c) CP 1949, Poetry of RF 1969, RF: P and P 1972
  d) see items: 15, 22, 29, 30

Does No One at All Ever Feel This Way in the Least?
  a) as "Does No One But Me at All Ever Feel This
     Way in the Least?" in booklet form as RF's
     Christmas poem, 1952
  b) In the Clearing
  c) Poetry of RF 1969
  d) see items: 27, 29

Doom to Bloom see Our Doom to Bloom

Door in the Dark, The
    b) West-Running Brook
    c) CP 1930, CP 1939, CP 1949, Poetry of RF 1969,
       RF: P and P 1972
    d) see items: 7, 9, 14, 22, 29, 30

Draft Horse, The
    b) In the Clearing
    c) Poetry of RF 1969, RF: P and P 1972
    d) see items: 27, 29, 30

Dream Pang, A
    b) A Boy's Will
    c) CP 1930, CP 1939, CP 1949, Poetry of RF 1969,
       RF: P and P 1972
    d) see items: 2, 9, 14, 22, 29, 30

Drumlin Woodchuck, A
    a) in The Atlantic Monthly, June 1936
    b) A Further Range
    c) CP 1939, Come In 1943, Poems 1946, CP 1949,
       RNT 1951, Aforesaid 1954, SP 1955, YCT 1959,
       SP 1963, Poetry of RF 1969, RF: P and P 1972
    d) see items: 12, 14, 16, 18, 22, 23, 24, 25, 26,
       28, 29, 30

Dust in the Eyes
    a) in broadside form as advertisement for West-
       Running Brook
    b) West-Running Brook
    c) CP 1930, CP 1939, Poems 1946, CP 1949, SP
       1963, Poetry of RF 1969
    d) see items: 7, 9, 14, 18, 22, 28, 29

Dust of Snow
    a) as "A Favour" in The London Mercury, Dec
       1920, and as "Snow Dust" in The Yale Review,
       Jan 1921
    b) New Hampshire
    c) SP 1928, CP 1930, AB 1932, SP 1934, SP 1936,
       CP 1939, Come In 1943, Poems 1946, CP 1949,
       RNT 1951, Aforesaid 1954, SP 1955, YCT 1959,
       SP 1963, Poetry of RF 1969, RF: P and P 1972
    d) see items: 5, 8, 9, 10, 11, 13, 14, 16, 18, 22,
       23, 24, 25, 26, 28, 29, 30

Egg and the Machine, The
>   a) as "The Walker" in The Second American Cara-
>   van (New York, 1928), ed. by Alfred Kreymborg,
>   Lewis Mumford and Paul Rosenfeld; added to
>   contents of West-Running Brook in CP 1930
>   c) CP 1930, CP 1939, Poems 1946, CP 1949, SP
>   1955, Poetry of RF 1969
>   d) see items: 9, 14, 18, 22, 25, 29

Empty Threat, An
>   b) New Hampshire
>   c) CP 1930, CP 1939, Poems 1946, CP 1949, SP 1955,
>   SP 1963, Poetry of RF 1969, RF: P and P 1972
>   d) see items: 5, 9, 14, 18, 22, 25, 28, 29, 30

Encounter, An
>   a) in The Atlantic Monthly, Nov 1916
>   b) Mountain Interval
>   c) SP 1923, SP 1928, CP 1930, SP 1934, CP 1939,
>   Poems 1946, CP 1949, SP 1963, Poetry of RF 1969
>   d) see items: 4, 6, 8, 9, 11, 14, 18, 22, 28, 29

Ends
>   b) In the Clearing
>   c) SP 1963, Poetry of RF 1969, RF: P and P 1972
>   d) see items: 27, 28, 29, 30

Equalizer, An
>   b) A Witness Tree
>   c) CP 1949, Poetry of RF 1969
>   d) see items: 15, 22, 29

Escapist--Never
>   a) in The Massachusetts Review, Winter 1962
>   b) In the Clearing
>   c) Poetry of RF 1969, RF: P and P 1972
>   d) see items: 27, 29, 30

Etherealizing
>   a) in The Atlantic Monthly, April 1947
>   b) Steeple Bush
>   c) CP 1949, Aforesaid 1954, SP 1955, SP 1963,
>   Poetry of RF 1969
>   d) see items: 21, 22, 24, 25, 28, 29

Evening in a Sugar Orchard
>   a) in Whimsies (University of Michigan), Nov 1921
>   b) New Hampshire

c) CP 1930, CP 1939, Come In 1943, CP 1949,
   RNT 1951, Poetry of RF 1969
d) see items: 5, 9, 14, 16, 22, 23, 29

Evil Tendencies Cancel
a) as "Tendencies Cancel" in Poetry, April 1936
b) A Further Range
c) CP 1939, Poems 1946, CP 1949, SP 1955, SP
   1963, Poetry of RF 1969
d) see items: 12, 14, 18, 22, 25, 28, 29

Exposed Nest, The
b) Mountain Interval
c) CP 1930, CP 1939, CP 1949, YCT 1959, Poetry
   of RF 1969
d) see items: 4, 9, 14, 22, 26, 29

Favour, A see Dust of Snow

Fear, The
a) in Poetry and Drama, Dec 1913
b) North of Boston
c) CP 1930, CP 1939, Poems 1946, CP 1949, RNT
   1951, SP 1955, SP 1963, Poetry of RF 1969, RF:
   P and P 1972
d) see items: 3, 9, 14, 18, 22, 23, 25, 28, 29, 30

Fear of God, The
b) Steeple Bush
c) CP 1949, SP 1963, Poetry of RF 1969, RF: P and P 1972
d) see Items: 21, 22, 28, 29, 30

Fear of Man, The
b) Steeple Bush
c) CP 1949, SP 1963, Poetry of RF 1969
d) see items: 21, 22, 28, 29

Figure in the Doorway, The
a) in The Virginia Quarterly Review, April 1936
b) A Further Range
c) CP 1939, Come In 1943, Poems 1946, CP 1949,
   RNT 1951, SP 1955, Poetry of RF 1969
d) see items: 12, 14, 16, 18, 22, 23, 25, 29

Fire and Ice
a) in Harper's Magazine, Dec 1920

b) New Hampshire
c) SP 1928, CP 1930, SP 1934, CP 1939, Come In
1943, Poems 1946, CP 1949, RNT 1951, SP 1955,
YCT 1959, SP 1963, Poetry of RF 1969, RF: P
and P 1972
d) see items: 5, 8, 9, 11, 14, 16, 18, 22, 23, 25,
26, 28, 29, 30

Fireflies in the Garden
b) West-Running Brook
c) CP 1930, AB 1932, CP 1939, Come In 1943,
Poems 1946, CP 1949, RNT 1951, SP 1955, YCT
1959, SP 1963, Poetry of RF 1969
d) see items: 7, 9, 10, 14, 16, 18, 22, 23, 25,
26 28, 29, 30

Flood, The
a) as "Blood" in The Nation, Feb 8, 1928
b) West-Running Brook
c) CP 1930, CP 1939, Poems 1946, CP 1949, SP
1955, SP 1963, Poetry of RF 1969
d) see items: 7, 9, 14, 18, 22, 25, 28, 29

Flower Boat, The
a) in The Youth's Companion, May 20, 1909
b) West-Running Brook
c) CP 1930, CP 1939, Come In 1943, Poems 1946,
CP 1949, RNT 1951, Poetry of RF 1969
d) see items: 7, 9, 14, 16, 18, 22, 23, 29

Flower-Gathering
b) A Boy's Will
c) SP 1923, SP 1928, CP 1930, SP 1934, SP 1936,
CP 1939, Poems 1946, CP 1949, Poetry of RF
1969, RF: P and P 1972
d) see items: 2, 6, 8, 9, 11, 13, 14, 18, 22, 29,
30

For John F. Kennedy His Inauguration
a) in newspapers directly after Kennedy's inauguration, Jan 20, 1961
b) In the Clearing
c) Poetry of RF 1969
d) see items: 27, 29

For Once, Then, Something
a) in Harper's Magazine, July 1920

     b) New Hampshire
     c) CP 1930, CP 1939, Come In 1943, Poems 1946,
        CP 1949, RNT 1951, Aforesaid 1954, SP 1955,
        SP 1963, Poetry of RF 1969, RF: P and P 1972
     d) see items: 5, 9, 14, 16, 18, 22, 23, 24, 25,
        28, 29, 30

[Forgive, O Lord ...]
     a) as "The Preacher" in RF's A Remembrance Col-
        lection of New Poems (New York, 1959)
     b) In the Clearing
     c) SP 1963, Poetry of RF 1969, RF: P and P 1972
     d) see items: 27, 28, 29, 30

Fountain, a Bottle, a Donkey's Ears, and Some Books, A
     a) in The Bookman, Oct 1923
     b) New Hampshire
     c) CP 1930, CP 1939, CP 1949, Poetry of RF 1969
     d) see items: 5, 9, 14, 22, 29

[Four-Room Shack ...]
     b) In the Clearing
     c) SP 1963, Poetry of RF 1969, RF: P and P 1972
     d) see items: 27, 28, 29, 30

Fragmentary Blue
     a) in Harper's Magazine, July 1920
     b) New Hampshire
     c) SP 1928, CP 1930, SP 1934, CP 1939, Poems
        1946, CP 1949, SP 1955, SP 1963, Poetry of RF
        1969
     d) see items: 5, 8, 9, 11, 14, 18, 22, 25, 28, 29

Freedom of the Moon, The
     b) West-Running Brook
     c) CP 1930, CP 1939, Poems 1946, CP 1949, YCT
        1959, Poetry of RF 1969
     d) see items: 7, 9, 14, 18, 22, 26, 29

From a Milkweed Pod see Pod of the Milkweed

From Iron
     a) as "The Sage" in RF's A Remembrance Collection
        of New Poems (New York, 1959)
     b) In the Clearing
     c) Poetry of RF 1969, RF: P and P 1972
     d) see items: 27, 29, 30

From Plane to Plane
    a) in What's New (Abbot Laboratories, Chicago); in
       "Afterword" of CP 1949
    c) CP 1949, Poetry of RF 1969
    d) see items: 22, 29

Gathering Leaves
    a) in The Measure, Aug 1923
    b) New Hampshire
    c) CP 1930, CP 1939, Come In 1943, Poems 1946,
       CP 1949, RNT 1951, YCT 1959, SP 1963, Poetry
       of RF 1969
    d) see items: 5, 9, 14, 16, 18, 22, 23, 26, 28,
       29

Generations of Men, The
    b) North of Boston
    c) CP 1930, CP 1939, Poems 1946, CP 1949, SP
       1963, Poetry of RF 1969
    d) see items: 3, 9, 14, 18, 22, 28, 29

Geode see All Revelation

Ghost House
    a) in The Youth's Companion, March 15, 1906
    b) A Boy's Will
    c) CP 1930, CP 1939, Come In 1943, Poems 1946,
       CP 1949, RNT 1951, SP 1955, SP 1963, Poetry
       of RF 1969, RF: P and P 1972
    d) see items: 2, 9, 14, 16, 18, 22, 23, 25, 28,
       29, 30

Gift Outright, The
    a) in The Virginia Quarterly Review, Spring 1942
    b) A Witness Tree
    c) Come In 1943, Poems 1946, CP 1949, RNT 1951,
       SP 1955, SP 1963, Poetry of RF 1969, RF: P and
       P 1972
    d) see items: 15, 16, 18, 22, 23, 25, 28, 29, 30

Girl's Garden, A
    b) Mountain Interval
    c) CP 1930, CP 1939, CP 1949, YCT 1959, SP
       1963, Poetry of RF 1969
    d) see items: 4, 9, 14, 22, 26, 28, 29

Going for Water
  b) A Boy's Will
  c) SP 1923, SP 1928, CP 1930, SP 1934, SP 1936,
     CP 1939, Poems 1946, CP 1949, RNT 1951, YCT
     1959, Poetry of RF 1969
  d) see items: 2, 6, 8, 9, 11, 13, 14, 18, 19, 22,
     23, 26, 29

Gold Hesperidee, The
  a) in Farm and Fireside, Sept 1921
  b) A Further Range
  c) CP 1939, Poems 1946, CP 1949, Poetry of RF
     1969
  d) see items: 14, 18, 22, 29

Good Hours
  b) North of Boston
  c) CP 1930, CP 1939, Poems 1946, CP 1949, RNT
     1951, YCT 1959, Poetry of RF 1969
  d) see items: 3, 9, 14, 18, 22, 23, 26, 29

Good-bye and Keep Cold
  a) in Harper's Magazine, July 1920
  b) New Hampshire
  c) SP 1928, CP 1930, SP 1934, SP 1936, CP 1939,
     Come In 1943, Poems 1946, CP 1949, RNT 1951,
     SP 1955, YCT 1959, SP 1963, Poetry of RF 1969
  d) see items: 5, 6, 8, 9, 11, 13, 14, 16, 18, 22,
     23, 25, 26, 28, 29

Grindstone, The
  a) in Farm and Fireside, June 1921
  b) New Hampshire
  c) SP 1928, CP 1930, SP 1934, SP 1936, CP 1939,
     Come In 1943, Poems 1946, CP 1949, RNT 1951,
     SP 1955, SP 1963, Poetry of RF 1969
  d) see items: 5, 8, 9, 11, 13, 14, 16, 18, 22, 23,
     25, 28, 29

Gum-Gatherer, The
  a) in The Independent, Oct 9, 1916
  b) Mountain Interval
  c) SP 1923, SP 1928, CP 1930, SP 1934, SP 1936,
     CP 1939, Come In 1943, Poems 1946, CP 1949,
     SP 1955, SP 1963, Poetry of RF 1969
  d) see items: 4, 6, 8, 9, 11, 13, 14, 16, 18, 22,
     25, 28, 29

Haec Fabula Docet
    a) in Atlantic Monthly, Dec 1946
    b) Steeple Bush
    c) CP 1949, SP 1955, Poetry of RF 1969
    d) see items: 21, 22, 25, 29

Hannibal
    b) West-Running Brook
    c) CP 1930, CP 1939, Poems 1946, CP 1949, SP
       1955, SP 1963, Poetry of RF 1969
    d) see items: 7, 9, 14, 18, 22, 25, 28, 29

Happiness Makes Up in Height for What It Lacks in Length
    a) in Atlantic Monthly, Sept 1938
    b) A Witness Tree
    c) Poems 1946, CP 1949, RNT 1951, Aforesaid
       1954, SP 1955, SP 1963, Poetry of RF 1969, RF:
       P and P 1972
    d) see items: 15, 18, 22, 23, 24, 25, 28, 29, 30

Hardship of Accounting, The
    a) as "Money" in Poetry, April 1936
    b) A Further Range
    c) CP 1939, Poems 1946, CP 1949, RNT 1951,
       Aforesaid 1954, SP 1955, SP 1963, Poetry of RF
       1969, RF: P and P 1972
    d) see items: 12, 14, 18, 22, 23, 24, 25, 28, 29,
       30

Hill Wife, The
    a) in The Yale Review, April 1916; part III published
       in Poetry and Drama, Dec 1914; part I published
       by itself in SP 1955
    b) Mountain Interval
    c) SP 1923, SP 1928, CP 1930, SP 1934, SP 1936,
       CP 1939, Poems 1946, CP 1949, RNT 1951, SP
       1963, Poetry of RF 1969, RF: P and P 1972
    d) see items: 4, 6, 8, 9, 11, 13, 14, 18, 22, 23,
       28, 29, 30

Hillside Thaw, A
    a) in The New Republic, April 6, 1921
    b) New Hampshire
    c) SP 1928, CP 1930, SP 1934, CP 1939, Come In
       1943, CP 1949, RNT 1951, Poetry of RF 1969
    d) see items: 5, 6, 9, 11, 14, 16, 22, 23, 29

Home Burial
    b) North of Boston
    c) SP 1923, SP 1928, CP 1930, SP 1934, SP 1936,
       CP 1939, Come In 1943, Poems 1946, CP 1949,
       RNT 1951, Aforesaid 1954, SP 1955, SP 1963,
       Poetry of RF 1969, RF: P and P 1972
    d) see items: 3, 6, 8, 9, 11, 13, 14, 16, 18, 22,
       23, 24, 25, 28, 29, 30

Housekeeper, The
    b) North of Boston
    c) CP 1930, CP 1939, Poems 1946, CP 1949, RNT
       1951, Poetry of RF 1969, RF: P and P 1972
    d) see items: 3, 9, 14, 18, 22, 23, 29, 30

How Hard It Is to Keep from Being King When It's in You
    and in the Situation
    a) in Proceedings of the American Academy of Arts
       and Letters and the National Institute of Arts and
       Letters, 2nd series, no. 1, 1951
    b) In the Clearing
    c) Poetry of RF 1969
    d) see items: 27, 29

Hundred Collars, A
    a) in Poetry and Drama, Dec 1913
    b) North of Boston
    c) SP 1923, SP 1928, CP 1930, SP 1934, SP 1936
       CP 1939, Poems 1946, CP 1949, RNT 1951, SP
       1955, SP 1963, Poetry of RF 1969
    d) see items: 3, 6, 8, 9, 11, 13, 14, 18, 22, 23,
       25, 28, 29

Hyla Brook
    b) Mountain Interval
    c) SP 1923, SP 1928, CP 1930, SP 1934, SP 1936,
       CP 1939, Come In 1943, Poems 1946, CP 1949,
       RNT 1951, Aforesaid 1954, SP 1955, YCT 1959,
       Poetry of RF 1969, RF: P and P 1972
    d) see items: 4, 6, 8, 9, 11, 13, 14, 16, 18, 22,
       23, 24, 25, 26, 29, 30

I Could Give All to Time
    a) in The Yale Review, Autumn 1941
    b) A Witness Tree
    c) Poems 1946, CP 1949, RNT 1951, SP 1963,
       Poetry of RF 1969

  d) see items: 15, 18, 22, 28, 29

I Will Sing You One-O
    a) in The Yale Review, Oct 1923
    b) New Hampshire
    c) CP 1930, CP 1939, CP 1949, RNT 1951, SP 1955,
       Poetry of RF 1969, RF: P and P 1972
    d) see items: 5, 9, 14, 22, 23, 25, 29, 30

Immigrants
    a) as fourth stanza of "The Return of the Pilgrims"
       in G. P. Baker's The Pilgrim Spirit (Boston
       1921)
    b) West-Running Brook
    c) CP 1930, CP 1939, Poems 1946, CP 1949, SP
       1955, SP 1963, Poetry of RF 1969
    d) see items: 7, 9, 14, 18, 22, 23, 28, 29

Imposter, An
    a) as "The Imposter" in Atlantic Monthly, April
       1947
    b) Steeple Bush
    c) CP 1949, SP 1955, Poetry of RF 1969, RF: P and
       P 1972
    d) see items: 21, 22, 25, 29, 30

In a Disused Graveyard
    a) in The Measure, Aug 1923
    b) New Hampshire
    c) CP 1930, CP 1939, Come In 1943, CP 1949, RNT
       1951, SP 1963, Poetry of RF 1969
    d) see items: 5, 9, 14, 16, 22, 23, 28, 29

In a Glass of Cider
    b) In the Clearing
    c) Poetry of RF 1969, RF: P and P 1972
    d) see items: 27, 29, 30

In a Poem
    b) A Witness Tree
    c) CP 1949, RNT 1951, SP 1963, Poetry of RF 1969,
       RF: P and P 1972
    d) see items: 15, 22, 23, 28, 29, 30

In a Vale
    b) A Boy's Will
    c) CP 1930, CP 1939, CP 1949, Poetry of RF 1969

d) see items: 2, 9, 14, 22, 29

In Divés Dive
  a) in Poetry, April 1936
  b) A Further Range
  c) CP 1939, Poems 1946, CP 1949, SP 1955, SP
     1963, Poetry of RF 1969
  d) see items: 12, 14, 18, 22, 25, 28, 29

In Hardwood Groves
  a) as "The Same Leaves" in The Dearborn Independ-
     ent, Dec 18, 1926
  b) added to contents of A Boy's Will in CP 1930
  c) CP 1930, CP 1939, Come In 1943, CP 1949, RNT
     1951, Poetry of RF 1969
  d) see items: 9, 14, 16, 22, 23, 29

In Neglect
  b) A Boy's Will
  c) CP 1930, CP 1939, Poems 1946, CP 1949, RNT
     1951, SP 1955, SP 1963, Poetry of RF 1969, RF:
     P and P 1972
  d) see items: 2, 9, 14, 18, 22, 23, 25, 28, 29,
     30

In the Home Stretch
  a) in The Century, July 1916
  b) Mountain Interval
  c) SP 1923, SP 1928, CP 1930, SP 1934, CP 1939,
     CP 1949, Poetry of RF 1969
  d) see items: 4, 6, 8, 9, 11, 14, 22, 29

In the Long Night
  a) in Dartmouth in Portrait 1944 (College Calender,
     Hanover, 1943)
  b) Steeple Bush
  c) CP 1949, SP 1963, Poetry of RF 1969
  d) see items: 21, 22, 28, 29

In Time of Cloudburst
  a) in Virginia Quarterly Review, April 1936
  b) A Further Range
  c) CP 1939, Poems 1946, CP 1949, Aforesaid 1954,
     SP 1955, SP 1963, Poetry of RF 1969
  d) see items: 12, 14, 18, 22, 24, 25, 28, 29

[In Winter in the Woods ...]
        a) in holograph facsimile, Amherst College 1962
        b) In the Clearing
        c) Poetry of RF 1969, RF: P and P 1972
        d) see items: 27, 29, 30

Ingenuities of Debt, The
        a) in Atlantic Monthly, Dec 1946
        b) Steeple Bush
        c) CP 1949, SP 1963, Poetry of RF 1969
        d) see items: 21, 22, 28, 29

Innate Helium
        b) Steeple Bush
        c) CP 1949, Poetry of RF 1969
        d) see items: 21, 22, 29

Inscription for a Garden Wall   see   Atmosphere

Into My Own
        a) as "Into Mine Own" in New England Magazine,
           May 1909
        b) A Boy's Will
        c) SP 1923, SP 1928, CP 1930, SP 1934, SP 1936,
           CP 1939, Come In 1943, Poems 1946, CP 1949,
           RNT 1951, SP 1955, SP 1963, Poetry of RF 1969,
           RF: P and P 1972
        d) see items: 2, 6, 8, 9, 11, 13, 14, 16, 18, 22,
           23, 25, 28, 29, 30

Investment, The
        b) West-Running Brook
        c) CP 1930, CP 1939, Come In 1943, Poems 1946,
           CP 1949, RNT 1951, Aforesaid 1954, SP 1955,
           SP 1963, Poetry of RF 1969
        d) see items: 7, 9, 14, 16, 18, 22, 23, 24, 25,
           28, 29

Iota Subscript
        b) Steeple Bush
        c) CP 1949 Aforesaid 1954, SP 1955, SP 1963,
           Poetry of RF 1969, RF: P and P 1972
        d) see items: 21, 22, 24, 25, 28, 29, 30

It Bids Pretty Fair
        b) Steeple Bush
        c) CP 1949, RNT 1951, SP 1955, SP 1963, Poetry

of RF 1969, RF: P and P 1972
d) see items: 21, 22, 23, 25, 28, 29, 30

It Is Almost the Year 2000
b) A Witness Tree
c) Poems 1946, CP 1949, SP 1955, SP 1963, Poetry of RF 1969, RF: P and P 1972
d) see items: 15, 18, 22, 25, 28, 29, 30

[It Takes All Sorts ...]
a) as "The Poet" in RF's A Remembrance Collection of New Poems (New York, 1959)
b) In the Clearing
c) Poetry of RF 1969, RF: P and P 1972
d) see items: 27, 29, 30

Kitchen Chimney, The
a) in The Measure, Aug 1923
b) New Hampshire
c) CP 1930, CP 1939, Come In 1943, Poems 1946, CP 1949, RNT 1951, YCT 1959, SP 1963, Poetry of RF 1969
d) see items: 5, 9, 14, 16, 18, 22, 23, 26, 28, 29

Kitty Hawk
a) in booklet form as RF's Christmas poem, 1956
b) In the Clearing
c) SP 1963, Poetry of RF 1969
d) see items: 27, 28, 29

Last Mowing, The
b) West-Running Brook
c) CP 1930, CP 1939, Poems 1946, CP 1949, YCT 1959, SP 1963, Poetry of RF 1969
d) see items: 7, 9, 14, 18, 22, 26, 28, 29

Last Word of a Bluebird, The
b) added to contents of Mountain Interval with publication of CP 1930
c) CP 1930, CP 1939, Poems 1946, CP 1949, Aforesaid 1954, SP 1955, YCT 1959, Poetry of RF 1969
d) see items: 9, 14, 18, 22, 24, 25, 26, 29

Late Walk, A
b) A Boy's Will

    c) CP 1930, CP 1939, CP 1949, SP 1963, Poetry
of RF 1969
    d) see items: 2, 9, 14, 22, 28, 29

Leaf-Treader, A
    a) in The American Mercury, Oct 1935
    b) A Further Range
    c) CP 1939, Come In 1943, Poems 1946, CP 1949,
RNT 1951, SP 1955, Poetry of RF 1969
    d) see items: 12, 14, 16, 18, 22, 23, 25, 29

Leaves Compared with Flowers
    a) in The Saturday Review of Literature, Feb 2,
1935
    b) A Further Range
    c) CP 1939, Poems 1946, CP 1949, SP 1955, Poet-
ry of RF 1969
    d) see items: 12, 14, 18, 22, 25, 29

Lesson for Today, The
    b) A Witness Tree
    c) Poems 1946, CP 1949, SP 1955, SP 1963, Poetry
of RF 1969, RF: P and P 1972
    d) see items: 15, 18, 22, 25, 28, 29, 30

Line-Gang, The
    b) Mountain Interval
    c) CP 1930, CP 1939, Poems 1946, CP 1949, RNT
1951, SP 1955, SP 1963, Poetry of RF 1969
    d) see items: 4, 9, 14, 18, 22, 23, 25, 28, 29

Line-Storm Song, A
    a) in New England Magazine, Oct 1907
    b) A Boy's Will
    c) CP 1930, CP 1939, Poems 1946, CP 1949, RNT
1951, SP 1955, Poetry of RF 1969
    d) see items: 2, 9, 14, 18, 22, 23, 25, 29

Lines Written in Dejection on the Eve of Great Success
    a) in RF's A Remembrance Collection of New Poems
(New York, 1959)
    b) In the Clearing
    c) SP 1963, Poetry of RF 1969, RF: P and P 1972
    d) see items: 27, 28, 29, 30

Literate Farmer and the Planet Venus, The
    a) in Atlantic Monthly, March 1941

b) A Witness Tree
c) Poems 1946, CP 1949, Poetry of RF 1969
d) see items: 18, 22, 29

Locked Out
    a) in The Forge, Feb 1917
    b) added to contents of Mountain Interval with the
       publication of CP 1930
    c) CP 1930, CP 1939, CP 1949, Poetry of RF 1969
    d) see items: 9, 14, 22, 29

Lockless Door, The
    a) in A Miscellany of American Poetry 1920 (New
       York, 1920)
    b) New Hampshire
    c) CP 1930, CP 1939, CP 1949, SP 1963, Poetry of
       RF 1969, RF: P and P 1972
    d) see items: 5, 9, 14, 22, 28, 29, 30

Lodged
    a) in The New Republic, Feb 6, 1924
    b) West-Running Brook
    c) CP 1930, CP 1939, Poems 1946, CP 1949, SP
       1955, SP 1963, Poetry of RF 1969, RF: P and P
       1972
    d) see items: 7, 9, 14, 18, 22, 25, 28, 29, 30

Lone Striker, A
    a) as number eight of The Borzoi Chap Books (New
       York: Knopf, 1933)
    b) A Further Range
    c) CP 1939, Come In 1943, Poems 1946, CP 1949,
       RNT 1951, SP 1955, SP 1963, Poetry of RF 1969
    d) see items: 12, 14, 16, 18, 22, 23, 25, 28, 29

Looking for a Sunset Bird in Winter
    b) New Hampshire
    c) CP 1930, CP 1939, Poems 1946, CP 1949, RNT
       1951, Aforesaid 1954, SP 1955, YCT 1959, SP
       1963, Poetry of RF 1969
    d) see items: 5, 9, 14, 18, 22, 23, 24, 25, 26, 28,
       29

Loose Mountain, A
    b) A Witness Tree
    c) Poems 1946, CP 1949, CP 1955, Poetry of RF
       1969

    d) see items: 15, 18, 22, 25, 29

Lost Follower, The
    a) in The Boston Herald, Sept 13, 1936
    b) A Witness Tree
    c) Poems 1946, CP 1949, Aforesaid 1954, SP 1955,
       SP 1963, Poetry of RF 1969
    d) see items: 15, 18, 22, 24, 25, 28, 29

Lost in Heaven
    a) in The Saturday Review of Literature, Nov 30,
       1935
    b) A Further Range
    c) CP 1939, Poems 1946, CP 1949, SP 1963, Poetry
       of RF 1969
    d) see items: 12, 14, 18, 22, 28, 29

Love and a Question
    b) A Boy's Will
    c) CP 1930, CP 1939, Come In 1943, Poems 1946,
       CP 1949, RNT 1951, Aforesaid 1954, SP 1955,
       SP 1963, Poetry of RF 1969, RF: P and P 1972
    d) see items: 2, 9, 14, 16, 18, 22, 23, 24, 25,
       28, 29, 30

Lovely Shall Be Choosers, The
    a) as part of The Poetry Quartos series (New York:
       Random House, 1929)
    b) added to contents of West-Running Brook with the
       publication of CP 1930
    c) CP 1930, CP 1939, Poems 1946, CP 1949,
       Aforesaid 1954, SP 1955, SP 1963, Poetry of
       RF 1969, RF: P and P 1972
    d) see items: 9, 14, 18, 22, 24, 25, 28, 29, 30

Lucretius versus the Lake Poets
    b) Steeple Bush
    c) CP 1949, Poetry of RF 1969
    d) see items: 21, 22, 29

Maple
    a) in The Yale Review, Oct 1921
    b) New Hampshire
    c) CP 1930, CP 1939, CP 1949, Poetry of RF 1969
    d) see items: 5, 9, 14, 22, 29

Master Speed, The
    a) in The Yale Review, Winter 1936
    b) A Further Range
    c) CP 1939, Come In 1943, Poems 1946, CP 1949,
       RNT 1951, SP 1963, Poetry of RF 1969
    d) see items: 12, 14, 16, 18, 22, 23, 28, 29

Meeting and Passing
    b) Mountain Interval
    c) CP 1930, CP 1939, CP 1949, Poetry of RF 1969
    d) see items: 4, 9, 14, 22, 29

Mending Wall
    b) North of Boston
    c) SP 1923, SP 1928, CP 1930, AB 1932, SP 1934,
       SP 1936, CP 1939, Come In 1943, Poems 1946,
       CP 1949, RNT 1951, Aforesaid 1954, SP 1955,
       YCT 1959, SP 1963, Poetry of RF 1969, RF: P
       and P 1972
    d) see items: 3, 6, 8, 9, 10, 11, 13, 14, 16, 18,
       22, 23, 24, 25, 26, 28, 29, 30

Middleness of the Road, The
    a) in Virginia Quarterly Review, Winter 1946
    b) Steeple Bush
    c) CP 1949, SP 1955, SP 1963, Poetry of RF 1969
    d) see items: 21, 22, 25, 28, 29

Milky Way Is a Cowpath, The
    b) In the Clearing
    c) Poetry of RF 1969
    d) see items: 27, 29

Minor Bird, A
    a) in The Islander (U of Michigan) Jan 1926
    b) West-Running Brook
    c) CP 1930, CP 1939, Come In 1943, Poems 1946,
       CP 1949, RNT 1951, SP 1955, YCT 1959, SP
       1963, Poetry of RF 1969, RF: P and P 1972
    d) see items: 7, 9, 14, 16, 18, 22, 23, 25, 26,
       28, 29, 30

Misgiving
    a) in The Yale Review, Jan 1921
    b) New Hampshire
    c) CP 1930, CP 1939, Poems 1946, CP 1949, SP
       1955, SP 1963, Poetry of RF 1969

d) see items: 5, 9, 14, 18, 22, 25, 28, 29

Money see Hardship of Accounting, The

Mood Apart, A
 a) in Fifty Years of Robert Frost, ed. Ray Nash
  (Dartmouth College Library: Hanover, 1944)
 b) Steeple Bush
 c) CP 1949, Aforesaid 1954, SP 1955, SP 1963,
  Poetry of RF 1969, RF: P and P 1972
 d) see items: 21, 22, 24, 25, 28, 29, 30

Moon Compasses
 a) in The Yale Review, Autumn 1934
 b) A Further Range
 c) CP 1939, Poems 1946, CP 1949, Poetry of RF
  1969
 d) see items: 12, 14, 18, 22, 29

Most of It, The
 b) A Witness Tree
 c) Poems 1946, CP 1949, Aforesaid 1954, SP 1955,
  SP 1963, Poetry of RF 1969, RF: P and P 1972
 d) see items: 15, 18, 22, 24, 25, 28, 29, 30

Mountain, The
 b) North of Boston
 c) SP 1923, SP 1928, CP 1930, SP 1934, SP 1936,
  CP 1939, Come In 1943, Poems 1946, CP 1949,
  RNT 1951, Aforesaid 1954, SP 1955, SP 1963,
  Poetry of RF 1969, RF: P and P 1972
 d) see items: 3, 6, 8, 9, 11, 13, 14, 16, 18, 22,
  23, 24, 25, 28, 29, 30

Mowing
 b) A Boy's Will
 c) SP 1923, SP 1928, CP 1930, SP 1934, SP 1936,
  CP 1939, Come In 1943, Poems 1946, CP 1949,
  RNT 1951, SP 1955, SP 1963, Poetry of RF 1969,
  RF: P and P 1972
 d) see items: 2, 6, 8, 9, 11, 13, 14, 16, 18, 22,
  23, 25, 28, 29, 30

My Butterfly
 a) in The Independent, Nov 8, 1894; also included in
  Twilight
 b) A Boy's Will

c) CP 1930, CP 1939, CP 1949, RNT 1951, Poetry
of RF 1969, RF: P and P 1972
d) see items: 1, 2, 9, 14, 22, 23, 29, 30

My November Guest
a) in The Forum, Nov 1912
b) A Boy's Will
c) SP 1923, SP 1928, CP 1930, AB 1932, SP 1934,
SP 1936, CP 1939, Poems 1946, CP 1949, RNT
1951, Aforesaid 1954, SP 1955, SP 1963, Poetry
of RF 1969, RF: P and P 1972
d) see items: 2, 6, 8, 9, 10, 11, 13, 14, 18, 22,
23, 24 25, 28, 29, 30

My Objection to Being Stepped On see Objection to Being
Stepped on, The

Nature Note, A
a) as "A Nature Note on Whippoorwills" in The
Coolidge Hill Gazette (Cambridge, Mass.), Dec
1938
b) A Witness Tree
c) Poems 1946, CP 1949, YCT 1959, Poetry of RF
1969
d) see items: 15, 18, 22, 26, 29

Need of Being Versed in Country Things, The
a) in Harper's Magazine, Dec 1920
b) New Hampshire
c) SP 1928, CP 1930, AB 1932, SP 1934, SP 1936,
CP 1939, Come In 1943, Poems 1946, CP 1949,
RNT 1951, Aforesaid 1954, SP 1955, SP 1963,
Poetry of RF 1969, RF: P and P 1972
d) see items: 5, 8, 9, 10, 11, 13, 14, 16, 18, 22,
23, 24, 25, 28, 29, 30

Neither Out Far Nor In Deep
a) in The Yale Review, Spring 1934
b) A Further Range
c) CP 1939, Poems 1946, CP 1949, SP 1955, SP
1963, Poetry of RF 1969, RF: P and P 1973
d) see items: 12, 14, 18, 22, 25, 28, 29, 30

Never Again Would Birds' Song Be the Same
b) A Witness Tree
c) Come In 1943, Poems 1946, CP 1949, RNT 1951,
Aforesaid 1954, SP 1955, SP 1963, Poetry of RF

1969
d) see items: 15, 16, 18, 22, 23, 24, 25, 28, 29

Never Naught Song, A
      b) In the Clearing
      c) SP 1963, Poetry of RF 1969, RF: P and P 1972
      d) see items: 27, 28, 29, 30

New Hampshire
      b) New Hampshire
      c) CP 1930, CP 1939, Poems 1946, CP 1949, SP
         1955, SP 1963, Poetry of RF 1969, RF: P and P
         1972
      d) see items: 5, 9, 14, 18, 22, 25, 28, 29, 30

Night Light, The
      a) in The Yale Review, Autumn 1946
      b) Steeple Bush
      c) CP 1949, Aforesaid 1954, SP 1955, SP 1963,
         Poetry of RF 1969, RF: P and P 1972
      d) see items: 21, 22, 24, 25, 28, 29, 30

1946 see Courage to Be New, The

No Holy Wars for Them
      a) in The Atlantic Monthly, April 1947
      b) Steeple Bush
      c) CP 1949, SP 1955, SP 1963, Poetry of RF 1969,
         RF: P and P 1972
      d) see items: 21, 22, 25, 28, 29, 30

Not All There
      a) in Poetry, April 1936
      b) A Further Range
      c) CP 1939, Poems 1946, CP 1949, RNT 1951, SP
         1955, SP 1963, Poetry of RF 1969, RF: P and P
         1972
      d) see items: 12, 14, 18, 22, 23, 25, 28, 29, 30

Not of School Age
      b) A Witness Tree
      c) CP 1949, YCT 1959, Poetry of RF 1969
      d) see items: 15, 22, 26, 29

Not Quite Social
      a) in The Saturday Review of Literature, March 30,
         1935

b) A Further Range
c) CP 1939, Poems 1946, CP 1949, SP 1955, SP
   1963, Poetry of RF 1969, RF: P and P 1972
d) see items: 12, 14, 18, 22, 25, 28, 29 30

Not to Keep
a) in The Yale Review, Jan 1917
b) New Hampshire
c) CP 1930, CP 1939, Poems 1946, CP 1949, Poetry of RF 1969, RF: P and P 1972
d) see items: 5, 9, 14, 18, 22, 29, 30

Nothing Gold Can Stay
a) in The Yale Review, Oct 1923
b) New Hampshire
c) SP 1928, CP 1930, AB 1932, SP 1934, CP 1939,
   Come In 1943, Poems 1946, CP 1949, SP 1955,
   SP 1963, Poetry of RF 1969, RF: P and P 1972
d) see items: 5, 8, 9, 10, 11, 14, 16, 18, 22, 25,
   28, 29, 30

November
a) as "October" in The Old Farmer's Almanac 1939
   (Boston, 1938)
b) A Witness Tree
c) Poems 1946, CP 1949, SP 1963, Poetry of RF
   1969, RF: P and P 1972
d) see items: 15, 18, 22, 28, 29, 30

Now Close the Windows
b) A Boy's Will
c) CP 1930, CP 1939, CP 1949, Poetry of RF 1969
d) see items: 2, 9, 14, 22, 29

Objection to Being Stepped On, The
a) as "My Objection to Being Stepped On" in booklet
   form as RF's Christmas poem, 1957
b) In the Clearing
c) Poetry of RF 1969
d) see items: 27, 29

October [see also November]
a) in The Youth's Companion, Oct 3, 1912
b) A Boy's Will
c) SP 1923, SP 1928, CP 1930, SP 1934, SP 1936,
   CP 1939, Poems 1946, CP 1949, RNT 1951, SP
   1955, SP 1963, Poetry of RF 1969, RF: P and P
   1972

      d) see items: 2, 6, 8, 9, 11, 13, 14, 18, 22, 23,
         25, 28, 29, 30

Of a Winter Evening see Questioning Faces

Of the Stones of the Place
      a) as "Rich in Stones" in The Old Farmer's Almanac
         1942 (Dublin, New Hampshire, 1941)
      b) A Witness Tree
      c) Poems 1946, CP 1949, SP 1963, Poetry of RF
         1969
      d) see items: 15, 18, 22, 28, 29

Old Barn at the Bottom of the Fogs, The
      b) A Further Range
      c) CP 1939, CP 1949, Poetry of RF 1969
      d) see items: 12, 22, 29

Old Man's Winter Night, An
      b) Mountain Interval
      c) SP 1923, SP 1928, CP 1930, AB 1932, SP 1934,
         SP 1936, CP 1939, Come In 1943, Poems 1946,
         CP 1949, RNT 1951, Aforesaid 1954, SP 1955,
         SP 1963, Poetry of RF 1969, RF: P and P 1972
      d) see items: 4, 6, 8, 9, 10, 11, 13, 14, 16, 18,
         22, 23, 24, 25, 28, 29, 30

On a Bird Singing in Its Sleep
      a) in Scribner's Magazine, Dec 1934
      b) A Further Range
      c) CP 1939, Poems 1946, CP 1949, RNT 1951, SP
         1955, SP 1963, Poetry of RF 1969, RF: P and P
         1972
      d) see items: 12, 14, 18, 22, 23, 25, 28, 29, 30

On a Star-Bright Night see Canis Major

On a Tree Fallen Across the Road
      a) in Farm and Fireside, Oct 1921
      b) New Hampshire
      c) CP 1930, CP 1939, Come In 1943, Poems 1946,
         CP 1949, RNT 1951, SP 1955, SP 1963, Poetry
         of RF 1969
      d) see items: 5, 9, 14, 16, 18, 22, 23, 25, 28,
         29

On Being Chosen Poet of Vermont
      a) in newspapers following RF's becoming Poet
         Laureate of Vermont, July 22, 1961
      b) In the Clearing
      c) SP 1963, Poetry of RF 1969
      d) see items: 27, 28, 29

On Being Idolized
      b) Steeple Bush
      c) CP 1949, SP 1955, SP 1963, Poetry of RF 1969
      d) see items: 21, 22, 25, 28, 29

On Going Unnoticed
      a) as "Unnoticed" in The Saturday Review of Litera-
         ture, March 28, 1925
      b) West-Running Brook
      c) CP 1930, CP 1939, Poems 1946, CP 1949, RNT
         1951, SP 1955, SP 1963, Poetry of RF 1969, RF:
         P and P 1972
      d) see items: 7, 9, 14, 18, 22, 23, 25, 28, 29,
         30

On Looking Up by Chance at the Constellations
      b) West-Running Brook
      c) CP 1930, SP 1934, SP 1936, CP 1939, Poems
         1946, CP 1949, Aforesaid 1954, SP 1955, SP
         1963, Poetry of RF 1969, RF: P and P 1972
      d) see items: 7, 9, 11, 13, 14, 18, 22, 24, 25,
         28, 29, 30

On Making Certain Anything Has Happened
      a) in booklet form as RF's Christmas poem, 1945
      b) Steeple Bush
      c) CP 1949, SP 1955, SP 1963, Poetry of RF 1969
      d) see items: 21, 22, 25, 28, 29

On Our Sympathy with the Under Dog
      b) A Witness Tree
      c) Poems 1946, CP 1949, SP 1963, Poetry of RF
         1969
      d) see items: 15, 18, 22, 28, 29

On Taking from the Top to Broaden the Base
      b) A Further Range
      c) CP 1939, CP 1949, Poetry of RF 1969
      d) see items: 12, 14, 22, 29

On the Heart's Beginning to Cloud the Mind
        a) in Scribner's Magazine, April 1934
        b) A Further Range
        c) CP 1939, Poems 1946, CP 1949, SP 1955, SP 1963, Poetry of RF 1969
        d) see items: 12, 14, 18, 22, 25, 28, 29

Once by the Pacific
        a) in The New Republic, Dec 29, 1926
        b) West-Running Brook
        c) CP 1930, AB 1932, SP 1934, SP 1936, CP 1939, Poems 1946, CP 1949, Aforesaid 1954, SP 1955, SP 1963, Poetry of RF 1969, RF: P and P 1972
        d) see items: 7, 9, 10, 11, 13, 14, 18, 22, 24, 25, 28, 29, 30

One Guess
        b) A Further Range
        c) CP 1939, Poems 1946, CP 1949, SP 1955, YCT 1959, SP 1963, Poetry of RF 1969
        d) see items: 12, 14, 18, 22, 25, 26, 28, 29

One More Brevity
        a) in booklet form as RF's Christmas poem, 1953
        b) In the Clearing
        c) Poetry of RF 1969, RF: P and P 1972
        d) see items: 27, 29, 30

One Step Backward Taken
        a) in The Book Collector's Packet, Jan 1946
        b) Steeple Bush
        c) CP 1949, SP 1955, SP 1963, Poetry of RF 1969
        d) see items: 21, 22, 25, 28, 29

Onset, The
        a) in The Yale Review, Jan 1921
        b) New Hampshire
        c) SP 1928, CP 1930, AB 1932, SP 1934, SP 1936, CP 1939, Come In 1943, Poems 1946, CP 1949, RNT 1951, Aforesaid 1954, SP 1955, SP 1963, Poetry of RF 1969, RF: P and P 1972
        d) see items: 5, 8, 9, 10, 11, 13, 14, 16, 18, 22, 23, 24, 25, 28, 29, 30

Our Doom to Bloom
        a) as 'Doom to Bloom" in booklet form as RF's Christmas poem, 1950 (without Robinson Jeffers

       quote)
- b) In the Clearing
- c) SP 1963, Poetry of RF 1969
- d) see items: 27, 28, 29

Our Getaway see Why Wait for Science

Our Hold on the Planet
- a) in booklet form as RF's Christmas poem, 1940
- b) A Witness Tree
- c) Poems 1946, CP 1949, RNT 1951, SP 1955, SP 1963, Poetry of RF 1969, RF: P and P 1972
- d) see items: 15, 18, 22, 23, 25, 28, 29, 30

Our Singing Strength
- a) in The New Republic, May 2, 1923
- b) New Hampshire
- c) CP 1930, CP 1939, Come In 1943, Poems 1946, CP 1949, RNT 1951, SP 1963, Poetry of RF 1969
- d) see items: 5, 9, 14, 16, 18, 22, 23, 28, 29

"Out, Out--"
- a) in McClure's, July 1916
- b) Mountain Interval
- c) SP 1923, SP 1928, CP 1930, SP 1934, SP 1936, CP 1939, Poems 1946, CP 1949, SP 1955, SP 1963, Poetry of RF 1969, RF: P and P 1972
- d) see items: 4, 6, 8, 9, 11, 13, 14, 18, 22, 25, 28, 29, 30

Oven Bird, The
- b) Mountain Interval
- c) SP 1923, SP 1928, CP 1930, SP 1934, SP 1936, CP 1939, Come In 1943, Poems 1946, CP 1949, RNT 1951, Aforesaid 1954, SP 1955, YCT 1959, SP 1963, Poetry of RF 1969, RF: P and P 1972
- d) see items: 4, 6, 8, 9, 11, 13, 14, 16, 18, 22, 23, 24, 25, 26, 28, 29, 30

Pan with Us
- b) A Boy's Will
- c) CP 1930, CP 1939, CP 1949, Poetry of RF 1969
- d) see items: 2, 9, 14, 22, 29

Passing Glimpse, A
- a) as "The Passing Glimpse" in The New Republic, April 21, 1926

   b) West-Running Brook
   c) CP 1930, CP 1939, Come In 1943, Poems 1946,
      CP 1949, RNT 1951, SP 1955, YCT 1959, SP
      1963, Poetry of RF 1969, RF: P and P 1972
   d) see items: 7, 9, 14, 16, 18, 22, 23, 25, 26,
      28, 29, 30

Pasture, The
   b) North of Boston
   c) SP 1923, SP 1928, CP 1930, SP 1934, SP 1936,
      CP 1939, Come In 1943, Poems 1946, CP 1949,
      RNT 1951, SP 1955, YCT 1959, SP 1963, Poetry
      of RF 1969, RF: P and P 1972
   d) see items: 3, 6, 8, 9, 11, 13, 14, 16, 18, 22,
      23, 25, 26, 28, 29, 30

Patch of Old Snow, A
   b) Mountain Interval
   c) CP 1930, CP 1939, CP 1949, RNT 1951, Poetry
      of RF 1969
   d) see items: 4, 9, 14, 22, 23, 29

Paul's Wife
   a) in The Century Magazine, Nov 1921
   b) New Hampshire
   c) CP 1930, CP 1939, Come In 1943, Poems 1946,
      CP 1949, RNT 1951, Aforesaid 1954, SP 1955,
      SP 1963, Poetry of RF 1969
   d) see items: 5, 9, 14, 16, 18, 22, 23, 24, 25,
      28, 29

Pauper Witch of Grafton, The
   a) in The Nation, April 13, 1921
   b) New Hampshire
   c) CP 1930, CP 1939, CP 1949, SP 1963, Poetry
      of RF 1969
   d) see items: 5, 9, 14, 22, 28, 29

Pea Brush
   b) Mountain Interval
   c) CP 1930, CP 1939, Poems 1946, CP 1949, RNT
      1951, YCT 1959, Poetry of RF 1969
   d) see items: 4, 9, 14, 18, 22, 23, 26, 29

Peaceful Shepherd, The
   a) in The New York Herald Tribune Books, March
      22, 1925

b) West-Running Brook
c) CP 1930, AB 1932, CP 1939, Poems 1946, CP 1949, SP 1955, SP 1963, Poetry of RF 1969, RF: P and P 1972
d) see items: 7, 9, 10, 14, 18, 22, 25, 28, 29, 30

Peck of Gold, A
a) as "The Common Fate" in The Yale Review, July 1927
b) West-Running Brook
c) CP 1930, SP 1934, SP 1936, CP 1939, Poems 1946, CP 1949, SP 1955, YCT 1959, SP 1963, Poetry of RF 1969
d) see items: 7, 9, 11, 13, 14, 18, 22, 25, 26, 28, 29

Peril of Hope
b) In the Clearing
c) SP 1963, Poetry of RF 1969, RF: P and P 1972
d) see items: 27, 28, 29, 30

Pertinax
a) in Poetry, April 1936
b) A Further Range
c) CP 1939, Poems 1946, CP 1949, SP 1955, SP 1963, Poetry of RF 1969
d) see items: 12, 14, 18, 22, 25, 28, 29

Place for a Third
a) in Harper's Magazine, Dec 1920
b) New Hampshire
c) CP 1930, CP 1939, CP 1949, Poetry of RF 1969
d) see items: 5, 9, 14, 22, 29

Planners, The
a) in The Atlantic Monthly, Dec 1946
b) Steeple Bush
c) CP 1949, SP 1955, SP 1963, Poetry of RF 1969
d) see items: 21, 22, 25, 28, 29

Plowmen
a) in A Miscellany of American Poetry 1920 (New York, 1920)
b) New Hampshire
c) CP 1930, CP 1939, Poems 1946, CP 1949, Poetry of RF 1969
d) see items: 5, 9, 14, 18, 22, 29

Pod of the Milkweed
    a) as From a Milkweed Pod in booklet form as RF's
       Christmas poem, 1954
    b) In the Clearing
    c) SP 1963, Poetry of RF 1969
    d) see items: 27, 28, 29

Poet, The see [It Takes All Sorts ...]

Prayer in Spring, A
    b) A Boy's Will
    c) CP 1930, CP 1939, Come In 1943, Poems 1946,
       CP 1949, RNT 1951, SP 1955, SP 1963, Poetry
       of RF 1969, RF: P and P 1972
    d) see items: 2, 9, 14, 16, 18, 22, 23, 25, 28,
       29, 30

Preacher, The see [Forgive, O Lord ...]

Precaution
    a) in Poetry, April 1936
    b) A Further Range
    c) CP 1939, Poems 1946, CP 1949, RNT 1951,
       Aforesaid 1954, SP 1955, SP 1963, Poetry of RF
       1969, RF: P and P 1972
    d) see items: 12, 14, 18, 22, 23, 24, 25, 28, 29,
       30

Provide, Provide
    a) in The New Frontier, Sept 1934
    b) A Further Range
    c) CP 1939, Poems 1946, CP 1949, Aforesaid 1954,
       SP 1955, SP 1963, Poetry of RF 1969, RF: P and
       P 1972
    d) see items: 12, 14, 18, 22, 24, 25, 28, 29, 30

Putting in the Seed
    a) in Poetry and Drama, Dec 1914
    b) Mountain Interval
    c) SP 1923, SP 1928, CP 1930, SP 1934, SP 1936,
       CP 1939, Poems 1946, CP 1949, RNT 1951, SP
       1955, SP 1963, Poetry of RF 1969
    d) see items: 4, 6, 8, 9, 11, 13, 14, 18, 22, 23,
       25, 28, 29

Quandary
    a) as "Somewhat Dietary" in The Massachusetts

Review, Fall 1959
- b) In the Clearing
- c) Poetry of RF 1969
- d) see items: 27, 29

Quest of the Purple-Fringed, The
- a) as "The Quest of the Orchis" in The Independent, June 27, 1901
- b) A Witness Tree
- c) Poems 1946, CP 1949, SP 1963, Poetry of RF 1969
- d) see items: 15, 18, 22, 28, 29

Question, A
- b) A Witness Tree
- c) Poems 1946, CP 1949, SP 1963, Poetry of RF 1969, RF: P and P 1972
- d) see items: 15, 18, 22, 28, 29, 30

Questioning Faces
- a) as "of a Winter Evening" in The Saturday Review, April 12, 1958
- b) In the Clearing
- c) SP 1963, Poetry of RF 1969
- d) see items: 27, 28, 29

Rabbit-Hunter, The
- b) A Witness Tree
- c) Poems 1946, CP 1949, SP 1963, Poetry of RF 1969
- d) see items: 15, 18, 22, 28, 29

Range-Finding
- b) Mountain Interval
- c) SP 1923, SP 1928, CP 1930, SP 1934, SP 1936, CP 1939, Poems 1946, CP 1949, SP 1955, SP 1963, Poetry of RF 1969
- d) see items: 4, 6, 8, 9, 11, 13, 14, 18, 22, 25, 28, 29

Record Stride, A
- a) in The Atlantic Monthly, May 1936
- b) A Further Range
- c) CP 1939, Poems 1946, CP 1949, SP 1955, YCT 1959, SP 1963, Poetry of RF 1969
- d) see items: 12, 14, 18, 22, 25, 26, 28, 29

Reflex, A
      b) In the Clearing
      c) Poetry of RF 1969
      d) see items: 27, 29

Reluctance
      a) in The Youth's Companion, Nov 7, 1912
      b) A Boy's Will
      c) SP 1923, SP 1928, CP 1930, AB 1932, SP 1934,
         SP 1936, CP 1939, Poems 1946, CP 1949, Afore-
         said 1954, SP 1955, SP 1963, Poetry of RF 1969,
         RF: P and P 1972
      d) see items: 2, 4, 6, 9, 10, 11, 13, 14, 18, 22,
         24, 25, 28, 29, 30

Return of the Pilgrims see Immigrants

Revelation
      b) A Boy's Will
      c) SP 1923, SP 1928, CP 1930, SP 1934, SP 1936,
         CP 1939, Poems 1946, CP 1949, SP 1955, SP
         1963, Poetry of RF 1969, RF: P and P 1972
      d) see items: 2, 4, 6, 9, 11, 13, 14, 18, 22, 25,
         28, 29, 30

Rich in Stones see Of the Stones of the Place

Riders
      b) West-Running Brook
      c) CP 1930, CP 1939, Come In 1943, Poems 1946,
         CP 1949, RNT 1951, SP 1955, SP 1963, Poetry
         of RF 1969, RF: P and P 1972
      d) see items: 7, 9, 14, 16, 18, 22, 23, 25, 28,
         29, 30

Ring Around see Secret Sits, The

Road Not Taken, The
      a) in The Atlantic Monthly, Aug 1915
      b) Mountain Interval
      c) SP 1923, SP 1928, CP 1930, AB 1932, SP 1934,
         SP 1936, CP 1939, Come In 1943, Poems 1946,
         CP 1949, RNT 1951, Aforesaid 1954, SP 1955,
         YCT 1959, SP 1963, Poetry of RF 1969, RF: P
         and P 1972
      d) see items: 4, 6, 8, 9, 10, 11, 13, 14, 16, 18,
         22, 23, 24, 25, 26, 28, 29, 30

Roadside Stand, A
    a) in The Atlantic Monthly, June 1936
    b) A Further Range
    c) CP 1939, Poems 1946, CP 1949, Poetry of RF
       1969
    d) see items: 12, 14, 18, 22, 29

Rogers Group, A
    a) in The Atlantic Monthly, Dec 1946
    b) Steeple Bush
    c) CP 1949, SP 1963, Poetry of RF 1969
    d) see items: 21, 22, 28, 29

Rose Family, The
    a) in The Yale Review, July 1927; also in The Lon-
       don Mercury, July 1927
    b) West-Running Brook
    c) CP 1930, CP 1939, CP 1949, YCT 1959, Poetry
       of RF 1969
    d) see items: 7, 9, 14, 22, 26, 29

Rose Pogonias
    b) A Boy's Will
    c) CP 1930, CP 1939, Poems 1946, CP 1949, SP
       1963, Poetry of RF 1969
    d) see items: 2, 9, 14, 18, 22, 28, 29

Runaway, The
    a) in The Amherst Monthly, June 1918
    b) New Hampshire
    c) SP 1923, SP 1928, CP 1930, AB 1932, SP 1934,
       SP 1936, CP 1939, Come In 1943, Poems 1946,
       CP 1949, RNT 1951, SP 1955, YCT 1959, SP
       1963, Poetry of RF 1969, RF: P and P 1972
    d) see items: 5, 6, 8, 9, 10, 11, 13, 14, 16, 18,
       22, 23, 25, 26, 28, 29, 30

Sage, The see From Iron

Same Leaves, The see In Hardwood Groves

Sand Dunes
    a) in The New Republic, Dec 15, 1926
    b) West-Running Brook
    c) CP 1930, CP 1939, Come In 1943, Poems 1946,
       CP 1949, RNT 1951, SP 1955, SP 1963, Poetry of
       RF 1969, RF: P and P 1972
    d) see items: 7, 9, 14, 16, 18, 22, 23, 25, 28, 29, 30

Secret Sits, The
   a) as "Ring Around" in Poetry, April 1936
   b) A Witness Tree
   c) Poems 1946, CP 1949, RNT 1951, Aforesaid
      1954, SP 1955, SP 1963, Poetry of RF 1969, RF:
      P and P 1972
   d) see items: 15, 18, 22, 23, 24, 25, 28, 29, 30

Self-Seeker, The
   b) North of Boston
   c) SP 1923, SP 1928, CP 1930, SP 1934, SP 1936,
      CP 1939, CP 1949, Poetry of RF 1969
   d) see items: 3, 6, 8, 9, 11, 13, 14, 22, 29

Semi-Revolution, A
   b) A Witness Tree
   c) Poems 1946, CP 1949, SP 1963, Poetry of RF
      1969
   d) see items: 15, 18, 22, 28, 29

Serious Step Lightly Taken, A
   b) A Witness Tree
   c) Come In 1943, Poems 1946, CP 1949, RNT 1951,
      SP 1955, SP 1963, Poetry of RF 1969, RF: P
      and P 1972
   d) see items: 15, 16, 18, 22, 23, 25, 28, 29, 30

Servant to Servants, A
   b) North of Boston
   c) SP 1923, SP 1928, CP 1930, SP 1934, SP 1936,
      CP 1939, Poems 1946, CP 1949, SP 1955, Poetry
      of RF 1969, RF: P and P 1972
   d) see items: 3, 6, 8, 9, 11, 13, 14, 18, 22, 25,
      29, 30

Silken Tent, The
   a) in The Virginia Quarterly Review, Winter 1939
   b) A Witness Tree
   c) Come In 1943, Poems 1946, CP 1949, RNT 1951,
      Aforesaid 1954, SP 1955, SP 1963, Poetry of RF
      1969, RF: P and P 1972
   d) see items: 15, 16, 18, 22, 23, 24, 25, 28, 29,
      30

Sitting by a Bush in Broad Sunlight
   b) West-Running Brook
   c) CP 1930, SP 1934, CP 1939, Come In 1943,

Poems 1946, CP 1949, RNT 1951, Aforesaid
1954, SP 1955, SP 1963, Poetry of RF 1969, RF:
P and P 1972

d) see items: 7, 11, 14, 16, 18, 22, 23, 24, 25,
28, 29, 30

Skeptic

b) Steeple Bush
c) CP 1949, SP 1963, Poetry of RF 1969
d) see items: 21, 22, 28, 29

Snow

a) in Poetry, Nov 1916
b) Mountain Interval
c) SP 1923, SP 1928, CP 1930, SP 1934, SP 1936,
CP 1939, Poems 1946, CP 1949, RNT 1951, SP
1955, Poetry of RF 1969
d) see items: 4, 6, 8, 9, 11, 13, 14, 18, 22, 23,
25, 29

Snow Dust see Dust of Snow

Soldier, A

a) as "The Soldier" in McCall's, May 1927
b) West-Running Brook
c) CP 1930, AB 1932, SP 1934, SP 1936, CP 1939,
Poems 1946, CP 1949, Aforesaid 1954, SP 1955,
SP 1963, Poetry of RF 1969, RF: P and P 1972
d) see items: 7, 9, 10, 11, 13, 14, 18, 22, 24,
25, 28, 29, 30

Some Science Fiction

a) in booklet form as RF's Christmas poem, 1955
(without final quatrain)
b) In the Clearing
c) Poetry of RF 1969
d) see items: 27, 29

Something for Hope

a) in The Atlantic Monthly, Dec 1946
b) Steeple Bush
c) CP 1949, SP 1955, SP 1963, Poetry of RF 1969
d) see items: 21, 22, 25, 28, 29

Somewhat Dietary see Quandary

Sound of Trees, The
    a) in Poetry and Drama, Dec 1914
    b) Mountain Interval
    c) SP 1923, SP 1928, CP 1930, SP 1934, CP 1939,
       Come In 1943, Poems 1946, CP 1949, RNT 1951,
       SP 1955, SP 1963, Poetry of RF 1969, RF: P
       and P 1972
    d) see items: 4, 6, 8, 9, 11, 14, 16, 18, 22, 23,
       25, 28, 29, 30

Span of Life, The
    a) in Poetry, April 1936
    b) A Further Range
    c) CP 1939, Poems 1946, CP 1949, SP 1955, SP
       1963, Poetry of RF 1969, RF: P and P 1972
    d) see items: 12, 14, 18, 22, 25, 28, 29, 30

Spring Pools
    a) in The Dearborn Independent, April 23, 1927
    b) West-Running Brook
    c) CP 1930, AB 1932, SP 1934, SP 1936, CP 1939,
       Come In 1943, Poems 1946, CP 1949, RNT 1951,
       Aforesaid 1954, SP 1955, SP 1963, Poetry of RF
       1969, RF: P and P 1972
    d) see items: 7, 9, 10, 11, 13, 14, 16, 18, 22,
       23, 24, 25, 28, 29, 30

Star in a Stoneboat, A
    a) in The Yale Review, Jan 1921
    b) New Hampshire
    c) CP 1930, CP 1939, Poems 1946, CP 1949, SP
       1955, SP 1963, Poetry of RF 1969, RF: P and P
       1972
    d) see items: 5, 9, 14, 18, 22, 25, 28, 29, 30

Star-Splitter, The
    a) in The Century Magazine, Sept 1923
    b) New Hampshire
    c) CP 1930, CP 1939, Poems 1946, CP 1949, RNT
       1951, SP 1955, SP 1963, Poetry of RF 1969, RF:
       P and P 1972
    d) see items: 5, 9, 14, 18, 22, 23, 25, 28, 29,
       30

Stars
    b) A Boy's Will
    c) CP 1930, CP 1939, Poems 1946, CP 1949, Poet-

ry of RF 1969
d) see items: 2, 9, 14, 18, 22, 29

Steeple on the House, A
   b) Steeple Bush
   c) CP 1949, SP 1955, SP 1963, Poetry of RF 1969
   d) see items: 21, 22, 25, 28, 29

Stopping by Woods on a Snowy Evening
   a) in The New Republic, March 7, 1923
   b) New Hampshire
   c) SP 1928, CP 1930, AB 1932, SP 1934, SP 1936,
      CP 1939, Come In 1943, Poems 1946, CP 1949,
      RNT 1951, Aforesaid 1954, SP 1955, YCT 1959,
      SP 1963, Poetry of RF 1969, RF: P and P 1972
   d) see items: 5, 8, 9, 10, 11, 13, 14, 16, 18, 22,
      23, 24, 25, 26, 28, 29, 30

Storm Fear
   b) A Boy's Will
   c) SP 1923, SP 1928, CP 1930, AB 1932, SP 1934,
      SP 1936, CP 1939, Poems 1946, CP 1949, RNT
      1951, SP 1955, SP 1963, Poetry of RF 1969, RF:
      P and P 1972
   d) see items: 2, 6, 8, 9, 10, 11, 13, 14, 18, 22,
      23, 25, 28, 29, 30

Strong Are Saying Nothing, The
   a) in The American Mercury, May 1936
   b) A Further Range
   c) CP 1939, Poems 1946, CP 1949, SP 1955, SP
      1963, Poetry of RF 1969
   d) see items: 12, 14, 18, 22, 25, 28, 29

Subverted Flower, The
   b) A Witness Tree
   c) CP 1949, SP 1955, SP 1963, Poetry of RF 1969,
      RF: P and P 1972
   d) see items: 15, 22, 25, 28, 29, 30

Sycamore
   b) A Witness Tree
   c) Poems 1946, CP 1949, SP 1963, Poetry of RF
      1969
   d) see items: 15, 18, 22, 28, 29

Take Something Like a Star
    c) Come In 1943, CP 1949, Aforesaid 1954, SP
       1955, SP 1963, Poetry of RF 1969
    d) see items: 16, 22, 24, 25, 28, 29, 30

Telephone, The
    a) in The Independent, Oct 9, 1916
    b) Mountain Interval
    c) CP 1930, CP 1939, Poems 1946, CP 1949, SP
       1955, YCT 1959, SP 1963, Poetry of RF 1969,
       RF: P and P 1972
    d) see items: 4, 9, 14, 18, 22, 25, 26, 28, 29,
       30

Tendencies Cancel see Evil Tendencies Cancel

Thatch, The
    b) West-Running Brook
    c) CP 1930, CP 1939, CP 1949, Poetry of RF 1969,
       RF: P and P 1972
    d) see items: 7, 9, 14, 22, 29, 30

There Are Roughly Zones
    b) A Further Range
    c) CP 1939, Poems 1946, CP 1949, SP 1955, SP
       1963, Poetry of RF 1969
    d) see items: 12, 14, 18, 22, 25, 28, 29

They Were Welcome to Their Belief
    a) in Scribner's Magazine, Aug 1934
    b) A Further Range
    c) CP 1939, Poems 1946, CP 1949, SP 1963, Poet-
       ry of RF 1969, RF: P and P 1972
    d) see items: 12, 14, 18, 22, 28, 29, 30

Time Out
    a) in The Virginia Quarterly Review, Spring 1942
    b) A Witness Tree
    c) Poems 1946, CP 1949, SP 1963, Poetry of RF
       1969
    d) see items: 15, 18, 22, 28, 29

Time to Talk, A
    a) in The Prospect (Plymouth, New Hampshire),
       June 1916
    b) Mountain Interval
    c) SP 1923, SP 1928, CP 1930, SP 1934, SP 1936,

CP 1939, Poems 1946, CP 1949, RNT 1951, SP
1955, YCT 1959, SP 1963, Poetry of RF 1969
    d) see items: 4, 6, 8, 9, 11, 13, 14, 18, 22, 23,
       25, 26, 28, 29

Times Table, The
    a) in The New Republic, Feb 9, 1927
    b) West-Running Brook
    c) CP 1930, CP 1939, Poems 1946, CP 1949, SP
       1963, Poetry of RF 1969
    d) see items: 7, 9, 14, 18, 22, 28, 29

To a Moth Seen in Winter
    a) in The Virginia Quarterly Review, Spring 1942
    b) A Witness Tree
    c) Poems 1946, CP 1949, SP 1963, Poetry of RF
       1969
    d) see items: 15, 18, 22, 28, 29

To a Thinker
    a) as "To a Thinker in Office" in The Saturday Re-
       view of Literature, Jan 11, 1936
    b) A Further Range
    c) CP 1939, CP 1949, Poetry of RF 1969
    d) see items: 12, 14, 22, 29

To a Young Wretch
    a) in booklet form as RF's Christmas poem, 1937
       (without subtitle)
    b) A Witness Tree
    c) Come In 1943, Poems 1946, CP 1949, RNT 1951,
       SP 1963, Poetry of RF 1969
    d) see items: 15, 16, 18, 22, 23, 28, 29

To an Ancient
    a) in The Atlantic Monthly, Dec 1946
    b) Steeple Bush
    c) CP 1949, SP 1955, SP 1963, Poetry of RF 1969
    d) see items: 21, 22, 25, 28, 29

To E. T.
    a) in The Yale Review, April 1920
    b) New Hampshire
    c) CP 1930, CP 1939, Poems 1946, CP 1949, SP
       1955, Poetry of RF 1969
    d) see items: 5, 9, 14, 18, 22, 25, 29

To Earthward
  a) in The Yale Review, Oct 1923
  b) New Hampshire
  c) SP 1928, CP 1930, AB 1932, SP 1934, SP 1936,
     CP 1939, Poems 1946, CP 1949, Aforesaid 1954,
     SP 1955, SP 1963, Poetry of RF 1969, RF: P and
     P 1972
  d) see items: 5, 8, 9, 10, 11, 13, 14, 18, 22, 24,
     25, 28, 29, 30

To the Right Person
  a) in The Atlantic Monthly, Oct 1946 (with subtitle
     "Fourteen Lines")
  b) Steeple Bush
  c) Poems 1946, CP 1949, SP 1955, SP 1963, Poet-
     ry of RF 1969
  d) see items: 18, 21, 22, 25, 28, 29

To the Thawing Wind
  b) A Boy's Will
  c) SP 1923, SP 1928, CP 1930, SP 1934, SP 1936,
     CP 1939, Poems 1946, CP 1949, RNT 1951, SP
     1955, SP 1963, Poetry of RF 1969, RF: P and
     P 1972
  d) see items: 2, 4, 6, 9, 11, 13, 14, 18, 22, 23,
     25, 28, 29, 30

Too Anxious for Rivers
  b) Steeple Bush
  c) CP 1949, Poetry of RF 1969
  d) see items: 21, 22, 29

Tree at My Window
  a) in The Yale Review, July 1927
  b) West-Running Brook
  c) CP 1930, AB 1932, SP 1934, SP 1936, CP 1939,
     Come In 1943, Poems 1946, CP 1949, RNT 1951,
     Aforesaid 1954, SP 1955, YCT 1959, SP 1963,
     Poetry of RF 1969, RF: P and P 1972
  d) see items: 7, 9, 10, 11, 13, 14, 16, 18, 22, 23,
     24, 25, 26, 28, 29, 30

Trespass
  a) in American Prefaces, April 1939
  b) A Witness Tree
  c) Poems 1946, CP 1949, SP 1963, Poetry of RF 1969
  d) see items: 15, 18, 22, 28, 29

Trial by Existence, The
    a) in The Independent, Oct 11, 1906
    b) A Boy's Will
    c) CP 1930, CP 1939, CP 1949, SP 1955, SP 1963,
       Poetry of RF 1969, RF: P and P 1972
    d) see items: 2, 9, 14, 22, 25, 28, 29, 30

Trial Run, A
    a) in The Atlantic Monthly, June 1936
    b) A Further Range
    c) CP 1939, Poems 1946, CP 1949, SP 1955, Poetry
       of RF 1969
    d) see items: 12, 14, 18, 22, 25, 29

Triple Bronze
    a) as Triple Plate in booklet form as RF's Christmas
       poem, 1939
    b) A Witness Tree
    c) Poems 1946, CP 1949, RNT 1951, SP 1955, SP
       1963, Poetry of RF 1969
    d) see items: 15, 18, 22, 23, 25, 28, 29

Tuft of Flowers, The
    a) in The Derry Enterprise, March 9, 1906
    b) A Boy's Will
    c) SP 1923, SP 1928, CP 1930, AB 1932, SP 1934,
       SP 1936, CP 1939, Come In 1943, Poems 1946,
       CP 1949, RNT 1951, Aforesaid 1954, SP 1955,
       YCT 1959, SP 1963, Poetry of RF 1969, RF: P
       and P 1972
    d) see items: 2, 6, 8, 9, 10, 11, 13, 14, 16, 18,
       22, 23, 24, 25, 26, 28, 29, 30

Two Leading Lights
    a) in Christmas booklet of Earle J. Bernheimer,
       1944
    b) Steeple Bush
    c) CP 1949, Poetry of RF 1969
    d) see items: 21, 22, 29

Two Look at Two
    b) New Hampshire
    c) SP 1928, CP 1930, AB 1932, SP 1934, SP 1936,
       CP 1939, Come In 1943, Poems 1946, CP 1949,
       RNT 1951, SP 1955, Poetry of RF 1969
    d) see items: 5, 8, 9, 10, 11, 13, 14, 16, 18, 22,
       23, 25, 29

Two Tramps in Mud Time
    a) in The Saturday Review of Literature, Oct 6,
       1934
    b) A Further Range
    c) CP 1939, Come In 1943, Poems 1946, CP 1949,
       RNT 1951, Aforesaid 1954, SP 1955, YCT 1959,
       SP 1963, Poetry of RF 1969, RF: P and P 1972
    d) see items: 12, 14, 16, 18, 22, 23, 24, 25, 26,
       28, 29, 30

U.S. 1946 King's X
    a) in The Atlantic Monthly, Dec 1946
    b) Steeple Bush
    c) CP 1949, SP 1963, Poetry of RF 1969
    d) see items: 21, 22, 28, 29

Unharvested
    a) in The Saturday Review of Literature as "Un-
       gathered Apples, " Nov 10, 1934
    b) A Further Range
    c) CP 1939, Poems 1946, CP 1949, SP 1963, Poet-
       ry of RF 1969
    d) see items: 12, 14, 18, 22, 28, 29

Unnoticed see On Going Unnoticed

Unstamped Letter in Our Rural Letter Box, An
    a) in booklet form as RF's Christmas poem, 1944
    b) Steeple Bush
    c) CP 1949, Poetry of RF 1969
    d) see items: 21, 22, 29

Untried see Waspish

Valley's Singing Day, The
    a) in Harper's Magazine, Dec 1920
    b) New Hampshire
    c) CP 1930, CP 1939, CP 1949, Poetry of RF 1969
    d) see items: 5, 9, 14, 22, 29

Vanishing Red, The
    a) in The Craftsman, July 1916
    b) Mountain Interval
    c) CP 1930, CP 1939, Come In 1943, Poems 1946,
       CP 1949, RNT 1951, SP 1963, Poetry of RF 1969
    d) see items: 4, 9, 14, 16, 18, 22, 23, 28, 29

Vantage Point, The
>   b) A Boy's Will
>   c) SP 1923, SP 1928, CP 1930, SP 1934, CP 1939,
>   Poems 1946, CP 1949, SP 1963, Poetry of RF
>   1969
>   d) see items: 2, 6, 8, 9, 11, 13, 14, 18, 22, 28,
>   29

Version
>   b) In the Clearing
>   c) Poetry of RF 1969
>   d) see items: 27, 29

Vindictives, The
>   b) A Further Range
>   c) CP 1939, Poems 1946, CP 1949, RNT 1951, SP
>   1955, SP 1963, Poetry of RF 1969
>   d) see items: 12, 14, 18, 22, 23, 25, 28, 29

Voice Ways
>   a) in The Yale Review, Winter 1936
>   b) A Further Range
>   c) CP 1939, Poems 1946, CP 1949, SP 1955, SP
>   1963, Poetry of RF 1969
>   d) see items: 12, 14, 18, 22, 25, 28, 29

Waiting
>   b) A Boy's Will
>   c) CP 1930, CP 1939, Poems 1946, CP 1949, SP
>   1963, Poetry of RF 1969
>   d) see items: 2, 9, 14, 18, 22, 28, 29

Walker, The see Egg and the Machine, The

Waspish
>   a) as "Untried" in Poetry, April 1936
>   b) A Further Range
>   c) CP 1939, Come In 1943, Poems 1946, CP 1949,
>   RNT 1951, SP 1955, SP 1963, Poetry of RF 1969
>   d) see items: 12, 13, 16, 18, 22, 23, 25, 28, 29

[We Vainly Wrestle ...]
>   b) In the Clearing
>   c) Poetry of RF 1969
>   d) see items: 27, 29

Were I in Trouble
     a) as "Were I in Trouble with the Night Tonight" in
       The Yale Review, Autumn 1946
     b) Steeple Bush
     c) CP 1949, SP 1963, Poetry of RF 1969
     d) see items: 21, 22, 28, 29

West-Running Brook
     b) West-Running Brook
     c) CP 1930, SP 1934, SP 1936, CP 1939, Poems
       1946, CP 1949, RNT 1951, Aforesaid 1954, SP
       1955, SP 1963, Poetry of RF 1969, RF: P and P
       1972
     d) see items: 7, 9, 11, 13, 14, 18, 22, 23, 24, 25,
       28, 29, 30

What Fifty Said
     b) included in contents of West-Running Brook with
       publication of CP 1930
     c) CP 1930, CP 1939, Poems 1946, CP 1949, SP
       1963, Poetry of RF 1969
     d) see items: 9, 14, 18, 22, 28, 29

White-Tailed Hornet, The
     a) in The Yale Review, Spring 1936, (subtitled "or
       Doubts About an Instinct")
     b) A Further Range
     c) CP 1939, Come In 1943, Poems 1946, CP 1949,
       RNT 1951, Aforesaid 1954, SP 1955, SP 1963,
       Poetry of RF 1969
     d) see items: 12, 14, 16, 18, 22, 23, 24, 25, 28,
       29

Why Wait for Science
     a) as "Our Getaway" in The New Hampshire Trouba-
       dour, Nov 1946
     b) Steeple Bush
     c) CP 1949, Aforesaid 1954, SP 1955, SP 1963,
       Poetry of RF 1969, RF: P and P 1972
     d) see items: 21, 22, 24, 25, 28, 29, 30

Wild Grapes
     a) in Harper's Magazine, Dec 1920
     b) New Hampshire
     c) CP 1930, CP 1939, Come In 1943, Poems 1946,
       CP 1949, RNT 1951, SP 1963, Poetry of RF 1969,
       RF: P and P 1972

d) see items: 5, 9, 14, 16, 18, 22, 23, 28, 29, 30

Willful Homing
    a) in The Saturday Review of Literature, Feb 26, 1938
    b) A Witness Tree
    c) Poems 1946, CP 1949, RNT 1951, SP 1955, SP 1963, Poetry of RF 1969, RF: P and P 1972
    d) see items: 15, 18, 22, 23, 25, 28, 29, 30

Wind and the Rain, The
    b) A Witness Tree
    c) Poems 1946, CP 1949, Poetry of RF 1969
    d) see items: 15, 18, 22, 29

Wind and Window Flower
    b) A Boy's Will
    c) CP 1930, CP 1939, CP 1949, RNT 1951, Poetry of RF 1969
    d) see items: 2, 9, 14, 22, 23, 29

Winter Eden, A
    a) in The New Republic, Jan 12, 1927
    b) West-Running Brook
    c) CP 1930, CP 1939, Poems 1946, CP 1949, RNT 1951, Aforesaid 1954, SP 1955, SP 1963, Poetry of RF 1969, RF: P and P 1972
    d) see items: 7, 9, 14, 18, 22, 23, 24, 25, 28, 29, 30

Wish to Comply, A
    b) Steeple Bush
    c) CP 1949, Poetry of RF 1969
    d) see items: 21, 22, 29

Witch of Coös, The
    a) in Poetry, Jan 1922
    b) New Hampshire
    c) CP 1930, SP 1934, SP 1936, CP 1939, Come In 1943, Poems 1946, CP 1949, RNT 1951, Aforesaid 1954, SP 1955, SP 1963, Poetry of RF 1969, RF: P and P 1972
    d) see items: 5, 9, 11, 13, 14, 16, 18, 22, 23, 24, 25, 28, 29, 30

Wood-Pile, The
    b) North of Boston
    c) SP 1923, SP 1928, CP 1930, SP 1934, SP 1936,
       CP 1939, Come In 1943, Poems 1946, CP 1949,
       RNT 1951, Aforesaid 1954, SP 1955, SP 1963,
       Poetry of RF 1969, RF: P and P 1972
    d) see items: 3, 6, 8, 9, 11, 13, 14, 16, 18, 22,
       23, 24, 25, 28, 29, 30

Wright's Biplane, The
    b) A Further Range
    c) CP 1939, Poems 1946, CP 1949, RNT 1951, SP
       1955, SP 1963, Poetry of RF 1969
    d) see items: 12, 14, 18, 22, 23, 25, 28, 29

Young Birch, A
    a) in booklet form as RF's Christmas poem, 1946
    b) Steeple Bush
    c) CP 1949, Aforesaid 1954, SP 1955, YCT 1959,
       SP 1963, Poetry of RF 1969, RF: P and P 1972
    d) see items: 21, 22, 24, 25, 26, 28, 29, 30

N.   SELECTED ANTHOLOGIES
CONTAINING FROST POEMS

The following is a list of selected anthologies containing poems by Robert Frost.   Below each item are the poems published therein.

American Life in Literature II.   rev. ed. , ed. by Jay B. Hubbell.   New York: Harper & Brothers, 1949.
  The Death of the Hired Man
  Mending Wall
  Birches
  An Old Man's Winter Night
  The Need of Being Versed in Country Things
  A Brook in the City
  Stopping by Woods on a Snowy Evening
  Our Singing Strength
  Paul's Wife
  The Bear
  Desert Places
  On the Heart's Beginning to Cloud the Mind
  They Were Welcome to Their Belief
  On a Bird Singing in Its Sleep

American Literary Masters II, ed. by Charles R. Anderson, et al.   New York: Holt, Rinehart & Winston, 1955.
  The Pasture
  Mowing
  Mending Wall
  The Death of the Hired Man
  Home Burial
  The Black Cottage
  A Servant to Servants
  The Code
  After Apple-Picking
  The Wood-Pile
  An Old Man's Winter Night
  "Out, Out--"

The Ax-Helve
The Grindstone
The Witch of Coös
Fire and Ice
For Once, Then, Something
I Will Sing You One-O
Nothing Gold Can Stay
Stopping by Woods on a Snowy Evening
To Earthward
Two Look at Two
Acquainted with the Night
West-Running Brook
Desert Places
Design
Neither Out Far Nor in Deep
The Silken Tent
All Revelation
The Most of It
Beech
Sycamore
Directive
(includes an essay, "The Figure a Poem Makes")

American Literature: The Makers and the Making II, ed.
by Cleanth Brooks, R. W. B. Lewis, and Robert Penn
Warren. New York: St. Martin's Press, 1973.
The Pasture
The Death of the Hired Man
After Apple-Picking
The Oven Bird
Fire and Ice
Stopping by Woods on a Snowy Evening
The Onset
The Need of Being Versed in Country Things
Once by the Pacific
Acquainted with the Night
Two Tramps in Mud Time
Desert Places
Neither Out Far Nor in Deep
Design
Provide, Provide
Come In
The Most of It
Away

American Poetry, ed. by Gay Wilson Allen, Walter B. Ride-
out and James K. Robinson. New York: Harper & Row,

1965.
>
> The Tuft of Flowers
> Mending Wall
> Home Burial
> After Apple-Picking
> The Road Not Taken
> The Oven Bird
> The Witch of Coös
> Stopping by Woods on a Snowy Evening
> For Once, Then, Something
> The Onset
> To Earthward
> Two Look at Two
> Acquainted with the Night
> West-Running Brook
> Two Tramps in Mud Time
> Desert Places
> Neither Out Far Nor in Deep
> Design
> The Gift Outright
> Directive

American Poetry 1671-1928, ed. by Conrad Aiken. New
York: Modern Library, 1929.
>
> The Telephone
> The Road Not Taken
> My November Guest
> Home Burial
> The Sound of the Trees
> Hyla Brook
> Mowing
> To Earthward
> Fire and Ice
> Stopping by Woods on a Snowy Evening

American Poetry and Prose, 4th ed. , ed. by Norman
Foerster. Boston: Houghton Mifflin, 1957.
>
> Mowing
> The Tuft of Flowers
> Reluctance
> The Death of the Hired Man
> Dust of Snow
> Mending Wall
> The Pasture
> Home Burial
> The Black Cottage
> Birches

The Road Not Taken
An Old Man's Winter Night
The Oven Bird
"Out, Out--"
Fire and Ice
New Hampshire
Stopping by Woods on a Snowy Evening
Once by the Pacific
Tree at My Window
Desert Places
Two Tramps in Mud Time
Departmental
A Considerable Speck
The Gift Outright
Come In

Anthology of American Literature II, ed. by George McMi-
chael. New York: Macmillan, 1974.
Mending Wall
Home Burial
The Road Not Taken
The Oven Bird
For Once, Then, Something
Fire and Ice
Dust of Snow
The Onset
Design
Nothing Gold Can Stay
Stopping by Woods on a Snowy Evening
To Earthward
Once by the Pacific
Acquainted with the Night
West-Running Brook
Desert Places
Neither Out Far Nor in Deep
Provide, Provide
The Subverted Flower
Forgive, O Lord

An Anthology of Famous English and American Poetry, ed.
by William Rose Benét and Conrad Aiken. New York:
Modern Library, 1944.
Desert Places
Bereft
For Once, Then, Something
Once by the Pacific
The Telephone

The Road Not Taken
My November Guest
Home Burial
The Sound of the Trees
Hyla Brook
Mowing
To Earthward
Fire and Ice
Stopping by Woods on a Snowy Evening

Chief Modern Poets of England and America, 3d ed., ed.
by Gerald DeWitt Sanders and John Herbert Nelson. New
York: Macmillan, 1947.
Reluctance
The Pasture
Mending Wall
The Death of the Hired Man
The Road Not Taken
A Patch of Old Snow
Birches
The Hill Wife
The Sound of the Trees
The Star-Splitter
Fire and Ice
Dust of Snow
Stopping by Woods on a Snowy Evening
The Onset
Goodbye and Keep Cold
Acceptance
A Minor Bird
Acquainted with the Night
The Investment
The Armful
On Looking Up by Chance at the Constellations
Two Tramps in Mud Time
On the Heart's Beginning to Cloud the Mind
Desert Places
The Strong Are Saying Nothing
There Are Roughly Zones

Major American Writers, rev. & enl. ed., ed. by Howard
Mumford Jones and Ernest E. Leisy. New York: Har-
court, Brace & Co., 1945.
The Tuft of Flowers
Mending Wall
The Fear
The Road Not Taken

An Old Man's Winter Night
"Out, Out--"
Snow
New Hampshire
Paul's Wife
Wild Grapes
Fire and Ice
Nothing Gold Can Stay
To Earthward
Two Look at Two
Spring Pools
Once by the Pacific
Bereft
Tree at My Window
West-Running Brook
A Soldier
Two Tramps in Mud Time
Desert Places
Build Soil--A Political Pastoral
The Silken Tent
Happiness Makes Up in Height for What it Lacks in
    Length
Come In
The Gift Outright
To a Young Wretch (Boethian)
Neither Out Far Nor in Deep

Modern American Poetry, new & enl. ed. , ed. by Louis
    Untermeyer. New York: Harcourt, Brace & World, 1962.
                The Pasture
                The Onset
                The Tuft of Flowers
                Reluctance
                Mending Wall
                The Cow in Apple Time
                The Death of the Hired Man
                After Apple-Picking
                An Old Man's Winter Night
                Birches
                Brown's Descent
                The Runaway
                To Earthward
                Fire and Ice
                Two Look at Two
                Canis Major
                The Peaceful Shepherd
                Bereft

Tree at My Window
West-Running Brook
Once by the Pacific
The Bear
Sand Dunes
The Lovely Shall Be Choosers
The Egg and the Machine
Stopping by Woods on a Snowy Evening
Nothing Gold Can Stay
The Road Not Taken
A Leaf-Treader
Lost in Heaven
Desert Places
Two Tramps in Mud Time
Departmental
A Considerable Speck
Happiness Makes Up in Height for What It Lacks in
     Length
Come In
From Plane to Plane
Choose Something Like a Star
The Gift Outright
Directive
Acquainted with the Night

Modern Poetry: American and British, ed. by Kimon Friar
     and John Malcolm Brinnin.   New York: Appleton-Century-
     Crofts, 1951.
          After Apple-Picking
          Happiness Makes Up in Height for What It Lacks in
               Length
          All Revelation
          The Silken Tent
          A Soldier
          The Most of It
          To Earthward

Modern Verse in English: 1900-1950, ed. by David Cecil
     and Allen Tate.   New York: Macmillan, 1958.
          My November Guest
          Mending Wall
          After Apple-Picking
          An Old Man's Winter Night
          Birches
          Fire and Ice
          Stopping by Woods on a Snowy Evening
          To Earthward

Tree at My Window
Desert Places
Moon Compasses

The Norton Anthology of Poetry, ed. by Arthur M. Eastman,
  et al. New York: W. W. Norton, 1970.
The Tuft of Flowers
Mending Wall
The Wood-Pile
The Oven Bird
Birches
The Hill Wife
The Aim Was Song
Stopping by Woods on a Snowy Evening
To Earthward
Spring Pools
West-Running Brook
A Lone Striker
The White-Tailed Hornet
The Strong Are Saying Nothing
Neither Out Far Nor in Deep
Design
Never Again Would Birds' Song Be the Same
The Gift Outright
In Winter in the Woods Alone

The Oxford Anthology of American Literature II, ed. by
  William Rose Benét and Norman Holmes Pearson.   New
  York: Oxford University Press, 1938.
Mowing
The Tuft of Flowers
Mending Wall
The Death of the Hired Man
Home Burial
After Apple-Picking
The Road Not Taken
Birches
The Hill Wife: The Oft Repeated Dream
"Out, Out--"
The Sound of the Trees
The Grindstone
Fire and Ice
Dust of Snow
The Runaway
Stopping by Woods on a Snowy Evening
To Earthward
Goodbye and Keep Cold

Not to Keep
Acquainted with the Night
Canis Major
The Bear
Two Tramps in Mud Time
Neither Out Far Nor in Deep
A Lone Striker

The Oxford Book of American Verse, ed. by F. O. Matthies-
    sen. New York: Oxford University Press, 1950.
The Pasture
My November Guest
Storm Fear
To the Thawing Wind
The Vantage Point
Mowing
The Tuft of Flowers
The Demiurge's Laugh
Pan with Us
Reluctance
Mending Wall
The Death of the Hired Man
After Apple-Picking
The Road Not Taken
An Old Man's Winter Night
Meeting and Passing
The Oven Bird
Birches
Putting in the Seed
"Out, Out--"
The Sound of the Trees
The Axe-Helve
Fire and Ice
Dust of Snow
Stopping by Woods on a Snowy Evening
The Onset
To Earthward
Not to Keep
A Brook in the City
The Need of Being Versed in Country Things
Spring Pools
Acceptance
Bereft
Tree at My Window
The Lovely Shall Be Choosers
The Investment
The White-Tailed Hornet

Desert Places
The Subverted Flower
The Gift Outright

This Singing World: An Anthology of Modern Verse for
Young People, ed. by Louis Untermeyer.   New York:
Harcourt, Brace, 1923.
The Pasture
Stopping by Woods on a Snowy Evening
A Brook in the City
The Runaway
A Hillside Thaw
The Tuft of Flowers

Twelve American Poets, ed. by Stephen Whicher and Lars
Åhnebrink.   New York: Oxford University Press, 1961.
Home Burial
The Road Not Taken
Birches
Fire and Ice
Stopping by Woods on a Snowy Evening
Desert Places
Design
Provide, Provide
The Gift Outright

Twelve American Writers, ed. by William M. Gibson and
George Arms.   New York: Macmillan, 1962.
Into My Own
Reluctance
Mending Wall
Home Burial
After Apple-Picking
The Road Not Taken
Putting in the Seed
The Cow in Apple Time
"Out, Out--"
Fire and Ice
Dust of Snow
Nothing Gold Can Stay
Stopping by Woods on a Snowy Evening
For Once, Then, Something
To Earthward
Acceptance
Tree at My Window
West-Running Brook
Two Tramps in Mud Time

Desert Places
A Leaf-Treader
Come In
The Gift Outright
Directive
Choose Something Like a Star
(includes two essays by Frost, "The Constant Sym-
    bol" and "On Emerson"; also a review of North
    of Boston by Ezra Pound and "The Other Frost"
    by Randall Jarrell)

O. UNCOLLECTED FROST POEMS

The following list designates the first (and sometimes only) publication of Frost's uncollected poems. The reader should consult Thompson's biography or Lathem and Thompson's Robert Frost: Poetry and Prose (to cite only two sources) for reprints of most of these poems.

A No. 1 Sundown, An:
> in The New Hampshire Troubadour, Nov 1946, p. 15.

Across the Atlantic:
> in The Independent, March 26, 1908, p. 676.

Birds Do Thus, The:
> in The Independent, Aug 20, 1896, p. 1.

Caesar's Lost Transport Ships:
> in The Independent, Jan 14, 1897, p. 1.

Charter Oak at Hartford, The:
> in High School Bulletin 13 (Lawrence, Mass.) no. 4, p. 2.

Class Hymn:
> in Order of Exercise for the Forty-first Anniversary of the Lawrence High School, Friday, July 1st, 1892 (Lawrence, Mass.) 1892

Correction, A:
> in What Cheer: An Anthology of American and British Humorous and Witty Verse, ed. David McCord. (N.Y., 1945).

Despair:
> in Thompson's Robert Frost: The Early Years, 1874-1915, p. 267.

Down the Brook--And Back:
> in High School Bulletin 13 (Lawrence, Mass.) no. 4,
> p. 1.

Dream-Land:
> in High School Bulletin 12 (Lawrence, Mass.) no. 8,
> p. 1.

Fish-Leap Fall:
> in a letter to Louis Untermeyer dated June 30, 1919
> [see Letters of Robert Frost to Louis Unter-
> meyer, pp. 90-91].

Flower Guidance:
> in Thompson's Robert Frost: The Early Years,
> 1874-1915, p. 584.

For Travelers Going Sidereal:
> in Robert Frost: Poetry and Prose, p. 434.

God's Garden:
> in The Boston Evening Transcript, June 23, 1898,
> p. 6.

Good Relief:
> in Lesley Frost's anthology Come Christmas (N.Y.,
> 1935), pp. 4-5.

Greece:
> in The Boston Evening Transcript, April 23, 1897,
> p. 6.

Hail First President:
> in a letter to Amy Lowell dated May 21, 1915 [see
> Thompson's Selected Letters of Robert Frost, p.
> 175].

I Am a Mede and Persian:
> in Thompson's Selected Letters of Robert Frost [a
> parody of Ezra Pound contained in a letter to
> F. S. Flint], pp. 85-86.

In England:
> in a letter to Sidney Cox dated Dec 26, 1912.

Kitchen in School, Or, Goings On at a Staid Old New Hamp-
       shire Academy, A:
              in The Pinkerton Critic, May 1910, p. 5.

La Noche Triste:
              in High School Bulletin (Lawrence, Mass.) April
              1890, pp. 1-2.

Later Minstrel, The:
              in The Pinkerton Critic, March 1909, p. 14.

Lost Faith, The:
              in The Derry News (Derry, N H.) March 1, 1907,
              pp. 1, 4.

Lure of the West, The:
              in Anderson's Robert Frost and John Bartlett: The
              Record of a Friendship, pp. 29-30.

Man Is as Tall, A:
              used by Yale University Press on fly leaf on Thomas
              Hornsby Ferril's book of poems, Westering (19   ).

Middletown Murder, The:
              in The Sautrday Review of Literature, Oct 13, 1928,
              p. 216.

My Giving:
              in Thompson's Robert Frost: The Early Years,
              1874-1915, p. 380.

My Olympic Record Stride:
              in a letter to Louis Untermeyer dated Dec 1932 [see
              Letters of Robert Frost to Louis Untermeyer, pp.
              232-233].

Nose-Ring, The:
              in a letter to Louis Untermeyer dated Feb 1, 1922
              [see Letters of Robert Frost to Louis Unter-
              meyer, p. 143]

Offer, The:
              in a letter to Louis Untermeyer dated Aug 20, 1932
              [see Letters of Robert Frost to Louis Unter-
              meyer, p. 228].

On the Sale of My Farm:
> in Thompson's Robert Frost: The Early Years,
> 1874-1915, p. 368.

Parlor Joke, The:
> in A Miscellany of American Poetry, 1920 (N. Y.,
> 1920) pp. 25-28.

Parting. To _____ _____:
> in High School Bulletin (Lawrence, Mass.) Dec
> 1891, p. 3.

Poets Are Born Not Made:
> in Thompson's Robert Frost: The Early Years,
> 1874-1915, p. 420.

Pride of Ancestry:
> in Thompson's Robert Frost: The Years of Tri-
> umph, 1915-1938, p. 473.

Prophets Really Prophecy as Mystics, The Commentators
Merely by Statistics:
> in Poetry, Oct-Nov 1962.

Somewhat Dietary:
> in The Massachusetts Review 1 (Oct 1959) 24.

Song of the Wave:
> in High School Bulletin (Lawrence, Mass.) May
> 1890, p. 3.

To Prayer I Think I Go:
> final version in a letter to Louis Untermeyer dated
> Jan 15, 1942 [see Letters of Robert Frost to
> Louis Untermeyer, p. 331].

Traitor, The:
> in The Phillips Andover Mirror (Andover, Mass.)
> June 1892, p. 24.

Tutelary Elves:
> in Christmas booklet sent to Susan Hayes Ward,
> 1911; Printed in Thompson's Robert Frost: The
> Early Years, 1874-1915, pp. 557-558.

Warning:
> in The Independent, Sept 9, 1897, p. 1.

When the Speed Comes:
>   in Thompson's <u>Robert Frost: The Early Years</u>,
>   <u>1874-1915</u>, p. 158.

Winter Ownership:
>   in <u>New York Herald Tribune Magazine</u>, March 4,
>   1934, p. 12.

INDEX OF CRITICS
(Authors of Secondary Material)

(Reviews of works by Robert Frost and about him have been given omnibus numbers that refer to the material reviewed. For example, number 108 refers to reviews of A Boy's Will; any author's name followed by number 108 signifies that he/she reviewed this book of poems.)